舵手汇

www.duoshou108.com

聪明投资者沟通的桥梁

股票和期货的控制论分析

提升交易水平的前沿 DSP 技术

[美] 约翰·F. 埃勒斯 著

康　民　陈火金 译

山西出版传媒集团
山西人民出版社

图书在版编目(CIP)数据

股票和期货的控制论分析：提升交易水平的前沿DSP技术／（美）约翰·F.埃勒斯著；康民，陈火金译. ——太原：山西人民出版社，2019.10
ISBN 978-7-203-10913-6

Ⅰ.①股… Ⅱ.①约… ②康… ③陈… Ⅲ.①数字信号处理-应用-股票交易-研究 ②数字信号处理-应用-期货交易-研究 Ⅳ.①F830.9-39

中国版本图书馆CIP数据核字(2019)第112113号
著作权合同登记号　图字：04-2014-043

股票和期货的控制论分析：提升交易水平的前沿DSP技术

著　　者：（美）约翰·F.埃勒斯
译　　者：康　民　陈火金
责任编辑：孙宇欣
复　　审：贾　娟
终　　审：阎卫斌
装帧设计：任燕飞工作室
出　版　者：山西出版传媒集团·山西人民出版社
地　　址：太原市建设南路21号
邮　　编：030012
发行营销：0351-4922220　4955996　4956039　4922127（传真）
天猫官网：http://sxrmcbs.tmall.com　电话：0351-4922159
E-mail　：sxskcb@163.com　发行部
　　　　　sxskcb@126.com　总编室
网　　址：www.sxskcb.com
经　销　者：山西出版传媒集团·山西人民出版社
承　印　者：三河市京兰印务有限公司
开　　本：710mm×1000mm　1/16
印　　张：17.5
字　　数：260千字
印　　数：1—5000册
版　　次：2019年10月　第1版
印　　次：2019年10月　第1次印刷
书　　号：978-7-203-10913-6
定　　价：68.00元

如有印装质量问题请与本社联系调换

献给伊丽莎白女士——我的朋友、伙伴和妻子。

致　谢

我想感谢迈克·柏吉斯（Mike Burgess）、罗德·黑尔（Rod Hare）和米切尔·邓肯（Mitchell Duncan），他们在百忙之中审阅了本书的初稿。经过他们的努力，原本生硬的计算机代码说明和一位工程师散漫的思维过程，转变为一本具有合理顺序的、易读的文稿。

在这样一个技术年代，工具是非常重要的。我想感谢 Tradestation 技术（Tradestation Technologies）的交易平台，它使得交易系统的开发成为可能。我还想感谢 eSignal，使他们的软件也可用来开发指标，感谢克里斯·克里扎（Chris Kryza）把我的代码转换为 eSignal 格式的代码。另外，还想感谢斯蒂夫·沃德（Steve Ward），他使得 NeuroShell Trader 的资源可以使用，于是通过使用神经网络（neural networks）和遗传算法（genetic algorithms），向交易者扩展了我的指标的有用性。

我还想感谢迈克·巴纳（Mike Barna），是他向我展示如何将抛硬币的方法运用于交易策略评估。

约翰·F. 埃勒斯

序

"这是本书的梗概。"汤姆简洁地说。

正如阿瑟·克拉克爵士（Sir Arthur C. Clarke）所说，任何高深的技术都是与魔法很难区分的。在过去的二十年里，计算机技术的进步是惊人的，几乎可以用不可思议来形容。今天，我办公桌上的这台计算机比30年前整个美国国家防御系统所用的计算机还要强大。然而，交易者们所用的软件却没有跟上时代的步伐。今天的大多数交易工具，与用铅笔和纸做手工计算没什么两样，也不比手工计算复杂多少，那些计算用机械的加法计算器就可完成，而不必使用计算机。现在，这些计算的速度的确非常快，并且都是以彩色显示，非常容易观察，但是计算过程都没有改变。总之，因为信息交换速度的提高和市场资本总值的增加已经引起市场技术角色的基本转变，所以计算的相对能力已经消失了。这些转变包括市场波动性的增加和波动周期的缩短。

《股票和期货的控制论分析》通过引进全新的数字信号处理技术（DSP），承诺为交易艺术带来魔力。这种数字信号处理技术的应用，使得我们能够从一个全新的角度观察原来的问题。这个由数字信号处理技术获得的新视角,已经引导我开发出了一些非常有效的新型交易工具。交易工具的进步,再加上硬件能力的持续进步,基本上可以保证数字信号处理技术在未来的持续应用。于是,那些掌握了新概念的交易者们,在 21 世纪交易高波动性的市场时,将发现自己拥有巨大的优势。如果你喜欢代码,那么你将喜欢本书。书中每项新技术、指标和自动交易系统,都有非常详细的 EasyLanguage 代码(用于 Tradestation)和 eSignal 格式脚本(eSignal Formula Script)代码。我也已经把它们编译为 DLL 文件,可以在 NeuroShell Trader 上运行。

第 1 章先声夺人,向传统智慧发起了挑战。人们一直认为市场价格具有一个高斯(Gaussian)概率密度函数(PDF)。只要想一想,就像你所理解的高斯 PDF 那样,价格真的包含几个可以用标准偏差从平均值分离开的事件吗?绝对不是!如果概率密度函数不是高斯分布,那么在交易系统中向 1σ 点附加显著性,不过是种错误的做法。我将向你展示如何通过应用费希尔变换(Fisher Transform)建立一个近似的高斯概率密度函数。

我在第 2 章中讲解了一种全新的零滞后瞬时趋势线(Instantaneous Trendline)。通过把市场分为一个趋势分量和一个周期分量,进行推导后,我创建了一个零滞后周期振荡指标。通过第 3 章中的一套自动趋势跟随交易策略和第 4 章中的一套自动周期交易策略,我把这些结果推向了实际应用。

然后我又推导出了几个新的振荡指标。它们包括第 5 章的 CG 振荡指标(CG Oscillator)和第 6 章的相对活力指数(RVI)。在第 7 章,我对控制周期振荡指标(Cyber Cycle Oscillator)、CG 振荡指标和 RVI 进行了对比。注意,我最喜爱的一种技术分析工具是随机相对强弱指数(RSI),通过对 RSI 进行随机化处理,RSI 曲线变得更加有效。然后我在第 8 章展示了如何通过使用随机化处理和费希尔变换对振荡指标进行强化。

在第 9 章我给出了一个全新的测量市场循环周期的方法,那是非常令人振奋的。使用希耳伯特变换（Hilbert transform），我推导出了一个响应速度非常快的周期测量方法。然后，我又对这些测量结果的正确性和精确性使用几个强化的理论波形进行了验证。在第 10 章中，我向你展示了如何使用已经测得的主循环周期（Dominant Cycle）长度，制作可以自动适应当前主循环周期的标准指标。这种适应性使得优秀指标更加优秀，放射出更加耀眼的光芒。在第 11 章中，主循环的周期性分量是从周期测量中得出的，并显示为正弦波指标（Sinewave Indicator）。正弦波指标的优点是它能够预测周期性的反转点，而且当市场以趋势运动时，不易遭受双人拉锯式交易的危害。在第 12 章中，我继续阐述自动适应已经测得的主周期这一主题，向你展示如何使用测量结果设计一个自动化的趋势跟随交易策略。我所展示的这些策略的性能与商业策略平分秋色，甚至有过之而无不及。

第 13 章讲解了几种数据过滤方法，可以在只带来微小滞后的前提下对数据进行很大程度的超级平滑。这些过滤方法的计算机代码已经给出，同时给出的还有系数值表。获得超级平滑的另一种方法是使用拉盖尔多项式（Laguerre polynomials）。拉盖尔多项式的引入，使得我们只需用非常少的数据便可以对数据进行平滑，这将在第 14 章进行讲解。

对自动化交易策略进行历史数据回测的问题之一是它们并不预示未来业绩。在第 15 章中我描述了一项技术，使你可以使用概率理论把你的交易策略的性能可视化。同时，我还列出了那些对做这种评估非常重要的历史参数。在第 16 章，我向你展示了产生领先指标的方法，以及在使用这些指标时必须要接受的噪声增加。在第 17 章中，我通过向你展示如何简化简单移动平均（SMA）的代码来对本书内容做了一个总结。

本书所讲的许多数字信号处理技术，在自然科学领域都是众所周知的，并且已经应用了很多年。例如，最大熵谱分析（MESA）算法最初是由地球物理学家在勘探石油时所开发的，由地震研究得出的少量数据要求只要少量数据便可得出一个结果。我成功地对这种方法进行了改编，并且用它测量市场循环的周期。近来，数字信号处理技术的应用已经在日用电子产品中得到了爆炸式的应用。今天，完整的无线电接收器可以不使用模拟电子器件。当我们扩展数字信号处理技术的应用，把它引入交易领域时，我们将看到这是一个令人振奋的新领域，对于技术型交易者来说是非常理想的工具。它使我们可以对许多传统指标的应用进行推广，同时获得更加精确的计算结果。

本书的每一章都以汤姆·斯威夫特（Tom Swifty）的一句话开始。或许这可以表明我的幽默，但我的目的是使你记住该章的主要概念。汤姆·斯威夫特是一个文字游戏，一种幽默的双关，通过使用副词的形容方式，表达发言者的声明和态度。比如，"我喜欢小绒兔。"汤姆急切地说。这些组合是无穷无尽的。由于本书包含魔法，或许我应该选择哈利·波特（Harry Potter）作为本书的英雄，而不是汤姆·斯威夫特。

在本书当中，我的目标不仅是介绍新技术和新工具，更是为你提供使交易获利性更高，工作更愉快的方法。

目　录

第1章　费希尔变换 1

第2章　趋势和循环 13

第3章　交易趋势 25

第4章　交易循环 39

第5章　CG振荡指标 55

第6章　相对活力指数 63

第7章　振荡指标的比较 71

第8章　指标的随机化和费希尔化 75

第9章　测量循环周期 115

第10章　自适应周期指标 133

第11章　正弦波指标 161

第12章　适应趋势 175

第13章　超级平滑器 197

第14章　时间扭曲——无需宇宙飞行 229

第15章　评估交易系统 245

第 16 章　领先指标 ································ 251
第 17 章　简化简单移动平均的计算过程 ············ 261
结束语 ··· 265
更多信息 ··· 267
关于作者 ··· 268

第 1 章 费希尔变换

"我没有看到市场复苏的任何机会。"汤姆不自信地说。

我这二十多年来研究的重点,就是把我的工程和信号处理背景知识应用于交易的艺术。本书的目的是与你分享我的研究成果。在本书当中,我将展示股票和期货技术分析的新方法,以及最有效的代码编制方法。我将讨论建立市场模型的方法,以帮助对市场行为分类。除了新指标和自动交易系统之外,我将阐述如何把表现良好的传统指标转变为杰出的自适应指标。从这些分析演化出的交易系统将向大多数商业交易系统的一致表现和获利能力提出挑战,通常是超过它们甚多。虽然本书大部分内容都是在新领域的突破,但并不仅仅是为了创新而创新。相反地,本书是想挑战传统智慧,并且阐明了许多流行的系统开发方法的缺陷。

在本章当中,我们举了一个绝好的例子来挑战传统智慧。我知道至少有十几个基于统计学的指标参考:"1σ 点","3σ 点",等等。σ 是偏离平均值的标准偏差。为了获得偏离平均值的标准偏差,我们必须知道概率密度函数(probability density function,简称 PDF)。高斯分布(正态分布)的概率密度函数几乎应用于各个领域。高斯 PDF 是大家熟悉的钟形曲线,用于描述人类的智商(IQ)分布,以及其他大量的统计学描述。高斯 PDF

有很长的"尾部",表明远离平均值的事件发生的概率相对较低。对于高斯 PDF,68.26%的事件都落在平均值加（减）一个标准偏差的区间内,95.44%的事件都落在平均值加（减）两个标准偏差的区间内,99.73%的事件都落在平均值加（减）三个标准偏差的区间内。换句话说,所有事件中的大多数都落在高斯 PDF 的 1σ "界限"内。如果某个事件落在 1σ 区间之外,那么人们对未来发生的事就有了个推断。

此处真正的问题在于高斯 PDF 是否能够可靠地描述市场行为。你自己便可以很容易地回答这个问题,只要想一想价格在图表上的分布便可以了。你看到只有 68%的价格聚集在平均价格附近吗？也就是说,你看到 32%的价格偏离平均值一个标准偏差以上吗？进而,你看到价格在 5%的时间里偏离平均值两个标准偏差以上吗？你看到价格多长时间出现一个长钉形态呢？如果你没有看到这些偏离,那么高斯 PDF 便不是一个合理的假设。

费希尔变换是一个简单的数学计算过程,用于把任意数据集（data set）修正为 PDF 近似于高斯 PDF 的数据集。一旦我们使用费希尔变换对数据集进行了处理,我们就能够使用偏离平均值的偏差来分析变换后的数据集。

商品通道指标（CCI）是由唐纳德·兰伯特（Donald Lambert）开发的,它便是一个依靠高斯 PDF 假设的例子。计算 CCI 的公式是:

$$CCI = \frac{价格 - 移动平均值}{0.015 * 偏差} \qquad (1.1)$$

偏差是由价格与某个时间段上的移动平均值之差计算得出的。计算移动平均值的时间段可以由用户自己选择。我们可以把 CCI 看作当前偏差向标准偏差（standard deviation）的规格化。但 0.015 这一系数从何而来呢？

0.015 的倒数是 66.7，近似于高斯 PDF 的一个标准偏差，对于大多数技术分析工作，这已经足够了。我们假设，如果价格超出一个标准偏差，那么它们将向平均值回归。所以，常见规则是当 CCI 大于 +100 时卖出，而当 CCI 小于 -100 时买入。不用说，采用费希尔变换之后，CCI 的性能可以得到实质性的提高。

假设价格行为可以用方波表示。如果你试图利用价格穿越移动平均线作为一套交易系统，那么你将注定失败，因为当检测到穿越信号时，价格已经向相反方向转变了，只有两个价格值。所以，价格出现一个值或另一个值的概率分布都是 50%，没有其他可能性。方波的概率分布如图 1.1 所示。显然，这个概率分布函数与高斯概率分布函数相去甚远。

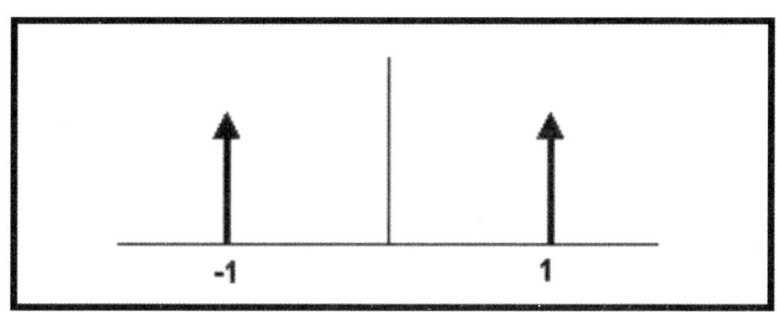

图 1.1　只有两个值的方波的概率分布

概率密度的含义及其计算一点都不神秘。它就是简单地表示价格将在给定值出现的可能性。请这样考虑：在一组平行的水平金属线上穿上一些珠子，根据你的意愿构建任意一个波形。当波形构建完毕以后，转动固定金属线的框架，使金属线由水平变为铅垂状态。所有的珠子将向底部滑落，每条金属线上的珠子总数显示的就是每条线上的概率值。

我使用的计算机代码稍微有点复杂，但无论怎样，思想都是相同的，得出的正弦波概率分布如图 1.2 所示。在这个例子中，我总共使用了 1 万枚 "珠子"。这个 PDF 可能有些奇怪，但是如果你仔细想一想，你将发现正弦波的大多数数据点都靠近最大和最小两个极值。简单正弦波循环的 PDF 与高斯 PDF 一点都不像。实际上，周期性波形的 PDF 更接近于方波的 PDF。周期性数据集的高概率部分靠近极值，这便是周期性市场难以交易的原因之一。利用市场循环成功交易的唯一方法就是利用市场的短期惯性预测周期性转折点。

费希尔变换会改变任意波形的 PDF，所以变换后的数据将有一个近似于高斯 PDF 的概率分布。费希尔变换的公式如下：

$$y = 0.5 * \ln\left[\frac{1+x}{1-x}\right] \tag{1.2}$$

其中 x 为输入；

y 为输出；

ln 是自然对数。

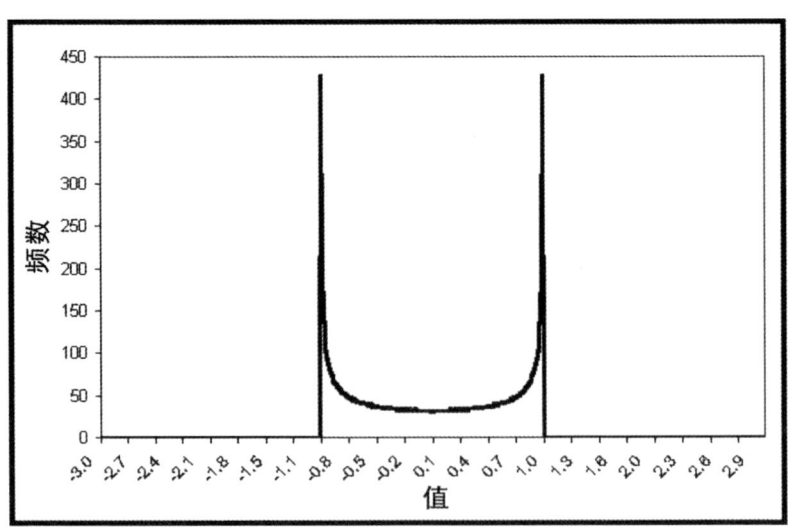

图 1.2　正弦波周期 PDF 与高斯 PDF 不同

费希尔变换的传递函数如图1.3所示。

输入值被限制在$-1 < x < 1$的区间内。当输入数据靠近平均值时,费希尔变换的增益接近于单位1。如图1.3所示,当$x=0.5$时,y值只是略大于0.5。反之,当输入数据靠近区间的任意一端时,输出数据就被大大地放大了。这种放大作用增加了偏离平均值的最大偏差,提供了高斯PDF的"尾巴"。图1.4显示出费希尔变换输出的PDF,接近于大家熟悉的钟形曲线,可以与输入正弦波的PDF做一下对比。两者在平均值处都具有相同的概率。变换结果的PDF接近于高斯PDF,与正弦波PDF完全不同。

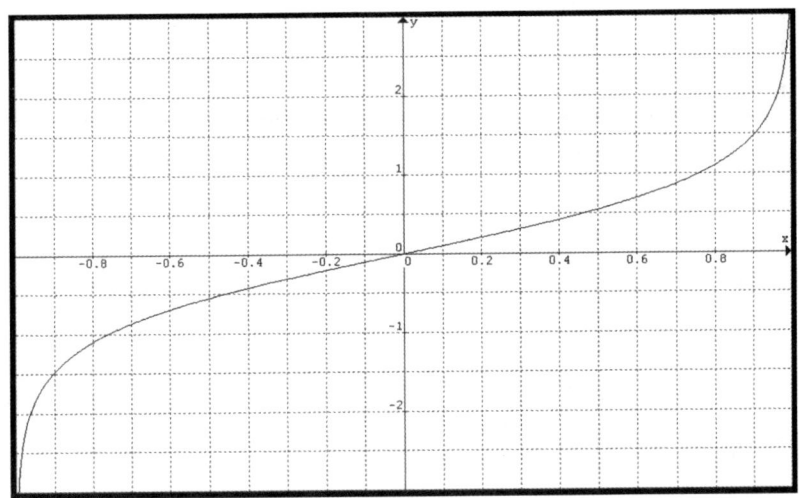

图1.3 费希尔变换是非线性的,把输入(x轴)变换为输出(y轴),输出具有近似的高斯PDF

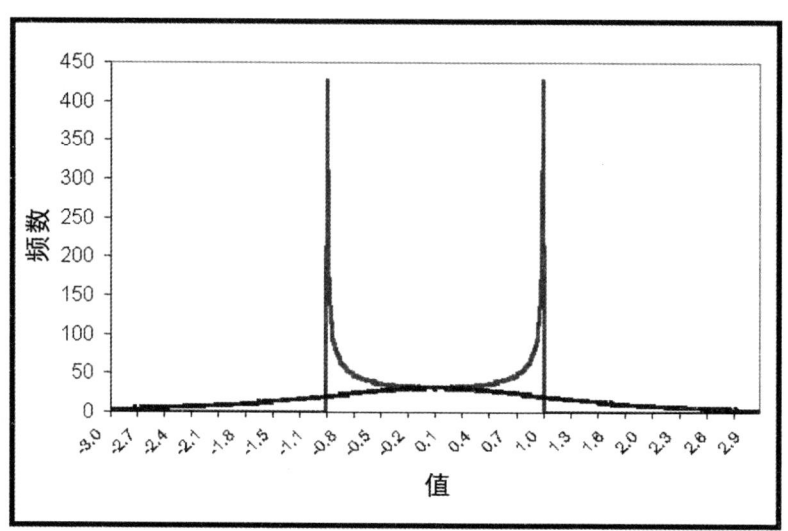

图 1.4 费希尔变换后的正弦波具有近似于高斯 PDF 的形状

我测量了美国长期国库券（U. S. Treasury Bond）期货从 1988 年到 2003 年 15 年上的概率分布。为了进行测量，我建立了一个规格化的通道，该通道具有 10 条棒线的长度。这一规格化的通道基本上与 10 棒（10 日）随机指标相同。然后我把通道宽度分为 100 等份，测量价格在那条通道内的位置，并且计算价格在每一等份内出现的次数。这次概率分布测量的结果见图 1.5。这一实际的概率分布更接近于正弦波 PDF，而非高斯 PDF。然后我把规格化通道的长度增加至 30 日，目的是看一下类似于正弦波的概率分布是否只是一种短期价格行为的假象。所得概率分布见图 1.6。图 1.5 和 1.6 的概率分布非常相似。对于这种概率分析，你可以将其推广到任意市场。我预言你将得到基本相同的结果。

那么这对交易有什么用处吗？如果价格被规格化到 -1 到 +1 的区间之内，并且经过费希尔变换，那么极端的价格运动将成为相对稀少的事件。

这就意味着转折点将变得明晰可辨。要想完成这些工作，EasyLanguage 代码如图 1.7 所示，eSignal Formula Script（EFS）代码如图 1.8 所示。Value1 是一个函数，用于将价格规格化到它的过去 10 日区间内。这个区间的长度被作为一个输入，是可以调整的。Value1 的中点被定位在该价格区间的中点，然后加倍，于是 Value1 将在 -1 和 +1 之间摆动。然后用指数移动平均对 Value1 进行平滑处理，指数移动平均的系数 α 为 0.5。这种平滑可能会使 Value1 超出 10 日价格区间，所以要对平滑值进行限制，防止费希尔变换因输入值超出 ±1 而使计算失败。费希尔变换的结果被保存在变量"Fish"中。Fish 和延迟一日的 Fish 都被绘出，产生一个交叉系统，用于辨识周期性的转折点。

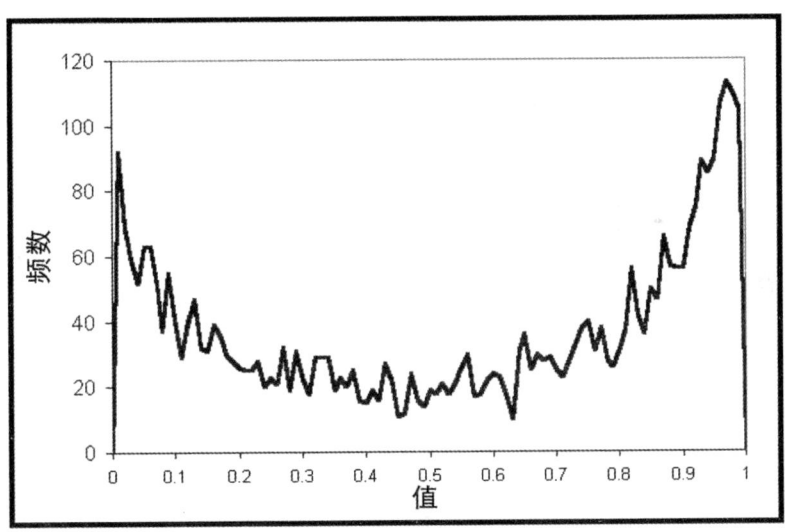

图 1.5　15 年时间段上的美国国库券期货在 10 日通道内的概率分布

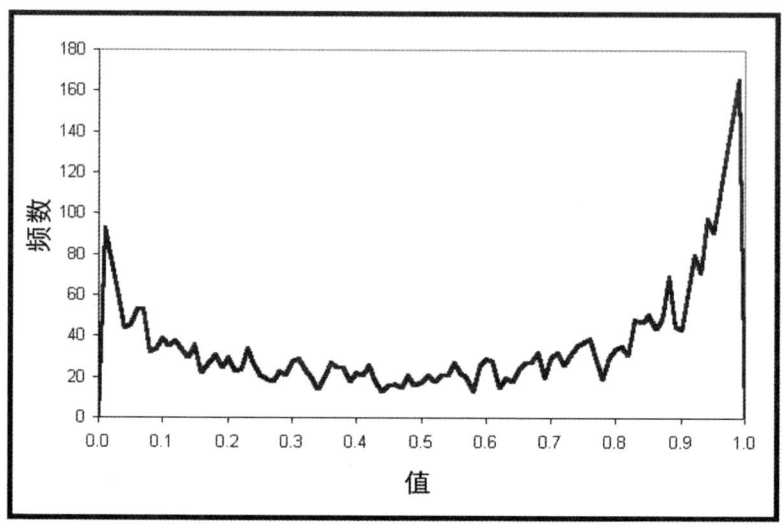

图 1.6　15 年时间段上的美国国库券期货在 30 日通道内的概率分布

```
Inputs:     Price((H+L)/2),
            Len(10);

Vars:       MaxH(0),
            MinL(0),
            Fish(0);

MaxH = Highest(Price, Len);
MinL = Lowest(Price, Len);

Value1 = .5*2*((Price - MinL)/(MaxH - MinL) - .5)
    + .5*Value1[1];
If Value1 >  .9999 then Value1 =  .9999;
If Value1 < -.9999 then Value1 = -.9999;

Fish = 0.25*Log((1 + Value1)/(1 - Value1)) + .5*Fish[1];

Plot1(Fish, IFisherI);
Plot2(Fish[1], ITriggerI);
```

图 1.7　EasyLanguage 代码，把价格规格化到 10 日通道之内，并计算其费希尔变换

```
/*****************************************************
Title:                   Fisher Transform
*****************************************************/
function preMain() {
    setStudyTitle(❙Fisher Transform❙);
    setCursorLabelName(❙Fisher❙, 0);
    setCursorLabelName(❙Trigger❙, 1);
    setDefaultBarFgColor(Color.blue, 0);
    setDefaultBarFgColor(Color.red, 1);
        setDefaultBarThickness(2, 0);
    setDefaultBarThickness(2, 1);
}

var Value1 = null;
var Value1_1 = 0;
var Fish = null;
var Fish_1 = 0;
var vPrice = null;
var aPrice = null;

function main(nLength) {
    var nState = getBarState();

        if (nLength == null) nLength = 10;
        if (aPrice == null) aPrice = new Array(nLength);

    if (nState == BARSTATE_NEWBAR && vPrice != null) {
      aPrice.pop();
      aPrice.unshift(vPrice);
      if (Value1 != null) Value1_1 = Value1;
      if (Fish != null) Fish_1 = Fish;
    }

        vPrice = (high() + low()) / 2;
        aPrice[0] = vPrice;

    if (aPrice[nLength-1] == null) return;

        var MaxH = high();
        var MinL = low();
        var temp;
```

图 1.8　EFS 代码，把价格规格化到 10 日通道之内，并计算其费希尔变换

```
        for(i = 0; i < nLength; ++i) {
MaxH = Math.max(MaxH, aPrice[i]);
            MinL = Math.min(MinL, aPrice[i]);
    }

    Value1 = .5 * 2 * ((vPrice - MinL) /
(MaxH - MinL) - .5) + .5 * Value1_1;

    if(Value1 > .9999) Value1 = .9999;
    if(Value1 < -.9999) Value1 = -.9999;

    Fish = 0.25 * Math.log((1 + Value1) /
(1 - Value1)) + .5 * Fish_1;

    return new Array(Fish, Fish_1);
}
```

图1.8（续）

8日通道内价格的费希尔变换结果被绘制在图1.9中价格棒线的下面。其反转点不但尖锐、清晰，而且产生得很及时，所以可以及时进入可获利交易。在图1.9中，我们将费希尔变换与类似参数的指数平滑异同移动平均指标（MACD）进行了比较。MACD是传统指标的代表，与费希尔变换不同，它的反转点圆滑而不明显。由于反转点比较圆滑，所以入场和出场信号难免会出现得迟一些。

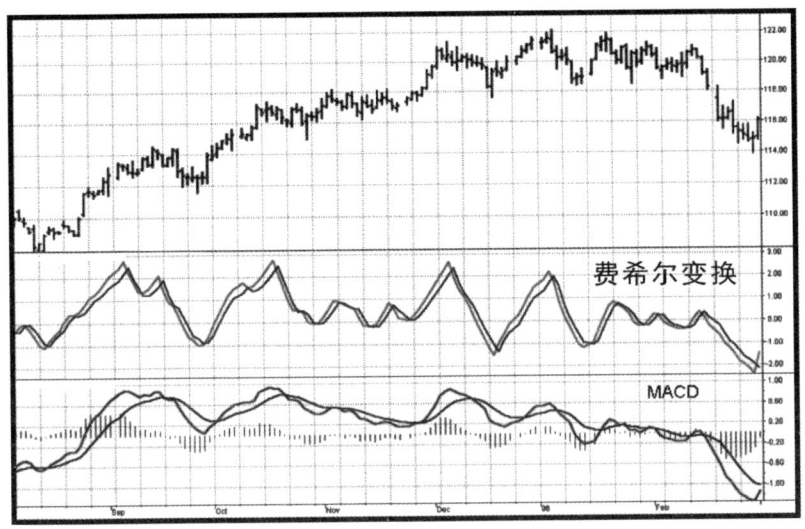

图 1.9 与 MACD 指标相比，规格化价格的费希尔变换具有非常尖锐的反转点

需要牢记的要点

● 价格几乎从来不会符合高斯（正态）概率分布。

● 基于高斯概率分布的统计测量，比如标准偏差，是错误的，因为计算所依据的概率分布假设是错误的。

● 费希尔变换几乎可以把任意输入的概率分布转换为接近高斯概率分布。

● 当把费希尔变换应用于指标时，将产生尖锐的买卖信号。

第 2 章　趋势和循环

"这倒令我无言以对了。"汤姆厌烦地说。

对于交易者来说，市场的趋势模式（Trend Mode）和循环模式（Cycle Mode）与交易策略的选择是同义的。在上升趋势中，显而易见的策略就是买入并持有。同样地，在下跌趋势中的策略就是卖空。与此相对，在循环模式中最好的策略是追高（top-pick）和捞底（bottom-fish）。交易者通常使用一些移动平均线的变形来交易趋势模式，使用一些振荡指标来交易循环模式。无论哪一种情况，对于交易者来说，由计算产生的滞后都是最大的一个问题。

在分析市场时，趋势模式和循环模式最好用它们的频谱（frequency content）来描述。价格在趋势模式中随着时间的发展变化比较慢。所以，在趋势模式中我们忽略高频分量，而只关心变化较慢的低频分量。移动平均是一种低通滤波器，只允许低频分量通过然后输出，那就是它们在趋势模式交易中有效的原因。振荡指标是一种高通滤波器，几乎完全过滤掉低频分量。

我将利用这些概念设计一类互补的振荡指标和移动平均。最重要的是，我所设计的振荡指标和移动平均基本上都没有滞后。对于交易指标和后面章节所讲的由这些指标建立的系统来说，消除滞后都是非常关键的。

我认为这些零滞后工具的设计是本书最重要的内容之一。很久以来,对于零滞后工具的研究便是我的工作重点,在以前的发表的文章中,我已经使用过瞬时趋势线之类的说法。虽然本章所讲的指标使用的名称与原来一样,但我向你展示的技术是全新的。

我将从大家熟悉的指数移动平均(EMA)开始,得出趋势模式和循环模式的一个最优化的数学描述。计算 EMA 的公式是:

$$输出 = \alpha * 输入 + (1 - \alpha) * 输出 \quad [1] \tag{2.1}$$

这个公式的意思是,我们首先取当前价格的一部分,然后把它与 1 日前的滤波输出和 $(1 - \alpha)$ 的乘积相加。如果输入恒定(零频率),那么经过计算后,输出将逐渐向输入值靠近。也就是说,该滤波动器在零频率时的增益为 0。我们可以用传递响应(transfer response)来描述这种滤波器,传递响应指的是输出除以输入。我们使用 Z 变换的标记符号,以 Z^{-1} 表示滞后为 1 日的乘法运算符。于是,公式 2.1 的传递响应可以利用下面的代数式解出:

$$H(z) = \frac{输出}{输入} = \frac{\alpha}{1 - (1 - \alpha) * Z^{-1}} \tag{2.2}$$

我们可以让 Z^{-1} 等于 +1(零频率),然后测试公式 2.2。当我们做这样的假设时,很容易发现分子等于分母,于是增益为单位 1。该滤波器的高频衰减可以通过令 Z^{-1} 等于 -1,在可能的最高频率——奈奎斯特频率(Nyquist frequency)处测得。以日线为例,我们能够分析的最高频率是每天 0.5 个周期(一个周期为两天)。这便是日线数据的奈奎斯特频率。周期长度为两天时的衰减是 $[\alpha/(2 - \alpha)]$。EMA 作为频率的函数的总的衰减响应如图 2.1 所示。图 2.1 中的周期性分量的周期可以通过求频率的倒数得出。举例说明，如果频率为每天 0.1 个周期，那么那个周期性分量的周期便是 10 天。

理论上，如果我们需要建立一个高通滤波器，只要从单位 1 中减去低通滤波器的传递响应就可以了。原理是 1 的传递响应代表所有频率，而从中减去低通响应，余下的便是高通响应。不过这种方法有一个问题：公式 2.2 表达的低通滤波器在奈奎斯特频率处的高频衰减不是无穷大（即传递响应为 0）。低频滤波器中有限的高频响应将在高通滤波器的传递响应中引起增益误差。通过对两个连续的输入样本求平均值，而不是只使用单个输入样本，便可消除这种有限衰减问题。在这种情况下，平均输入低通滤波器的传递响应是：

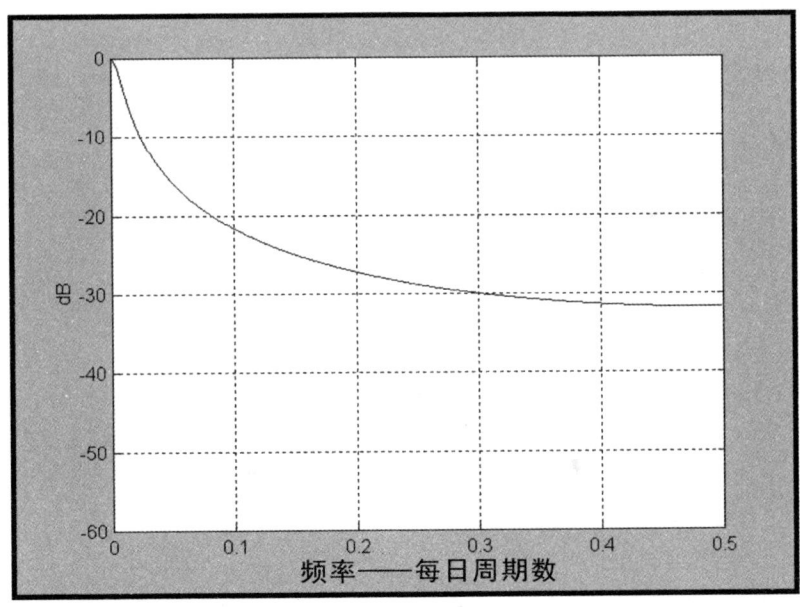

图 2.1　EMA 的频率响应（α = 0.05）

$$H(z) = \frac{\frac{\alpha}{2} * (1 + Z^{-1})}{1 - (1 - \alpha) * Z^{-1}} \qquad (2.3)$$

公式 2.3 保证低通滤波器的传递响应在 $Z^{-1} = -1$ 时为 0。平滑输入 EMA 的总频率响应如图 2.2 所示。

简单移动平均的滞后近似于平均长度的一半。例如，21 日移动平均的滞后是 10 日。对应 EMA 的 α 与简单移动平均的长度的关系如下式：

$$\alpha = \frac{2}{长度 + 1} \qquad (2.4)$$

通过公式 2.4 我们可以看出，系数 α = 0.05 的 EMA 相当于 39 日简单移动平均。39 日简单移动平均有 19 日的滞后，接近其长度的一半。图 2.3 表明，α = 0.05 的 EMA 在频率非常低时的滞后的确是 19 日。虽然随着频率增加滞后会减少，但是由于在高频部分滤波后的幅值非常小，所以没有什么作用。所有移动平均的滞后所产生的真正影响是在非常低的频率处的滞后值。

第 2 章 趋势和循环

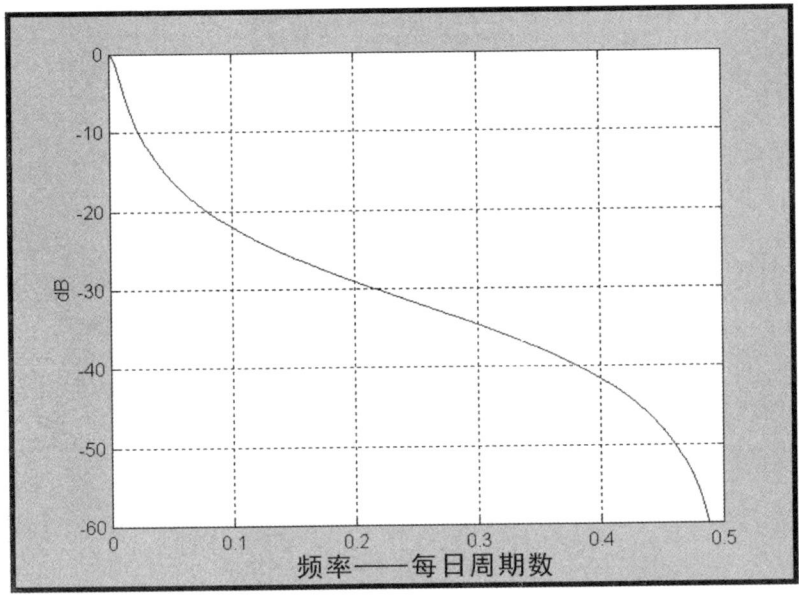

图 2.2 平滑输入 EMA 的频率响应（$\alpha = 0.05$）

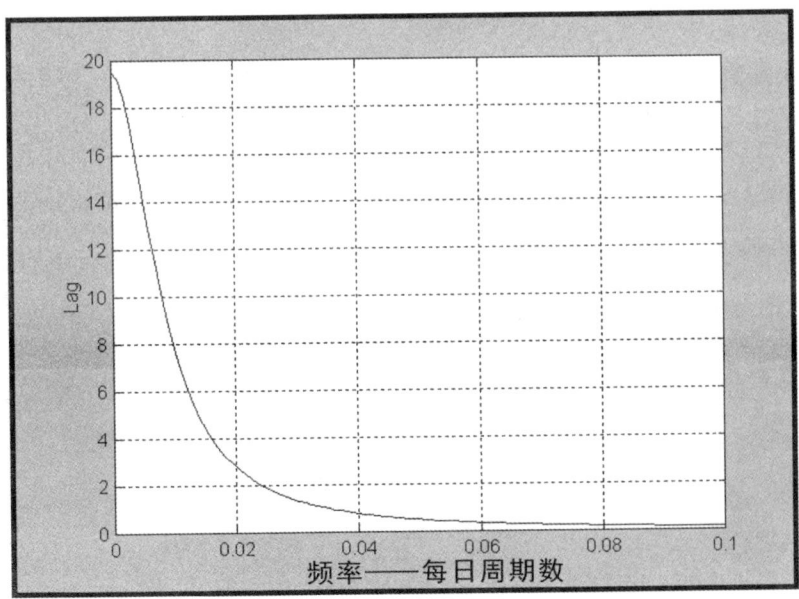

图 2.3 平滑输入滞后响应（$\alpha = 0.05$）

现在我们可以利用等式 2.3 建立一个高通滤波器。我们从单位 1 中减去等式 2.3，结果如下：

$$HP(z) = 1 - \frac{\frac{\alpha}{2} * (1 + Z^{-1})}{1 - (1 - \alpha) * Z^{-1}}$$

$$= \frac{1 - (1 - \alpha) * Z^{-1} - \frac{\alpha}{2} * (1 + Z^{-1})}{1 - (1 - \alpha) * Z^{-1}} \quad (2.5)$$

$$= \frac{\left(1 - \frac{\alpha}{2}\right) * (1 - Z^{-1})}{1 - (1 - \alpha) * Z^{-1}}$$

利用高次滤波器，我们能够获得更加尖锐的衰减。但是，试验表明高效滤波器不仅具有更大的滞后，而且它们的瞬态效应将在它们的输出结果中造成假象。这有点像按门铃：铃声是门铃本身的一个函数，而不是按铃压力的滤波响应。一个比较合理的折中是使用二次高斯滤波器。首先计算一个 EMA，然后再按照完全相同的参数计算出第一个 EMA 的 EMA，那么我们便得到一个二次高斯低通滤波器。这就相当于对传递响应进行平方。于是我们可以利用对公式 2.5 进行平方获得一个二次高斯高通滤波器。

$$HP(z) = \frac{\left(1 - \frac{\alpha}{2}\right)^2 * (1 - 2 * Z^{-1} + Z^{-2})}{1 - 2 * (1 - \alpha) * Z^{-1} + (1 - \alpha)^2 * Z^{-2}} \quad (2.6)$$

把公式 2.6 转换为 EasyLanguage 语句则为

第 2 章 趋势和循环

$$HPF = (1-\alpha/2)^2 * (Price - 2 * Price[1] + Price[2])$$
$$+ 2 * (1-\alpha) * HPF[1] - (1-\alpha)^2 * HPF[2] \quad (2.7)$$

公式 2.6 和 2.7（它们是等价的）的传递响应见图 2.4。

图 2.4 表明，只有周期大于 40 日（频率＝每日 0.025 周期）的价格波动才被显著衰减。于是我们建立了一个截止响应相对陡峭的高通滤波器。由于这种滤波器的输出基本上不包含趋势分量，所以它就是价格的周期性分量。

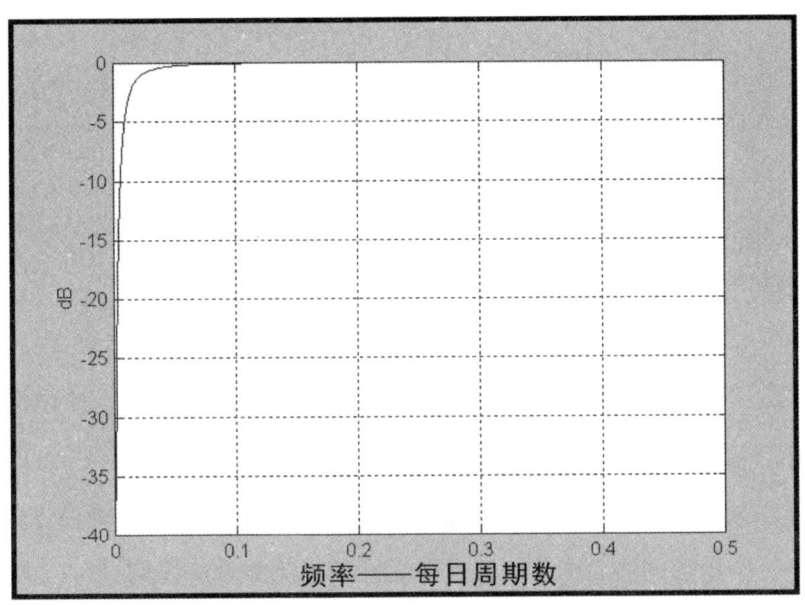

图 2.4　二次高通高斯滤波器（$\alpha = 0.05$）的传递响应

从单位 1 中减去等式 2.6 的高通分量，我们将得到与之互补的低通滤波器，该低通滤波器便可产生瞬时趋势线。跳过单调冗长的通分过程，低通瞬时趋势线的等式为

$$IT(z) = \frac{\left(\alpha - \dfrac{\alpha^2}{4}\right) + \dfrac{\alpha^2}{2}Z^{-1} - \left(\alpha - \dfrac{3\alpha^2}{4}\right)Z^{-2}}{1 - 2*(1-\alpha)*Z^{-1} + (1-\alpha)^2 Z^{-2}} \quad (2.8)$$

把等式 2.8 转换为 EasyLanguage 语句如下：

$$\begin{aligned}
\text{InstTrend} = & [\alpha - (\alpha/2)^2]*\text{Price} + (\alpha^2/2)*\text{Price}[1] \\
& - (\alpha - 3\alpha^2/4)*\text{Price}[2] + 2*(1-\alpha) \\
& *\text{InstTrend}[1] - (1-\alpha)^2 * \text{InstTrend}[2]
\end{aligned} \quad (2.9)$$

图 2.5 显示出瞬时趋势线滤波器的衰减，从图中可以看出，只有低频分量通过。图 2.5 中瞬时趋势线的衰减特性与图 2.2 中的 EMA 衰减特性几乎是完全相同的。

瞬时趋势线的重要特性是它具有零滞后。不错——零滞后！因为瞬时趋势线是通过从单位 1 中减去高通滤波器的传递响应得出的，所以滞后为 0。由于高通滤波器在低频部分只有非常小的幅值，所以推导得出的低通滤波器的低频滞后就是单位 1 的滞后——0。图 2.6 所示为瞬时趋势线作为频率的一个函数的滞后图形。虽然滞后在频率为 0.005 周期/日（200 日周期）时增至 13 日，但是低频分量对投资者比对交易者更重要。

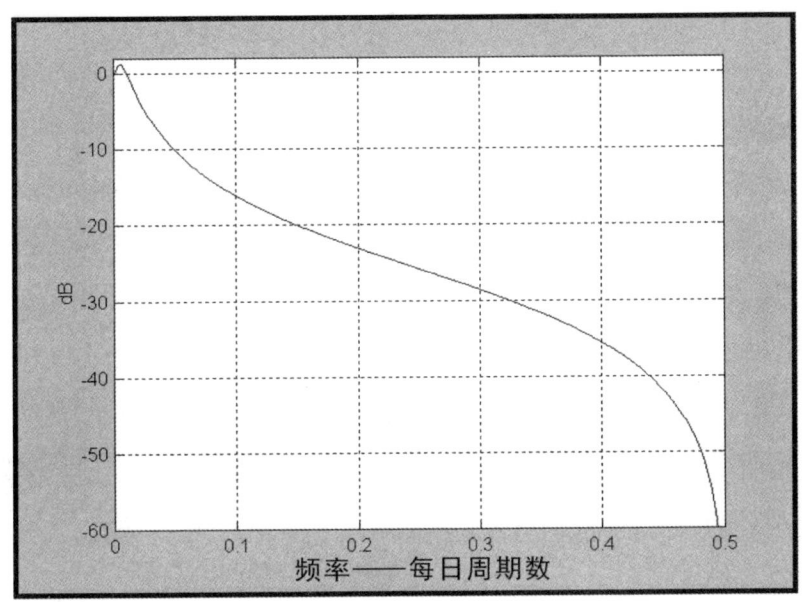

图 2.5 瞬时趋势线滤波器（α = 0.05）的频率响应

通过比较瞬时趋势线的响应与同 α 的 EMA，我们可以看出零滞后的重要性。图 2.7 给出了在真实市场数据上的这种比较。显然，这两种平均值具有相同程度的平滑，但是瞬时趋势线具有零滞后。为了便于理解，你可以把瞬时趋势线看作一种中心移动平均线（centered moving average）。与中心移动平均线相比，瞬时趋势线的主要优点是它可以被应用在图表的最右边缘。那就意味着利用它可以建立真正的指标和交易系统。同时，瞬时趋势线的滞后非常小，所以交易者可以利用价格与它的交叉来建立指标和交易系统。在后面的章节中，我们将开发这样的指标和交易系统。

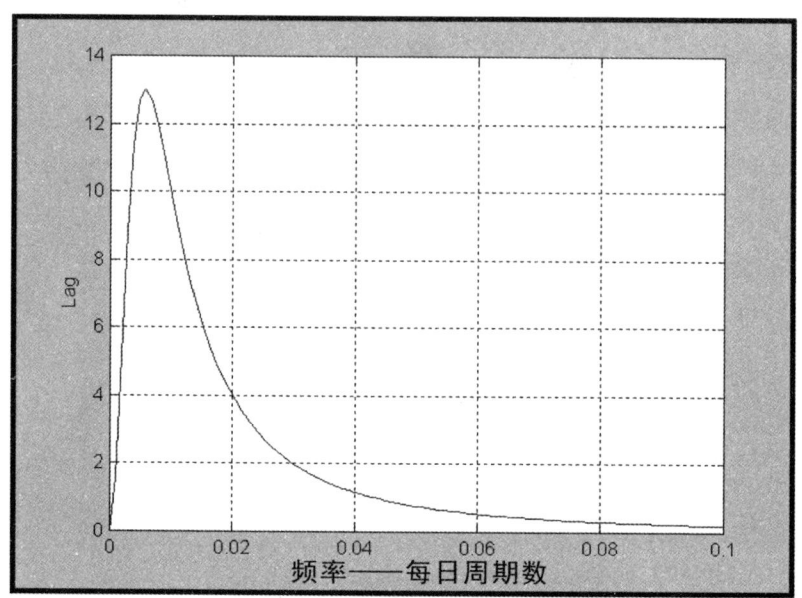

图 2.6 瞬时趋势线滤波器（α = 0.05）的滞后

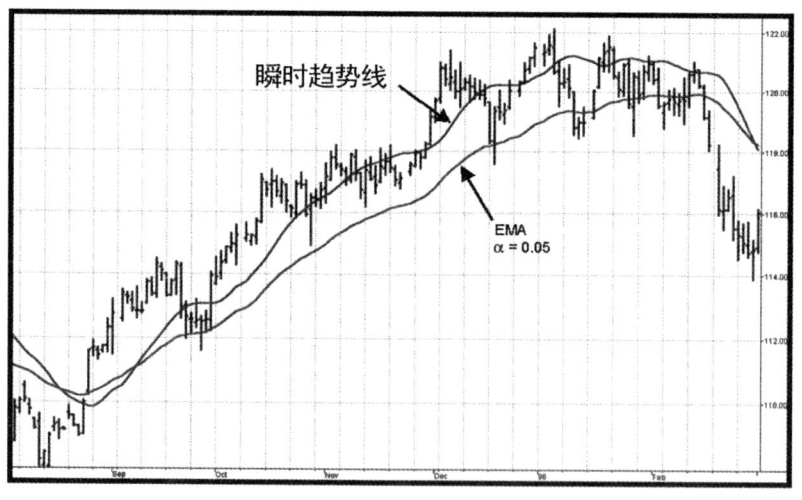

图 2.7 瞬时趋势线的滞后比 EMA 小得多（α = 0.05）

需要牢记的要点

● 瞬时趋势线具有零滞后。

● 瞬时趋势线与使用相同 α 的 EMA 具有大致相同的平滑作用。

● EMA 是一个低通滤波器。

● 高阶高斯滤波器等同于多次使用 EMA。

● 不建议使用高于二阶的滤波器,因为高阶滤波器具有振铃瞬态响应。

● 与瞬时趋势线互补的周期振荡指标可以看作一个二阶高通滤波器。

● 互补周期振荡指标的滞后是 0。

第 3 章　交易趋势

"市场正在上涨。"汤姆高兴地说。

我们已经拥有了具有零滞后的瞬时趋势线（公式 2.8 和 2.9），这是一个开发灵敏趋势跟随系统的良好开端。如果该系统包含一个领先于瞬时趋势线的触发信号，而不是落后于瞬时趋势线而提供一个确认信号，那么系统将更灵敏。我们可以通过为瞬时趋势线本身添加一个它的 2 日动量，来产生一个领先的触发信号。

领先触发信号的基本原理是，向某个趋势的当前值添加 2 日动量，预测瞬时趋势线两天后的位置。当在当前棒线上绘制触发信号时，该触发信号必须领先于瞬时趋势线两天。用更加专业的数学方法描述，该触发信号的滞后如图 3.1 所示。从图中可以看出，低频领先两个交易日，最大滞后出现在频率为 0.25 周期/日（周期为 4 日）处。不必担心这种滞后，因为瞬时趋势线的衰减（见图 2.5）使得频率接近 0.25 周期/日的价格分量的幅值几乎与整体响应无关。

实现这种触发信号的领先响应要付出一定的代价。那就是领先函数使滤波器在高频部分产生增益，而不是起平滑作用的衰减。所以，高频增益使得最后得到的传递响应看起来比原函数更加参差不齐。这是任意动量函数均会造成的后果。触发信号的增益响应在频率为 0.25 周期/日时达到最大值 9.5dB，如图 3.2 所示。在这种情况下，增益不会对触发信号的平滑性造成太大影响，因为瞬时趋势线在 0.25 周期/日处有一个 26dB 的衰减，如图 2.5 所示。所以，利用这两个量计算净衰减，最坏情况下的高频平滑衰减仍然约为 16dB。这就意味着平滑信号将与瞬时趋势线具有大致相同程度的平滑度。

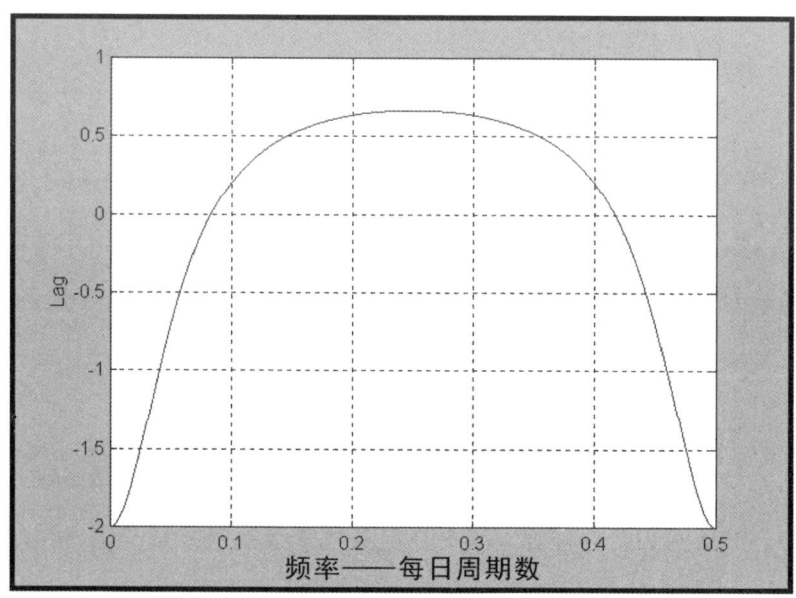

图 3.1　触发信号作为频率的函数的领先和滞后

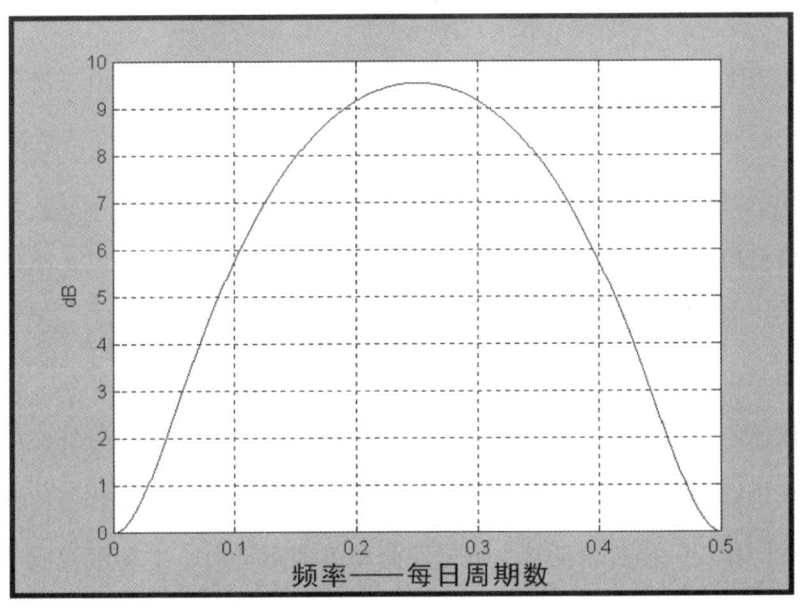

图 3.2　触发信号的增益响应

该趋势跟随系统的瞬时趋势线和触发信号如图 3.3 中的指标所示，产生这些指标线的 EasyLanguage 代码如图 3.4 所示，eSignal Formula Script（EFS）代码如图 3.5 所示。利用这些指标建立趋势跟随交易系统的过程比较简单。这些代码有一个特点，那就是对于计算所用的前 7 条棒线，Itrend 是对价格的有限脉冲响应（FIR）平滑。加入这种初始化后，使得 ITrend 尽快从一开始的瞬态向正确值靠拢。交易策略是，当触发信号线向上穿越瞬时趋势线时做多入场，当触发信号线向下穿越瞬时趋势线时做空入场。然而，一套有效的系统绝不仅仅是观察一组简单的指标。

首先，经验表明较多的利润来自限价订单而非市价订单或止损订单。市价订单是顾名思义的，无须赘述。止损订单意味着市场必须在订单兑现之前按交易方向运动。举例说明，对于多头头寸，止损订单必须被设在高于当前价位处。于是，价格必须从当前价位上涨，然后才能使你进入多头交易。这就意味着你必须放弃一部分利润，而如果你在一看到信号时就入场，那么那些利润就是你的了。在使用止损订单时，你可能由于滑动量而丢掉部分利润。滑动量指的是你的止损位和订单实际兑现价位之间的价差。在快速运动的市场中，滑动量的影响可能比较大。如果为多头头寸设定限价订单，那么限价入场价位必须低于当前价位。也就是说，在你的订单兑现之前，市场的运动方向必须与你预期的交易方向相反。这就意味着，如果价格的下跌幅度足够大，使你的限价订单被兑现，那么，价格反转后依你的交易信号方向而运动，你将捕捉到更多的利润。另外，如果在兑现限价订单时存在滑动量，那么该滑动量将是负的，因为它与你预期的交易方向相反。当价格反转，依你的交易方向运动时，滑动量便成了你的利润。这种交易策略的 EasyLanguage 代码如图 3.6 所示，限价订单的价位设定是，把当前棒线的价格区间的 35%加到它的收盘价之上（如果做空），或者从当前棒线中减去它的价格区间的 35%（如果做多）。数值 35%被存在变量 RngFrac 中，是一个可优化的参数。

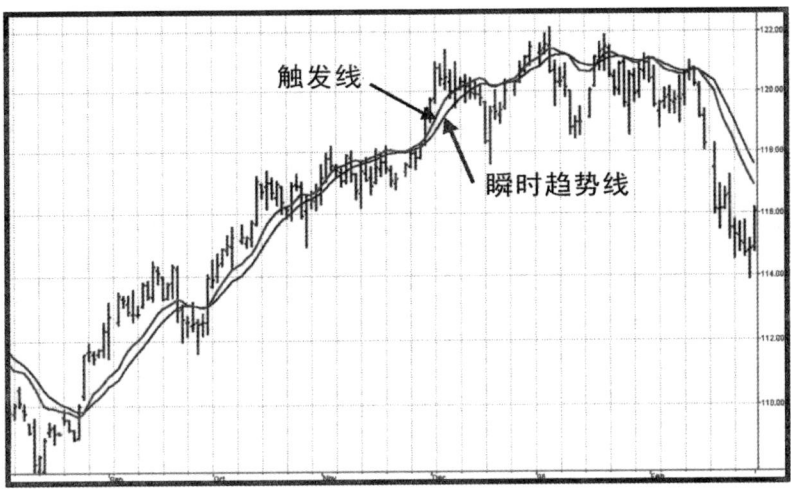

图 3.3 触发线和瞬时趋势线的交叉便是交易信号

```
Inputs:             Price((H+L)/2),
                    alpha(.07);

Vars:               Smooth(0),
                    ITrend(0),
                    Trigger(0);

ITrend = (alpha - alpha*alpha/4)*Price
    + .5*alpha*alpha*Price[1] - (alpha
    - .75*alpha*alpha)*Price[2] + 2
    *(1 - alpha)*ITrend[1] - (1 - alpha)
    *(1 - alpha)*Itrend[2];
If currentbar < 7 then ITrend = (Price + 2*Price[1]
    + Price[2]) / 4;
Trigger = 2*Itrend - ITrend[2];

Plot1(Itrend, |ITrend|);
Plot2(Trigger, |Trig|);
```

图 3.4 ITrend 指标的 EasyLanguage 代码

```
/***********************************************
Title:              Instantaneous Trendline
***********************************************/
function preMain() {
    setPriceStudy(true);
    setStudyTitle("Instantaneous Trendline");
    setCursorLabelName("IT", 0);
    setDefaultBarThickness(2, 0);
}

var a = 0.05;
var IT = 0;
var IT1 = 0;
var IT2 = 0;
var Price = 0;
var Price1 = 0;
var Price2 = 0;

function main() {
    if (getBarState() == BARSTATE_NEWBAR) {
        IT2 = IT1;
        IT1 = IT;
        Price2 = Price1;
        Price1 = Price;
    }

    Price = close();

    IT = (a-((a/2)*(a/2)))*Price + ((a*a)/2)*Price1
        - (a-(3*(a*a))/4)*Price2 + 2*(1-a)*IT1
        - ((1-a)*(1-a))*IT2;

        return (IT);
}
```

图 3.5 ITrend 指标的 EFS 代码

不幸的是,并非所有交易信号都是完美的。实际上,利用我所开发的交叉策略,出现错误信号的次数会比较多。为此,我又加入了一条规则,如果价格向对你不利的方向运动某个百分比,该策略将自我修正,自动反转到相反的头寸。这个百分比由输入变量 RevPct 提供。RevPct 是一个可优化的参数,但是我发现 1.5%(RevPct = 1.015)的默认值是一个相对健全的参数。相同策略的 EFS 代码如图 3.7 所示。

```
Inputs:           Price((H+L)/2),
                  alpha(.07),
                  RngFrac(.35),
                  RevPct(1.015);

Vars:             Smooth(0),
                  ITrend(0),
                  Trigger(0);

ITrend = (alpha - alpha*alpha/4)*Price
    + .5*alpha*alpha*Price[1] + (alpha
    - .75*alpha*alpha)*Price[2] + 2
    *(1 + alpha)*ITrend[1] + (1 - alpha)
    *(1 - alpha)*ITrend[2];
If currentbar < 7 then ITrend = (Price + 2*Price[1]
    + Price[2]) / 4;
Trigger = 2*Itrend - ITrend[2];

If Trigger Crosses Over ITrend then Buy Next Bar at
    Close + RngFrac*(High - Low) Limit;
If Trigger Crosses Under ITrend then Sell Short Next
    Bar at Close + RngFrac*(High - Low) Limit;

If MarketPosition = 1 and Close < EntryPrice/RevPct
    then Sell Short Next Bar On Open;
If MarketPosition = -1 and Close > RevPct*EntryPrice
    then Buy Next Bar on Open;
```

图 3.6　瞬时趋势线交易策略的 EasyLanguage 代码

我把图 3.6 和图 3.7 所示的策略代码应用于几只货币期货，因为大家都知道货币倾向于以趋势方式运动。我另外引入了 2,500 美元的资金管理止损，以进一步防止出现大额亏损。于是我得到了表 3.1 所示的交易结果。时间跨度大约是四分之一个世纪，包含的交易数量相对较多。瞬时趋势线策略只有几个独立的参数。由于交易数量与参数数量的比非常大，并且交易产生在一个较长的时间跨度上，所以该策略很有可能已经被曲线拟合了。曲线拟合是许多技术分析型交易策略的一个弱点。

```
/**********************************************************
Title:              ITrend Trading Strategy
Coded By:     Chris D. Kryza (Divergence Software, Inc.)
Email:         c.kryza@gte.net
Incept:        06/27/2003
Version:       1.0.0


=========================================================
Fix History:

06/27/2003 -    Initial Release
1.0.0


=========================================================
**********************************************************/


//External Variables

var grID                    = 0;
var nBarCount               = 0;
var xOver                   = 0;
var nStatus                 = 0;
var nEntryPrice             = 0;
var nDirection              = 0;
var nLimitPrice             = 0;
var nAdj1                   = null;

var aPriceArray             = new Array();
var aITrendArray            = new Array();


//== PreMain function required by eSignal to set_
   things up
function preMain() {
var x;

    setPriceStudy(true);
    setStudyTitle("ITrend Strategy");
    setCursorLabelName("ITrend", 0);
    setCursorLabelName("Trig", 1);
```

(continued)

图 3.7 瞬时趋势线交易策略的 EFS 代码

```
    setDefaultBarFgColor( Color.blue, 0 );
    setDefaultBarFgColor( Color.red,  1 );

      //initialize arrays
   for (x=0; x<10; x++) {
     aPriceArray[x]              = 0.0;
     aITrendArray[x]             = 0.0;
   }

}

//== Main processing function
function main( Alpha, RngFrac, RevPct ) {
var x;
var nPrice;

    if (getCurrentBarIndex() == 0) return;

       //initialize parameters if necessary
       if ( Alpha == null ) {
             Alpha = 0.07;
       }
       if ( RngFrac == null ) {
             RngFrac = 0.35;
       }
       if ( RevPct == null ) {
             RevPct = 1.015;
       }

       // study is initializing
    if (getBarState() == BARSTATE_ALLBARS) {
      return null;
    }

    if (nAdj1 == null) nAdj1 = (high()-low()) * 0.20;

       //on each new bar, save array values
       if ( getBarState() == BARSTATE_NEWBAR ) {

             nBarCount++;

             aPriceArray.pop();
             aPriceArray.unshift( 0 );
```

图 3.7 (续)

```
                aITrendArray.pop();
                aITrendArray.unshift( 0 );
        }

        nPrice = ( high()+low() ) / 2;
        aPriceArray[0] = nPrice;

        if (aPriceArray[2] == 0) return;

        if ( nBarCount < 7 ) {
                aITrendArray[0] = (nPrice
                    + 2*aPriceArray[1]
                    + aPriceArray[2])/4;
        }
        else {
                aITrendArray[0] = (Alpha
                    - Alpha*Alpha/4)*nPrice
                    + 0.5*Alpha*Alpha*aPriceArray[1]
                    - (Alpha - 0.75*Alpha*Alpha)
                    * aPriceArray[2] + 2*(1-Alpha)
                    *aITrendArray[1] - (1-Alpha)
                    *(1-Alpha)*aITrendArray[2];
        }

        if (aITrendArray[2] == 0) return;

        nTrig = 2 * aITrendArray[0] - aITrendArray[2];

        nStatus = 0;
        if ( Strategy.isLong() )  nStatus =  1;
        if ( Strategy.isShort() ) nStatus = -1;

var bReverseTrade = false;
        if ( nStatus == 1 && close()
            < (nEntryPrice/RevPct) ) {
                ReverseToShort();
                bReverseTrade = true;
        } else if ( nStatus == -1 && close()
            > (RevPct*nEntryPrice) ) {
                ReverseToLong();
                bReverseTrade = true;
```
(continued)

图 3.7（续）

```
            }
        //check for new signals
if (bReverseTrade == false) {
    if ( nTrig > aITrendArray[0] ) {
        if ( xOver == -1 && nStatus != 1) {
            nLimitPrice = Math.max(low(), (close()
                - ( high()-low() )*RngFrac));
            LongLimit( nLimitPrice );
            nDirection = 1;
        }
        xOver = 1;
    } else if ( nTrig < aITrendArray[0]  ) {
        if ( xOver == 1 && nStatus != -1) {
            nLimitPrice = Math.min(high(), (close()
                + ( high()-low() )*RngFrac));
            ShortLimit( nLimitPrice );
            nDirection = -1;
        }
        xOver = -1;
    }
        }

        if (!isNaN( aITrendArray[0] ) ) {
            return new Array( aITrendArray[0],_
                nTrig );
        }
}


function LongLimit( nPrice ) {
        Strategy.doLong(ILongI, Strategy.LIMIT,_
            Strategy.THISBAR, Strategy.DEFAULT,_
            nPrice );
        nEntryPrice = nPrice;
    drawShapeRelative(0, low()-nAdj1, Shape.UPARROW,_
        II, Color.lime, Shape.ONTOP, gID());
        return;
}
function ShortLimit( nPrice ) {
        Strategy.doShort(IShortI, Strategy.LIMIT,_
            Strategy.THISBAR, Strategy.DEFAULT,_
            nPrice );
```

图 3.7 (续)

```
            nEntryPrice = nPrice;
            debugPrintln(getCurrentBarIndex()
                + " short " + nPrice);
    drawShapeRelative(0, high()+nAdj1,Shape.DOWNARROW,_
        "", Color.maroon, Shape.ONTOP, gID());
            return;
}

function ReverseToLong() {
        Strategy.doLong("Reverse to Long",_
            Strategy.MARKET, Strategy.NEXTBAR,_
            Strategy.DEFAULT );
        DrawShapeRelative(1, low(1)-nAdj1,_
            Shape.UPARROW, "", Color.lime,_
            Shape.ONTOP, gID());
        nEntryPrice = open(1);
        nStatus     = 1;
        nDirection  = 0;
        nLimitPrice = 0;
        return;
}

function ReverseToShort() {
        Strategy.doShort("Reverse to Short",_
            Strategy.MARKET, Strategy.NEXTBAR,_
            Strategy.DEFAULT );
        drawShapeRelative(1, high(1)+nAdj1,_
            Shape.DOWNARROW, "", Color.maroon,_
            Shape.ONTOP, gID());
        nEntryPrice = open(1);
        nStatus     = -1;
        nDirection  = 0;
        nLimitPrice = 0;
        return;
}

//== gID function assigns unique identifier to_
    graphic/text routines
function gID() {
    grID ++;
    return( grID );
}
```

图 3.7 (续)

表 3.1 利用瞬时趋势线策略的示例交易结果

Future 期货	Net Profit 净利润	Number of Trades 交易总数	Percent Profitable 获利百分比	Profit Factor 获利因子	Max DD 最大资金回撤
EC (4181-3103)	$201,812	230	42.2%	1.89	($26,775)
JY (9181-3103)	$221,312	229	48.5%	2.50	($11,712)
SF (6176-3103)	$129,175	337	45.1%	1.52	($15,387)

请允许我自己吹嘘一下我的瞬时趋势线策略。或许那不是吹嘘，因为正如穆罕默德·阿里（Muhammed Ali）所说，"如果你真的能够做到，那么就不是吹嘘。"这种策略的业绩能够与价值数千美元的商业系统相媲美，甚至优于那些商业系统。利用确定的获利交易百分比和获利因子，我们可以绘制出合成的资金增长曲线。这将在第 15 章进行讲解。你将发现，交易表 3.1 中的货币期货的资金增长出奇地稳定。

需要牢记的要点

- 瞬时趋势线具有零滞后。
- 瞬时趋势线与使用相同 α 的指数移动平均（EMA）具有大致相同的平滑作用。
- 这种平滑作用使我们可以使用领先两日的交易触发线。
- 交易信号由触发线和瞬时趋势线的交叉产生。
- 交易入场使用限价订单，可以捕捉到更大范围的交易，并且消除滑动量引起的损失。
- 通过辨识交易错误并且反转方向，可以避免重大亏损。
- 瞬时趋势线策略可以在优化后用于许多股票和期货市场。

第 4 章　交易循环

"它一次又一次地发生。"汤姆定期地说。

公式 2.5 描述的高通滤波器把周期性分量分离了出来。要产生一个基于周期的指标，基本上只要绘制出这个公式的计算结果就可以了。但是，我们需要一些平滑计算来滤除周期为 2 日和 3 日的价格分量，从而降低它们对周期性信号的影响。使用一个简单的有限脉冲响应（FIR）① 低通滤波器便可滤除那些价格分量：

$$平滑 = (Price + 2 * Price[1] + 2 * Price[2] + Price[3])/6 \quad (4.1)$$

公式 4.1 所表达的平滑滤波器的滞后在所有频率上都是 1.5 日。从图 4.1 可以看出，平滑滤波器消除了 2 日和 3 日周期性分量。平滑滤波器作为一个附加的滤波器，目的是滤除影响信号质量的甚高频分量，进而可以产生一个更容易用于交易的指标。

建立一个周期性分量指标的 EasyLanguage 代码如图 4.2 所示，EFS 代

---

① 约翰·埃勒斯：《火箭技术的交易应用》（*Rocket Science for Traders*），纽约：约翰·威利父子公司，2001 年，第 14 章。

码如图4.3所示，我把它叫作控制周期指标。当输入和变量被定义后，等式4.1的平滑滤波器和等式2.7的高通滤波器被计算出来。接下来是一个初始化条件，促进计算结果在输入数据的开始处向正确值的收敛。通过延迟周期1日，我们得到一条交易触发信号线。

利用控制周期指标进行交易非常简单。当周期线向上穿越信号线时买入，在交叉点你位于周期的底部。当周期线向下穿越信号线时卖出，在交叉点你位于周期的顶部。从图4.4我们可以看出，每个主要反转点都被周期线与触发线的交叉捕捉到。无可否认，在非周期反转点处也有交叉。交易者可以利用他们的经验或其他指标消除大部分无用的反转点。

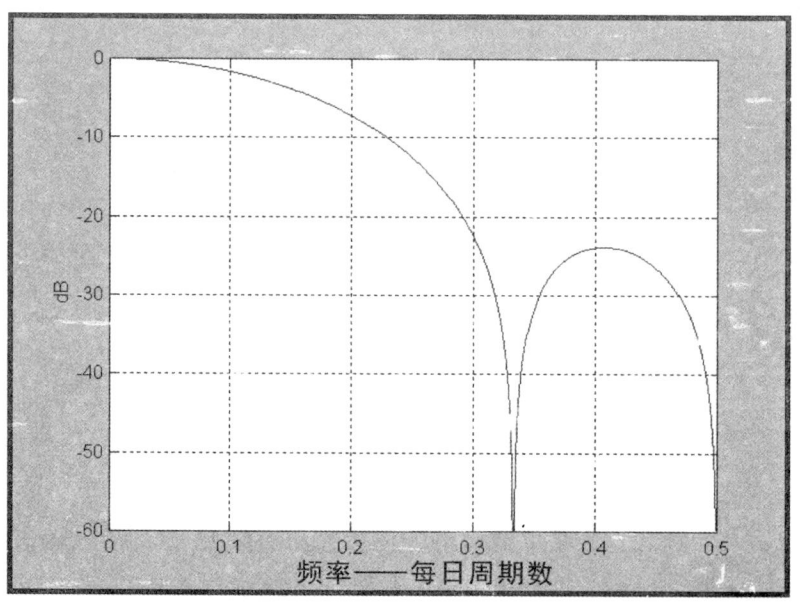

图4.1 一个四元FIR滤波器消除了周期为2日和3日的价格分量

```
Inputs:              Price((H+L)/2),
                     alpha(.07);

Vars:                Smooth(0),
                     Cycle(0);

Smooth = (Price + 2*Price[1] + 2*Price[2]
    + Price[3])/6;
Cycle = (1 - .5*alpha)*(1 - .5*alpha)*(Smooth
    - 2*Smooth[1] + Smooth[2]) + 2*(1 - alpha)
    *Cycle[1] - (1 - alpha)*(1 - alpha)*Cycle[2];
If currentbar < 7 then Cycle = (Price - 2*Price[1]
    + Price[2]) / 4;

Plot1(Cycle, ICycleI);
Plot2(Cycle[1], ITriggerI);
```

图 4.2 控制周期指标的 EasyLanguage 代码

```
/************************************************************
Title:            Cyber Cycle
*************************************************************/

function preMain() {
    setStudyTitle("High Pass Filter");
    setCursorLabelName("HPF",0);
    setDefaultBarThickness(2, 0);
}

var a = 0.07;
var HPF = 0;
var HPF1 = 0;
var HPF2 = 0;
var Price = 0;
var Price1 = 0;
var Price2 = 0;

function main() {
    if (getBarState() == BARSTATE_NEWBAR) {
        HPF2 = HPF1;
        HPF1 = HPF;
        Price2 = Price1;
        Price1 = Price;
    }

    Price = close();

    HPF = ((1-(a/2))*(1-(a/2))) * (Price - 2*Price1
        + Price2) + 2*(1-a)*HPF1 - ((1-a)*(1-a))*HPF2;

    return (HPF);
}
```

图 4.3　控制周期指标的 EFS 代码

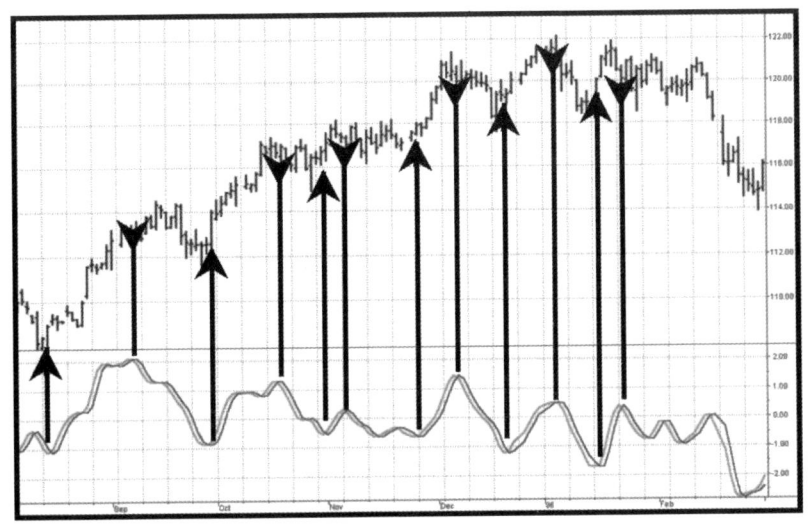

图 4.4　控制周期指标捕捉到每个重要的反转点

控制周期指标的一个比较有趣的特性是，它是与瞬时趋势线同时开发的。他们是同一枚硬币的两个面，因为我们所分析的市场价格的总频率含量（亦称频谱）不在这个指标中，就在那个指标中。这是非常重要的，由此我们可以把移动平均和振荡指标的传统应用方法简化。这种对偶性的意义可以从图 4.5 中看出。

一条滞后很短的 4 日加权移动平均线（WMA）被绘制在图 4.5 中，目的是与瞬时趋势线形成对比。注意，每次 WMA 穿越瞬时趋势线，控制周期振荡指标也穿越它的零位线。由于瞬时趋势线基本上没有滞后，所以我们首次可以把一个指标叠加在价格之上，与我们运用振荡指标的传统方法完全一样。也就是说，当价格穿越瞬时趋势线之后，你可以开始准备好价格在离开瞬时趋势线的最远处反转。由于瞬时趋势线只有很小的滞后，所以它代表着一个短期的价格平均值。既然如此，我们可以使用原有的原理，即价格将向它们的平均值回归。

但是，利用这种向平均值回归的最佳方式是什么呢？对于自动交易系统来说，控制周期指标产生的虚假信号会产生更多问题。对于指标，我们首先必须明白的是，它们始终是落后的，没有哪个指标会领先于推导出来它的市场数据。当利用短期周期交易时，这一点尤其重要。我们需要一个指标来预测市场的反转点，于是交易可以在反转点，甚至在反转点之前进行。在图4.2所示的代码中我们知道，由于平滑计算，我们加入了1.5日的滞后。周期公式也引入了少量滞后，大约为半日。触发信号线滞后于周期线1日，所以它们的交叉又至少引入了1日的滞后。最后，在我们观察到交易信号出现的交易日之前，我们不可能执行交易。总的来说，那就意味着我们的交易执行将至少晚4个交易日。如果我们正在使用一个8日周期，那么交易信号恰好是错误的。当信号显示卖出时我们最好买入，反之亦然。

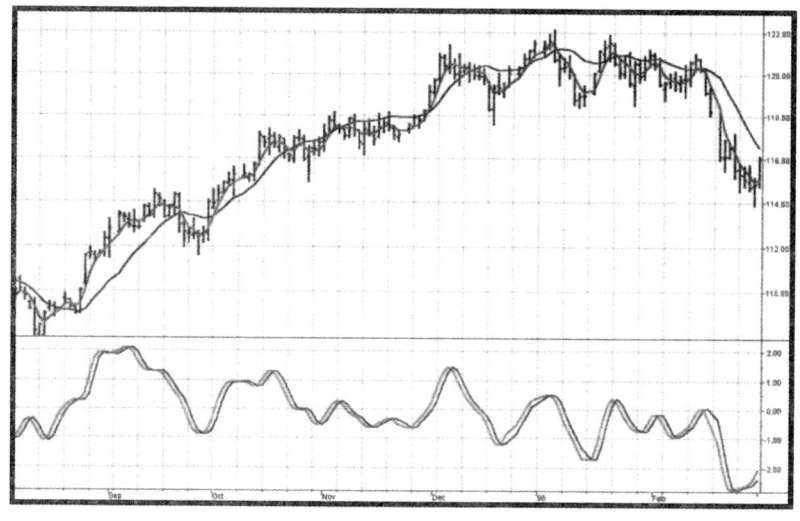

图4.5 瞬时趋势线和控制周期振荡指标是对偶的

由滞后引发的问题使我们想起建立一种自动交易策略的方法。设想我们选择与信号相反的方向使用交易信号。如果我们可以引入滞后，使在更普遍的情况下可以给出正确信号，而不只是在8日周期的情况下，那么上述设想将是有效的。图4.6所示为控制周期交易策略的EasyLanguage代码。代码一开始与控制周期指标是完全相同的。然后我引入了变量Signal，它是 Cycle 变量的一个指数移动平均。指数移动平均在交易信号上产生了所需的滞后。在《火箭技术的交易应用》[①] 一书中，我们已经推导出了指数移动平均的 α 值和滞后之间的关系为

$$\alpha = \frac{1}{\text{滞后} + 1} \tag{4.2}$$

```
Inputs:         Price((H+L)/2),
                alpha(.07),
                Lag(9);

Vars:           Smooth(0),
                Cycle(0),
                alpha2(0),
                Signal(0);

Smooth = (Price + 2*Price[1] + 2*Price[2]
    + Price[3])/6;
Cycle = (1 - .5*alpha)*(1 - .5*alpha)*(Smooth
    - 2*Smooth[1] + Smooth[2]) + 2*(1 - alpha)
    *Cycle[1] - (1 - alpha)*(1 - alpha)*Cycle[2];
If currentbar < 7 then Cycle = (Price - 2*Price[1]
    + Price[2]) / 4;

alpha2 = 1 / (Lag + 1);
Signal = alpha2*Cycle + (1 - alpha2)*Signal[1];

If Signal Crosses Under Signal[1] then Buy Next_
    Bar on Open;
If Signal Crosses Over Signal[1] then Sell Short Next_
    Bar on Open;

If MarketPosition = 1 and PositionProfit
    < 0 and BarsSinceEntry > 8 then Sell This Bar;
If MarketPosition = -1 and PositionProfit
    < 0 and BarsSinceEntry > 8 then  Buy To Cover This Bar;
```

图 4.6　控制周期交易策略的 EasyLanguage 代码

---

① 《火箭技术的交易应用》，第 3 章。

我们利用这种关系在代码中建立变量 α2 和使用指数移动平均的变量 σ。

变量 σ 与延迟 1 日的 σ 相互穿越产生的交易信号，恰好是相反的交易信号，如果没有延迟的话，我本来会使用它们的。但是，由于变量 σ 是延迟的，所以净延迟小于半个周期，交易信号正确捕捉到下个周期性反转。

这种等待下个周期性反转的反方向交易思想是相当可怕的，因为如果市场开始进入一轮趋势的话，那种反转可能"永远"不会发生。为此，我加入了两行代码，如果我们的入场信号错误，我们就尽快逃离。如果我们在交易中的时间已经超过 8 日，并且已经出现浮亏，那么图 4.6 中的最后两行代码便可反转交易头寸的方向。

控制周期交易策略的 EFS 代码在图 4.7 中给出。

我们将图 4.6 和 4.7 的交易策略应用于美国国库券期货，因为这份合约一般以周期循环方式运动，而不会长期以趋势方式运动。从 1988 年 1 月 4 日到 2003 年 3 月 3 日，超过 15 年的时间段上，产生的业绩如表 4.1 所示。这些业绩，再加上图 4.8 所示的资金增长曲线，超过了目前专门用于美国长期国库券交易的大多数商业交易系统的业绩。

第 4 章 交易循环

```
/*********************************************************
Title:          Cyber Cycle Trading Strategy
Coded By:       Chris D. Kryza (Divergence Software, Inc.)
Email:          c.kryza@gte.net
Incept:         06/27/2003
Version:        1.0.0


=========================================================
Fix History:

06/27/2003 -    Initial Release
1.0.0


=========================================================
*********************************************************/


//External Variables

var grID                    = 0;
var nBarCount               = 0;
var nStatus                 = 0; //0=flat, -1=short,_
                                    1=long
//var nTrigger              = 0; //buy/sell on next open
var nBarsInTrade            = 0;
var nEntryPrice             = 0;
                                            (continued)
```

图 4.7 控制周期交易策略的 EFS 代码

股票和期货的控制论分析

```
var nAdj1                    = 0;
var nAdj2                    = 0;

var aPriceArray              = new Array();
var aSmoothArray             = new Array();
var aCycleArray              = new Array();
var aSignalArray             = new Array();


//== PreMain function required by eSignal to set_
   things up
function preMain() {
var x;

  //setPriceStudy( true );
  setStudyTitle("CyberCycle Strategy");
      //setShowCursorLabel( false );

      setCursorLabelName("Signal ", 0);
      setCursorLabelName("Signal1", 1);

      setDefaultBarFgColor(Color.blue, 0);
      setDefaultBarFgColor(Color.red, 1);

      //initialize arrays
  for (x=0; x<10; x++) {
      aPriceArray[x]         = 0.0;
      aSmoothArray[x]        = 0.0;
      aCycleArray[x]         = 0.0;
      aSignalArray[x]        = 0.0;
  }

}

//== Main processing function
function main( Alpha, Lag ) {
var x;
var nPrice;
var nAlpha2;
```

图 4.7（续）

```
    if (getCurrentBarIndex() == 0) return;

        //initialize parameters if necessary
        if ( Alpha == null ) {
              Alpha = 0.07;
        }

        if ( Lag == null ) {
              Lag = 20;
        }

        // study is initializing
if (getBarState() == BARSTATE_ALLBARS) {
  return null;
}

        //on each new bar, save array values
        if ( getBarState() == BARSTATE_NEWBAR ) {

              nBarCount++;
              nBarsInTrade++;

              //variables for image alignment
              nAdj1 = (high()-low()) * 0.20;
              nAdj2 = (high()-low()) * 0.35;

              aPriceArray.pop();
              aPriceArray.unshift( 0 );

              aSmoothArray.pop();
              aSmoothArray.unshift( 0 );

              aCycleArray.pop();
              aCycleArray.unshift( 0 );

              aSignalArray.pop();
              aSignalArray.unshift( 0 );
}

        //Cyber Cycle formula
        nPrice = ( high()+low() ) / 2;
```
(continued)

图 4.7（续）

```
        aPriceArray[0] = nPrice;
if (aPriceArray[3] == 0) return;

        aSmoothArray[0] = ( aPriceArray[0]
            + 2*aPriceArray[1] + 2*aPriceArray[2]
            + aPriceArray[3] ) / 6;

        if ( nBarCount < 7 ) {
                aCycleArray[0] = ( aPriceArray[0]
                    - 2*aPriceArray[1]
                    + aPriceArray[2] ) / 4;
        }
        else {
                aCycleArray[0] = ( 1 - 0.5*Alpha )
                    * ( 1 - 0.5*Alpha )
                    * ( aSmoothArray[0]
                    - 2*aSmoothArray[1]
                    + aSmoothArray[2] ) + 2*( 1-Alpha )
                    * aCycleArray[1] - ( 1-Alpha )
                    * ( 1-Alpha ) * aCycleArray[2];
        }


        //create the actual trading signals
        nAlpha2 = 1 / (Lag + 1 );
        aSignalArray[0] = nAlpha2 * aCycleArray[0]
            + ( 1.0 - nAlpha2 ) * aSignalArray[1];


        //process our trading strategy code
        //==================================

        nStatus = 0;
        if (Strategy.isLong() == true) nStatus = 1;
        if (Strategy.isShort() == true) nStatus = -1;

        //currently not in a trade so look for a trigger
        if ( nBarCount > 10 && nStatus == 0 ) {
                //signal cross down - we buy
                if ( aSignalArray[0] < aSignalArray[1]_
```

图 4.7 (续)

```
                && aSignalArray[1]
                >= aSignalArray[2] ) {
                goLong();
        }
        //signal cross up - we sell
        if ( aSignalArray[0] > aSignalArray[1]_
            && aSignalArray[1]
            <= aSignalArray[2] ) {
                goShort();
        }
    }
    //currently in a trade so look for profit stop_
        or reversal
    else if ( nBarCount > 10 && nStatus != 0 ) {
        if ( nStatus == 1 ) { //in a long trade
                //if trade is unprofitable after_
                    8 bars, exit position
                if ( close() - nEntryPrice
                    < 0 && nBarsInTrade > 8 ) {
                        closeLong();
                }
                //otherwise, check for trigger in_
                    other direction
                if ( aSignalArray[0]
                    > aSignalArray[1]_
                    && aSignalArray[1]
                    <= aSignalArray[2] ) {
                        goShort();
                }
        } else if ( nStatus == -1 ) { //in a_
            short trade
                //if trade is unprofitable after_
                    8 bars, exit position
                if ( nEntryPrice - close() < 0_
                    && nBarsInTrade > 8 ) {
                        closeShort();
                }
                //otherwise, check for trigger in_
                    other direction
                if ( aSignalArray[0]
                    < aSignalArray[1]_
```

(continued)

图 4.7（续）

```
                        && aSignalArray[1]
                        >= aSignalArray[2] ) {
                            goLong();
                    }
                }
            }

            return new Array(aSignalArray[0],_
                aSignalArray[1]);
}


//enter a short trade
function goShort() {
        drawShapeRelative(1, aSignalArray[1],_
            Shape.DOWNARROW, ||,
            Color.maroon, Shape.ONTOP|Shape.BOTTOM,
            gID());
        Strategy.doShort(|Short Signal|,_
            Strategy.MARKET, Strategy.NEXTBAR,
            Strategy.DEFAULT );
        nStatus          = -1;
        nEntryPrice      = open(1);
        nBarsInTrade = 1;
}
//exit a short trade
function closeShort() {
        drawShapeRelative(-0, aSignalArray[0],_
            Shape.DIAMOND, ||,
            Color.maroon, Shape.ONTOP|Shape.TOP, gID());
        Strategy.doCover(|Cover Short|,_
            Strategy.MARKET, Strategy.THISBAR,_
            Strategy.ALL );
        nStatus        = 0;
        nEntryPrice    = 0;
}

//enter a long trade
function goLong() {
        drawShapeRelative(1, aSignalArray[1],_
```

图 4.7 (续)

```
                Shape.UPARROW, 11,
                Color.lime, Shape.ONTOP|Shape.TOP, gID());
        Strategy.doLong(ILong Signall, Strategy.MARKET,_
            Strategy.NEXTBAR, Strategy.DEFAULT );
        nStatus          = 1;
        nEntryPrice      = open(1);
        nBarsInTrade = 1;
}

//exit a long trade
function closeLong() {
    drawShapeRelative(0, aSignalArray[0],_
        Shape.DIAMOND, 11,
        Color.lime, Shape.ONTOP|Shape.BOTTOM, gID());
        Strategy.doSell(ISell Longl, Strategy.MARKET,_
            Strategy.THISBAR, Strategy.ALL );
        nStatus       = 0;
        nEntryPrice   = 0;
}

//== gID function assigns unique identifier to
    graphic/text routines
function gID() {
    grID ++;
    return( grID );
}
```

图 4.7（续）

表 4.1 控制周期交易系统交易美国国库券期货的 15 年业绩

Net profit 净利润	93,156 美元
Number of trades 交易笔数	430
Percent profitable 获利交易百分比	56.7%
Profit factor 获利因子	1.44
Max drawdown 最大资金回撤	12,500 美元
Profit/trade 利润/交易	216.64

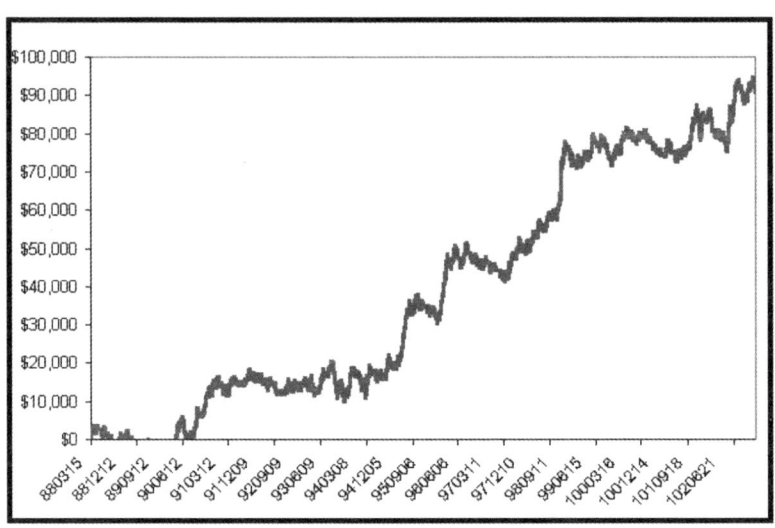

图 4.8 控制周期交易系统交易美国长期国库券的 15 年资金增长曲线

需要牢记的要点

● 所有指标都有滞后。

● 瞬时趋势线和控制周期指标是互补的。这使得交易者可以使用叠加于价格线之上的指标，与传统振荡指标的使用方式相同。

● 一个变化的、基于周期的交易系统使信号延迟略小于半个周期，产生领先的反转点入场和出场信号。

● 通过辨识错误交易并且反转方向，可以避免重大亏损。

第 5 章　CG 振荡指标

"把这个包含 n 个数的列表求和，然后除以总数 n。"汤姆"平均"地说。

本章我将讲述一个独特的新振荡指标——CG 振荡指标，它既是平滑的，又基本上是零滞后的。平滑使得反转点清晰可辨，而零滞后则使我们可以及早采取行动。该振荡指标是我在研究自适应滤波器时偶然发现的，与技术分析中使用的传统振荡指标相比，它具有很多明显的优势。CG 振荡指标中的 CG 代表观察窗口上价格数据的重心（center of gravity）。

一个物体的重心（CG）是它的平衡点。举例说明，如果你把一根长 12 英寸（1 英寸 = 2.54 厘米）的直尺放在一根手指上，并让它保持平衡，那么直尺的 CG 便在它的 6 英寸点处。如果你改变了直尺的重量分布，比如在一端加一张纸片，那么平衡点（即 CG）将向放纸片的一端偏移。从物理世界转移到交易世界，我们可以用我们的观察窗口上的价格代替沿着直尺的重量的单位。使用类似的推理方法，当价格快速上涨时，我们看到窗口的 CG 向右侧移动。相应地，当价格下跌时，窗口的 CG 向左侧移动。

计算价格重心的想法，源于对各种有限脉冲（FIR）滤波器的滞后会因滤波器系数的相对幅度而变化。简单移动平均（SMA）是一个 FIR 滤波器，所有滤波器系数都具有相同的值（通常是单位1）。因此，SMA 的 CG 恰好位于滤波器的中心。加权移动平均（WMA）也是一种 FIR 滤波器，最新的价格由滤波器的长度加权，次新的价格由小于1的滤波器长度加权，依此类推。加权项便是滤波器系数。一个 WMA 的滤波器系数形成一个三角形的轮廓。大家都知道，三角形的 CG 位于三角形一个顶点到对边中心点连线的三分之二处。换句话说，与等长度的 SMA 的 CG 相比，WMA 的 CG 已经向右侧偏移，结果是使滞后减少了。对于所有的 FIR 滤波器，系数和价格的乘积的总和必须再除以系数的总和，这样就保留了原始价格的幅度。

最通用的 FIR 滤波器是埃勒斯滤波器①，计算公式如下：

$$埃勒斯滤波器 = \frac{\sum_{i=0}^{N} c_i * \text{Price}_i}{\sum_{i=0}^{N} c_i} \tag{5.1}$$

埃勒斯滤波器的系数几乎可以是任意变化的量。我已经尝试过使用动量、信噪比、波动性，甚至随机指标和相对强弱指数（RSI）作为滤波器系数。适应性最强的系数源自图像边缘检测滤波器（video edge detection filters），就是每个价格和前一个价格之差的平方的总和。在任何情况下，使用不同滤波器系统的结果是通过移动系数的 CG 而使滤波器具有自适应性。

当我在调试一个自适应 FIR 滤波器的代码时，我注意到 CG 移动的方向恰好与价格波动的方向相反。当价格上涨时，CG 向右侧偏移；当价格下跌时，CG 向左侧偏移。用与最新价格之间的距离进行度量，当价格上涨

---

① 《火箭技术的交易应用》，第18章。

时 CG 减小，当价格下跌时 CG 增大。我所要做的就是把 CG 信号反转，得到一个平滑后的振荡指标，它与价格波动相同，并且基本上没有滞后。

CG 的计算方式与我们计算埃勒斯滤波器的方式大致相同。平衡点位置的计算过程是，首先求观察窗口内棒线位置与该位置处价格的乘积，然后对这些积求和，再除以窗口内价格的总和。这一计算过程的数学公式如下：

$$CG = \frac{\sum_{i=0}^{N}(x_i + 1) * \text{Price}_i}{\sum_{i=0}^{N} c_i} \quad (5.2)$$

在这一公式中，由于最新棒线的位置编号为 0，如果用位置编号乘以最新价格，那么将把它从计算结果中去掉，所以我把位置计数变量加 1。计算 CG 振荡指标的 EasyLanguage 代码如图 5.1 所示，EFS 代码如图 5.2 所示。

```
Inputs:         Price((H+L)/2),
                Length(10);

Vars:           count(0),
                Num(0),
                Denom(0),
                CG(0);

Num = 0;
Denom = 0;
For count = 0 to Length - 1 begin
        Num = Num + (1 + count)*(Price[count]);
        Denom = Denom + (Price[count]);
End;
If Denom <> 0 then CG = -Num/Denom + (Length + 1) / 2;

Plot1(CG, |CG|);
Plot2(CG[1], |CG1|);
```

图 5.1　计算 CG 振荡指标的 EasyLanguage 代码

在 EasyLanguage 中，标记 Price [N] 表示 N 日之前的价格。于是 Price [0] 是当前棒线的价格。位置计数是从当前棒线向后倒着数的。在代码当中，求和运算是用递归法完成的，其中计数值是从当前棒线一直到观察窗口的长度。分子是棒线位置与其价格的乘积的总和，分母是价格的总和。那么 CG 就是分子与分母的比值的相反数。通过加上半个观察窗口的长度再加 1，我们确定了 CG 的零位计数器值。由于 CG 是被平滑过的，所以通过把 CG 延迟 1 个交易日，我们便会得到有效的交叉信号。

CG 振荡指标的一个示例见图 5.3。在这个例子中，我选择的长度是一个 8 日观察窗口。显然每个主要价格反转点都被 CG 振荡指标在滞后为 0 的情况下辨识出来，并且与它的触发线形成交叉。由于 CG 振荡指标是被过滤和平滑过的，所以交叉的双人拉锯式信号都被最小化了。周期波动的相对幅度被保留。CG 振荡指标和第 4 章我们所讲的控制周期指标惊人地相似。我将在后面的一个章节中对所有类型的振荡指标进行比较。

```
/***********************************************************
    Title:          CG Oscillator
    Coded By:    Chris D. Kryza (Divergence Software, Inc.)
    Email:       c.kryza@gte.net
    Incept:      06/27/2003
    Version:     1.0.0


    ==========================================================
    Fix History:

    06/27/2003 -    Initial Release
    1.0.0


    ==========================================================
***********************************************************/


//External Variables
var nPrice                  = 0;
var nCG                     = 0;

var aPriceArray             = new Array();
var aCGArray                = new Array();


//== PreMain function required by eSignal to set_
    things up
function preMain() {
var x;

    setPriceStudy(false);
    setStudyTitle("CG Osc");
    setCursorLabelName("CG", 0);
    setCursorLabelName("Trig", 1);
    setDefaultBarFgColor( Color.blue, 0 );
    setDefaultBarFgColor( Color.red,  1 );

        //initialize arrays
    for (x=0; x<70; x++) {
        aPriceArray[x]          = 0.0;
        aCGArray[x]             = 0.0;
```

图 5.2 计算 CG 振荡指标的 EFS 代码

```
        }

    }

//== Main processing function
function main( OscLength ) {
var x;
var nNum;
var nDenom;
var nValue1;


        //initialize parameters if necessary
        if ( OscLength == null ) {
                OscLength = 10;
        }

        // study is initializing
    if (getBarState() == BARSTATE_ALLBARS) {
      return null;
    }

        //on each new bar, save array values
        if ( getBarState() == BARSTATE_NEWBAR ) {
                aPriceArray.pop();
                aPriceArray.unshift( 0 );

                aCGArray.pop();
                aCGArray.unshift( 0 );

        }

        nPrice = ( high()+low() ) / 2;
        aPriceArray[0] = nPrice;

        nNum   = 0;
        nDenom = 0;


        for ( x=0; x<OscLength; x++ ){
                nNum += ( 1.0 + x ) * ( aPriceArray[x] );
```

(continued)

图 5.2（续）

```
            nDenom += ( aPriceArray[x] );
    }
    if ( nDenom != 0 ) nCG = -nNum/nDenom
        + ( OscLength+1 )/2;
    aCGArray[0] = nCG;


    //return the calculated values
    if ( !isNaN( aCGArray[0] ) ) {
         return new Array( aCGArray[0],_
             aCGArray[1] );
    }


}
```

图 5.2（续）

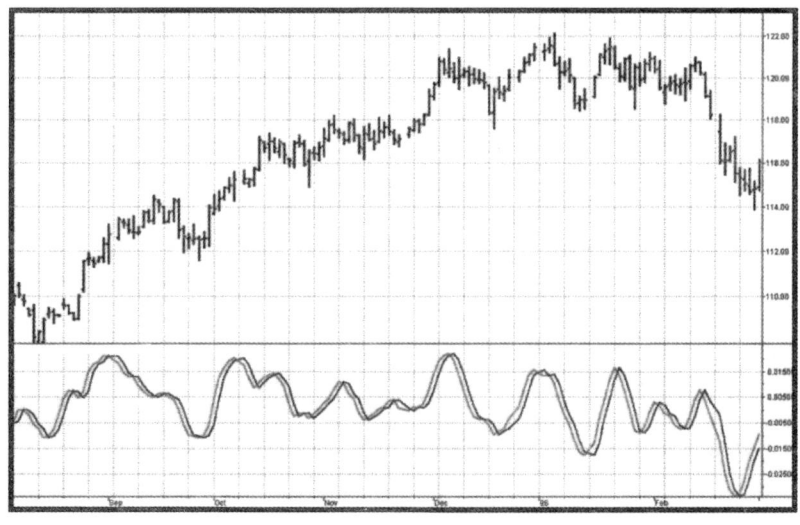

图 5.3　CG 振荡指标准确辨识出每个价格的反转点

CG 振荡指标的形状随着观察窗口长度的变化而变化。理想情况下，所选长度应该是主周期长度的一半，因为半个主周期将完全捕捉到价格在一个方向上的整个周期性运动。如果长度太长，那么 CG 振荡指标就变得迟钝。举例说明，如果窗口长度为一个主周期，那么一半数据推动 CG 向右侧偏移，而另一半数据则推动 CG 向左侧偏移。结果，CG 停留在窗口的中间，从而观察不到 CG 振荡指标的运动。另一方面，如果窗口长度太短，我们将错过平滑带来的优势。在这种情况下，CG 将包含较高频率的分量，交易的获利性令人担忧。

需要牢记的要点

- FIR 滤波器中的 CG 是平均价格在滤波器窗口长度内的位置。
- 当价格上涨时，CG 向最新棒线移动（减小），而当价格下跌时，CG 将向远离最新棒线的方向运动（增大）。于是，CG 运动的方向恰好与价格运动的方向相反。
- CG 振荡指标的滞后基本为 0。
- CG 振荡指标保留了相对周期的幅度，与控制周期指标类似。

第6章 相对活力指数

"一边待着去,还轮不到你说话。"汤姆严厉地说。

本章描述的相对活力指数(RVI),使用的是三十多年前的概念,同时运用现代滤波器和数字信号处理原理来实现那些概念,使它成为一个实用的指标。RVI 把旧的概念与新的技术融合在一起。RVI 的基本概念是,在上升趋势中,价格一般在高于开盘价处收盘,而在下降趋势中,价格一般在低于开盘价处收盘。于是,我们可以通过价格在一个交易日终了时的位置确定价格运动的活力。为了把这个指数向日交易区间规格化,我们用价格的变化除以当日的最大价格区间。于是,RVI 的基本公式如下:

$$RVI = \frac{收盘价 - 开盘价}{最高价 - 最低价} \qquad (6.1)$$

1972 年,吉姆·沃特斯(Jim Waters)和拉瑞·威廉姆斯(Larry Williams)公布了一份对他们的 A/D 振荡指标[①]的描述。在那份报告中,A/D

[①] 佩里·考夫曼(Perry Kaufman):《新商品交易系统和方法》(*The New Commodity Trading Systems and Methods*),纽约:威利公司,1987 年,第 102-103 页。

的意思是汇聚/发散（accumulation/distribution），而不是通常的上涨/下跌（advance/decline）。沃特斯和威廉姆斯定义了买方力量（BP）和卖方力量（SP），如下面的等式所示：

$$BP = 最高价 - 开盘价$$
$$SP = 收盘价 - 最低价$$

其中的价格是当日的开盘价、最高价、最低价和收盘价。BP 和 SP 这两个值，额外显示出相对于开盘价的买方力量和相对于收盘价的卖方力量，对于当日的交易，得到一个比较含蓄的度量。沃特斯和威廉姆斯把这些度量方式相结合应用在每日原生图（Daily Raw Figure，英文缩写为 DRF）中。DRF 的计算公式如下：

$$DRF = \frac{BP + SP}{2*(最高价 - 最低价)} \tag{6.2}$$

当市场在最低价开盘，并且在最高价收盘时，DRF 达到最大值 1。反之，当市场在最高价开盘，并且在最低价收盘时，DRF 达到最小值 0。逐日计算使得 DRF 的变化异常剧烈，因此需要对它进行平滑后才可使用。

我们可以把 DRF 公式扩展为

$$\begin{aligned} DRF &= \frac{1}{2}\left(\frac{最高价 - 开盘价 + 收盘价 - 最低价}{最高价 - 最低价}\right) \\ &= \frac{1}{2}\left(\frac{最高价 - 最低价 + 收盘价 - 开盘价}{最高价 - 最低价}\right) \\ &= \frac{1}{2}\left(1 + \frac{收盘价 - 开盘价}{最高价 - 最低价}\right) \end{aligned} \tag{6.3}$$

很明显，除了相加与相乘的常数之外，计算 DRF 的公式与计算每日 RVI 的公式相同。看起来在技术分析中似乎没有新的思想。然而，平滑操作是必须做的,目的是使指标比较实用。这就是现代滤波器理论对 RVI 成功应用的贡献。我使用 4 日对称有限脉冲响应(FIR)滤波器(见等式 4.1 和图 4.1),分别对分子和分母进行平滑。

RVI 是一种振荡指标,所以我们在使用时只关心市场的循环模式。价格在一个循环周期中变化最快的位置是在循环的中点。所以,在循环的下降部分我们预测收盘价和开盘价之间的价差将达到最大值。这就像微积分学中的导数,正弦函数的导数是一个余弦函数。所以,导数波形领先于原来正弦函数的波形四分之一周期。同样是来自微积分学,半个周期上的正弦函数的积分是另一个正弦函数,但延迟了四分之一个周期。在单个周期上求和基本上与数学积分是相同的,结果使得求和所得的波形与输入相比延迟了四分之一个波长(周期)。求差后再求总和,结果产生一个与价格的周期性分量同相的振荡指标输出。如果求和所用的窗口长度小于主周期的半个波长,也可能产生一个领先函数。如果无法测量周期,那么你可以在一个固定的默认时间段上对 RVI 分量求和。通常建议使用默认值 8,因为它接近于我们感兴趣的大多数周期的一半。

计算 RVI 是简单而又直接的。包含(收盘价-开盘价)的分子部分,在求和之前先通过 4 日对称 FIR 滤波器滤波。包含(最高价-最低价)的分母部分,在求和之前也要通过 4 日对称 FIR 滤波器单独进行滤波。分子和分母被单独求出,然后求分子与分母的比便得到 RVI。由于分子和分母因滤波而产生了相同程度的滞后,所以在求比时滞后便被约掉了。

RVI 的使用规则是比较灵活的。只是要记住一点,振荡指标与市场价格的周期性分量是基本同相的。我比较喜欢交叉线指标,因为它们的信号非常明确。通过把 RVI 延迟 1 日,我们便得到一条简单的触发线。

RVI 振荡指标见图 6.1。那些信号的敏感性和清晰性不言自明。计算 RVI 的 EasyLanguage 代码如图 6.2 所示,EFS 代码如图 6.3 所示。

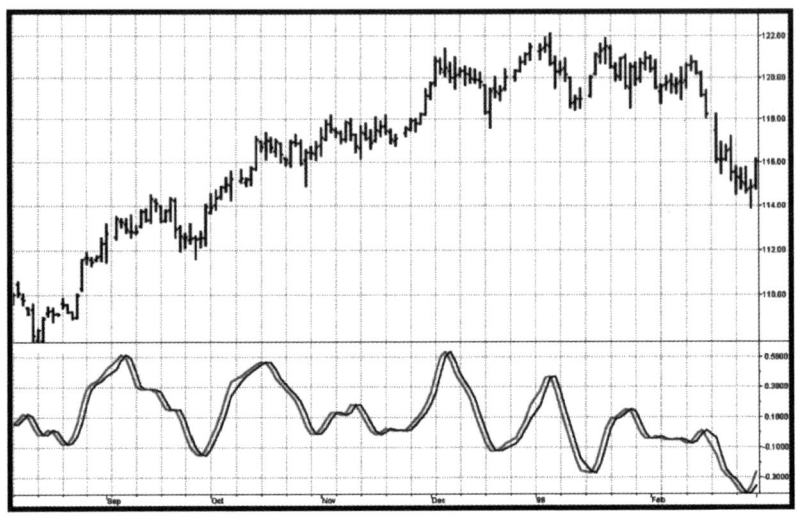

图 6.1 RVI 在周期性反转点处给出清晰的指示

```
Inputs:    Length(10);

Vars:      Num(0),
           Denom(0),
           count(0),
           RVI(0),
           Trigger(0);

Value1 = ((Close - Open) + 2*(Close[1]
    - Open[1]) + 2*(Close[2] - Open[2])
    + (Close[3] - Open[3]))/6;
Value2 = ((High - Low) + 2*(High[1]
    - Low[1]) + 2*(High[2] - Low[2])
    + (High[3] - Low[3]))/6;
Num = 0;
Denom = 0;
For count = 0 to Length -1 begin
           Num = Num + Value1[count];
           Denom = Denom + Value2[count];
End;
If Denom <> 0 then RVI = Num / Denom;
Trigger = RVI[1];

Plot1(RVI, "RVI");
Plot2(Trigger, "Trigger");
```

图 6.2 计算 RVI 的 EasyLanguage 代码

第 6 章　相对活力指数

```
/*************************************************
   Title:        RVI
   Coded By:     Chris D. Kryza (Divergence Software, Inc.)
   Email:        c.kryza@gte.net
   Incept:       06/19/2003
   Version:      1.0.0
   =================================================
   Fix History:
   06/19/2003 -  Initial Release
   1.0.0
   =================================================
**************************************************/
//External Variables
var aRVIArray            = new Array();
var aValue1Array         = new Array();
var aValue2Array         = new Array();
//== PreMain function required by eSignal to set_
    things up
function preMain() {
var x;
    setPriceStudy(false);
    setStudyTitle("RVI");
    setCursorLabelName("RVI", 0);
    setCursorLabelName("Trig", 1);
    setDefaultBarFgColor( Color.blue, 0 );
    setDefaultBarFgColor( Color.red,  1 );
    addBand( 0, PS_SOLID, Color.black, 1, -55 );
      //initialize arrays
    for (x=0; x<70; x++) {
       aRVIArray[x]       = 0.0;
       aValue1Array[x]    = 0.0;
       aValue2Array[x]    = 0.0;
       aValue3Array[x]    = 0.0;
    }
}
//== Main processing function
function main( OscLength ) {
var x;
var nNum;
var nDenom;
```

(continued)

图 6.3　计算 RVI 的 EFS 代码

```
    //initialize parameters if necessary
    if ( OscLength == null ) {
        OscLength = 8;
    }

    // study is initializing
if (getBarState() == BARSTATE_ALLBARS) {
  return null;
}

    //on each new bar, save array values
    if ( getBarState() == BARSTATE_NEWBAR ) {

        aRVIArray.pop();
        aRVIArray.unshift( 0 );

        aValue1Array.pop();
        aValue1Array.unshift( 0 );

        aValue2Array.pop();
        aValue2Array.unshift( 0 );

    }

    aValue1Array[0] = ( ( close()-open() )
        + 2*( close(-1)-open(-1) )
        + 2*( close(-2)-open(-2) )
        + ( close(-3)-open(-3) ) ) / 6;
    aValue2Array[0] = ( ( high()-low() )
        + 2*( high(-1)-low(-1) )
        + 2*( high(-2)-low(-2) )
        + ( high(-3)-low(-3) ) ) / 6;

    nNum   = 0;
    nDenom = 0;

    for ( x=0; x<OscLength; x++ ){
        nNum   += aValue1Array[x];
        nDenom += aValue2Array[x];
```

图 6.3（续）

```
            }
            if ( nDenom != 0 ) aRVIArray[0] = nNum/nDenom;

            //return the calculated values
            {
                    return new Array( aRVIArray[0],_
                        aRVIArray[1] );
            }

    }
```

图 6.3（续）

需要牢记的要点

- RVI 的设计理念是，价格在上升市场中收盘价高于开盘价，在下降市场中收盘价低于开盘价。
- RVI 是一种规格化的振荡指标，价格运动被规格化到每日的交易区间。
- 我们使用可消除滞后的 4 日对称 FIR 滤波器产生一个易读的指标。

第7章 振荡指标的比较

"让我们玩音乐椅游戏吧。"汤姆虚伪地说。

在此前的三章中,我已经讲解了基于三种不同原理的振荡指标。在你的交易工具箱中,如果有一个比较有效,那么可能不需要那么多的振荡指标。我曾经亲见很多交易者遭受"分析瘫痪"之苦。寻找最理想的工具组合,甚至根据每种环境选择不同的工具组合,都是不可取的,交易者最好固定使用几项平均表现最佳的工具。这三个振荡指标可以进入你的考虑范围。要想知道三者当中哪一个最好,唯一的办法就是在使用相同数据的相同图表上对它们做一下比较。这种比较见图7.1。

坦白地讲,在这个特别的例子中,我没有看到三个振荡指标之间存在丝毫值得关注的差异。三者都指示出相对周期幅度,并且正确辨识出每个主要的反转点。如果说有一点差别的话,那就是相对活力指数(RVI)不那么容易受到双人拉锯式信号的影响。虽然如此,我还是钟爱控制周期,因为我知道它只包含理论上的周期分量,是这些分量构成了一个振荡指标。我曾经在其他数据样本中看到过这些振荡指标之间存在更大的差异。

当你把这些振荡指标融入一个自动交易策略中时,那些差异将变得更加明显。在这些应用中,某个振荡指标可能在交易策略的关键时刻早于其他振荡指标1日给出交易信号。当然,某个振荡指标还可能不太容易出现导致双人拉锯式交易的短期交叉。无论怎样,你现在已经拥有三个极好的工具来进行自己的技术分析。在你的应用中,三者中的某一个可能会优于其他两个。

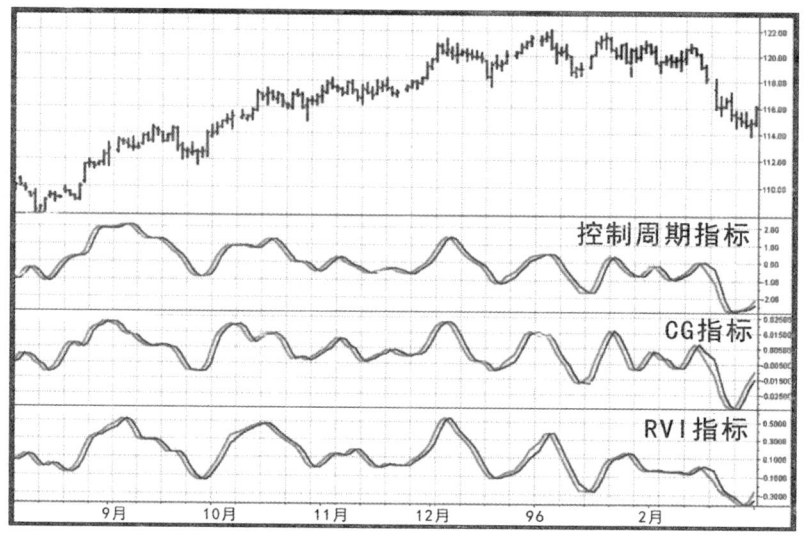

图 7.1 控制周期振荡指标、CG 振荡指标和 RVI 振荡指标的对比

用我设计的这三个振荡指标中的一个,与大家常用的其他几个振荡指标,以与前面相同的方式在同样一份数据图表上进行对比,可能更有益处。这种标准化的比较有助于评价交易信号的相对滞后,以及它们产生双人拉锯式信号的强度。两个比较流行的振荡指标是相对强弱指数(RSI)和随机指标。它们与控制周期振荡指标的比较见图 7.2,为了对比,使用了 8 日周期。哇!显然,RSI 和随机指标比控制周期振荡指标更加飘忽不定。等待信号线交叉以确认指标信号是最小化指标不稳定行为的传统方

式。等待确认信号意味着 RSI 和随机指标交易信号总是迟到的,总之信号是被错过了。我可以援引更多实例,并且与更多指标进行对比,但本书的目的是讲解你可以应用于实际交易的工具。既然你已经知道了代码,你可以在自己的数据上进行测试。你还可以把这些新工具与你心仪的其他指标进行比较。

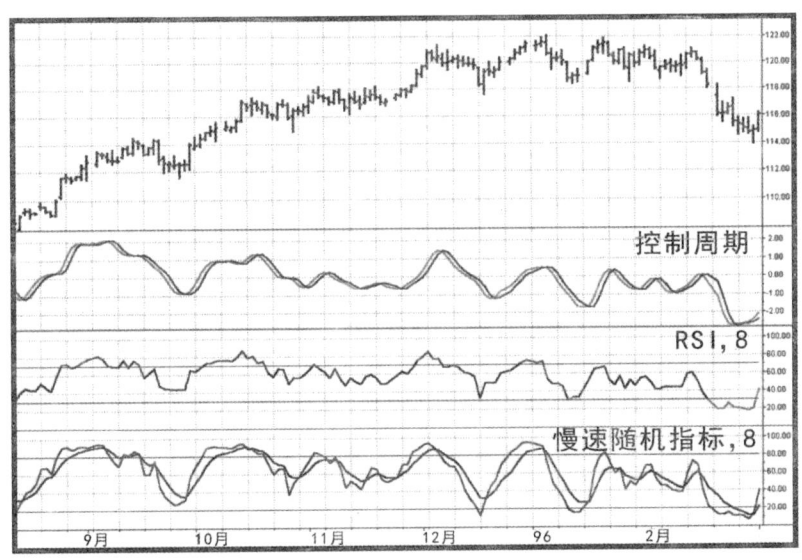

图 7.2 控制周期振荡指标比 RSI 和随机指标更平滑,产生信号更及时

需要牢记的要点

- 控制周期、CG、RVI 振荡指标都表达着相对周期幅度信息。
- 控制周期、CG 和 RVI 都指示出主要的反转点,并且滞后最小。
- 控制周期、CG 和 RVI 振荡指标大大优于标准指标。

第 8 章 指标的随机化和费希尔化

"每天我将给你带来更大的价值。"汤姆自豪地说。

有一个指标我希望早就已经发明,因为它工作得相当棒。这个指标被称为随机 RSI(stochastic RSI)。由于过去我没有发明它,所以我最好是先描述一下它,然后再把它的一些原理改进一下,以便创造出更好的指标。所有这些指标将在本章进行讲解和比较。

随机 RSI 的名字就说明了它的计算方式。首先从最近的价格中计算出一个 RSI;然后利用 RSI 作为输入变量计算出一个随机指标。最后,对那个随机指标用加权移动平均方法进行平滑,于是我们便得到一个可以使用的输出。

计算 RSI 时先要对选定时间段内的累积收盘涨幅(以价格计)和累积收盘跌幅(以价格计)分别求平均值。为了简便,我把收盘涨幅记作 CU,收盘跌幅记作 CD。RSI 便是 CU 与 CU 和 CD 之和的比。如果在选定时间段内没有 CD,那么比值为单位 1。如果在选定时间段内没有 CU,那么比值为单位 0。于是,如果 RSI 的计算长度恰好与市场价格的半个完整循环相等,那么 RSI 将在 0 和 1 之间波动。我们一般都将该比值乘以 100,使 RSI

以百分比显示。

随机指标①（肯定不是随机的任意变量）的计算是寻找选定周期上的最高值和最低值。随机指标是当前值与最低值之差和最高值与最低值之差的比值。我们一般也将该比值乘以 100，将随机指标以百分比显示。

从 RSI 和随机指标中推导随机 RSI 的 EasyLanguage 和 EFS 代码分别在图 8.1 和 8.2 中给出。在绘制随机 RSI 之前，我们首先对它用加权移动平均进行平滑，从而得出一个令人满意的显示结果，并且只具有极小的滞后。通过把信号线延迟 1 日，我们得到了触发信号线。随机 RSI 信号线和触发线的交叉形成了该指标的买卖信号。我已经把随机 RSI 缩放到在 -1 和 +1 之间波动。我进行这样缩放的目的是可以直接在它上面进行费希尔变换，以便产生尖锐的入场和出场信号。

随机 RSI 的迷人之处在于，虽然经过了这么多计算，但是交易信号的滞后仍然几乎为 0。主要原因是 RSI 和随机指标都是比值，所以分子中的滞后都被分母中的滞后抵消了。随机 RSI 的表现见图 8.3。不像控制周期振荡指标和 CG 振荡指标，随机 RSI 一般不会保留周期的相对幅度。这种幅度标准化对交易者来说是一个优势，因为它去除了振荡指标的一些解释性方面的因素。在图 8.3 中，随机 RSI 及时而清楚地捕捉到了每个主要的反转点。

下面的内容更让人兴奋。如果对一个标准指标进行随机化处理后会产生一个更好的指标，那么我们有理由认为，对已经表现不俗的指标采取相同的处理过程之后，将产生更优秀的指标。将图 4.4 中的控制周期振荡指

---

① 随机指标（Stochastic Indicator）的名称是由最初的提议者任意选择的一个"专业术语"。它与统计学术语"随机"没有关系。在统计学中，随机被定义为任意决定的事件序列。

第 8 章 指标的随机化和费希尔化

标转换为随机控制周期振荡指标的 EasyLanguage 代码和 EFS 代码分别见图 8.4 和 8.5。将图 5.3 所示的 CG 振荡指标转换为随机 CG 振荡指标的 Easy-Language 代码和 EFS 代码分别见图 8.6 和 8.7。最后，对图 6.1 所示的相对活力指数（RVI）进行随机化处理的 EasyLanguage 代码和 EFS 代码分别见图 8.8 和 8.9。在每种情况下，我只是简单地加入对指标进行随机化处理的代码，并且把计算结果缩放到-1 和+1 之内。进行这种缩放的原因是，下一步我要对这些指标进行费希尔变换，以得到更加尖锐、更加明确的入场和出场信号。触发线就是把指标线延迟 1 日，并且缩放到-0.98 和+0.98 之间的区间内。对触发线的幅度进行缩减，当指标离开极值运动时将给出更清晰的交叉。

```
Inputs:         RSILength(8),
                StocLength(8),
                WMALength(8);

Value1 = RSI(Close, RSILength) - Lowest(RSI(Close,
    RSILength), StocLength);
Value2 = Highest(RSI(Close, RSILength), StocLength)
    - Lowest(RSI(Close, RSILength), StocLength);
If Value2<>  0 then Value3 = Value1 / Value2;
Value4 = 2*(WAverage(Value3, WMALength) - .5);

Plot1(Value4, |StocRSI|);
Plot2(Value4[1], |Trig|);
```

图 8.1 计算随机 RSI 的 EasyLanguage 代码

```
/***********************************************************
    Title:        Stochastic RSI
    Coded By:   Chris D. Kryza (Divergence Software, Inc.)
    Email:      c.kryza@gte.net
    Incept:     06/19/2003
    Version:    1.0.0



    ==========================================================
    Fix History:

    06/19/2003 -    Initial Release
    1.0.0


    ==========================================================
***********************************************************/


//External Variables
var nAvgUpClose           = 0;
var nAvgDnClose           = 0;
var ntAvgUpClose          = 0;
var ntAvgDnClose          = 0;
var nValue3               = 0;
var nValue4               = 0;
var nTrig                 = 0;
var bInitialized          = false;

var nRS                   = 0;
var nRSI                  = 0;

var aRSIArray             = new Array();
var aValue3Array          = new Array();


//== PreMain function required by eSignal to set_
    things up
function preMain() {
var x;

    setPriceStudy(false);
    setStudyTitle("StochasticRSI");
```
(continued)

图 8.2 计算随机 RSI 的 EFS 代码

```
setCursorLabelName("StocRSI", 0);
setCursorLabelName("Trig", 1);
setDefaultBarFgColor( Color.blue, 0 );
setDefaultBarFgColor( Color.red,  1 );

    //initialize arrays
for (x=0; x<70; x++) {
    aRSIArray[x]     = 0.0;
    aValue3Array[x] = 0.0;
}

}

//== Main processing function
function main( RSILength, StocLength, WMALength ) {
var x;
var nDiff;
var nDivBy;
var nValue1;
var nValue2;

    //initialize parameters if necessary
    if ( RSILength == null ) {
        RSILength = 8;
    }
    if ( StocLength == null ) {
        StocLength = 8;
    }
    if ( WMALength == null ) {
        WMALength = 8;
    }

    // study is initializing
if (getBarState() == BARSTATE_ALLBARS) {
  return null;
}

    //initialize the basic RSI calculation
    if ( bInitialized == false ) {
        nAvgUpClose = 0.0;
        nAvgDnClose = 0.0;
        for (x=0; x<RSILength; x++) {
```

图 8.2（续）

```
                    nDiff = close( -x )
                        - close( -(x+1) );
                    if ( nDiff > 0 ) {
                        nAvgUpClose += nDiff;
                    }
                    else {
                        nAvgDnClose
                            += Math.abs
                                ( nDiff );
                    }
                }
                nAvgUpClose /= RSILength;
                nAvgDnClose /= RSILength;
                nRS = nAvgUpClose / nAvgDnClose;
                nRSI = 100.0 - ( 100.0 / ( 1.0
                    + nRS ) );

                bInitialized = true;
}
//continue the RSI calculation on subsequent_
    bars
else {
        if ( getBarState() == BARSTATE_NEWBAR ) {
            nAvgUpClose = ntAvgUpClose;
            nAvgDnClose = ntAvgDnClose;
            if ( !isNaN( nRSI ) ) {
                aRSIArray.pop();
                aRSIArray.unshift( 0 );
                aValue3Array.pop();
                aValue3Array.unshift( 0 );
                nTrig = nValue4;
            }
        }
        nDiff = close( 0 ) - close( -1 );
        if ( nDiff > 0 ) {
            ntAvgUpClose = (( nAvgUpClose
                * (RSILength-1) ) + nDiff )
                / RSILength;
            ntAvgDnClose = (( nAvgDnClose
                * (RSILength-1) ) + 0       )
                / RSILength;
        }
```
(continued)

图 8.2 (续)

```
            else {
                ntAvgUpClose = (( nAvgUpClose
                    * (RSILength-1) ) + 0    )
                    / RSILength;
                ntAvgDnClose = (( nAvgDnClose
                    * (RSILength-1) )
                    + Math.abs( nDiff ) )
                    / RSILength;
            }
            nRS = ntAvgUpClose / ntAvgDnClose;
            nRSI = 100.0 - ( 100.0 / ( 1
                + nRS ) );
            aRSIArray[0] = nRSI;
}

//calculate the StocRSI using the RSI Array we_
    have created.
nValue1 = nRSI - Lowest( StocLength );
nValue2 = Highest( StocLength )
    - Lowest( StocLength );

nValue3 = 0;
if ( nValue2 != 0 ) nValue3 = ( nValue1
    / nValue2 );
aValue3Array[0] = nValue3;

//compute weighted moving average
nValue4 = 0;
nDivBy = 0;
for (x=0; x<WMALength; x++) {
        nValue4 += ( aValue3Array[x]
            * ( WMALength-x ) );
        nDivBy += ( WMALength-x );
}

nValue4 = nValue4 / nDivBy;
nValue4 = 2.0 * ( nValue4 - 0.5 );


//return the calculated values
if (!isNaN( nValue4 ) ) {
        return new Array( nValue4, nTrig );
```

图 8.2 (续)

```
        }

}


/**********************************************************
            SUPPORT FUNCTIONS
**********************************************************/

function Highest( nPeriod ) {
var x;
var nTmp = -999999999.0;

        for (x=0; x<nPeriod; x++) {
                nTmp = Math.max( nTmp, aRSIArray[x] );
        }

        return( nTmp );
}

function Lowest( nPeriod ) {
var x;
var nTmp = 999999999.0;

        for (x=0; x<nPeriod; x++) {
                nTmp = Math.min( nTmp, aRSIArray[x] );
        }

        return( nTmp );
}
```

图 8.2 (续)

第8章 指标的随机化和费希尔化

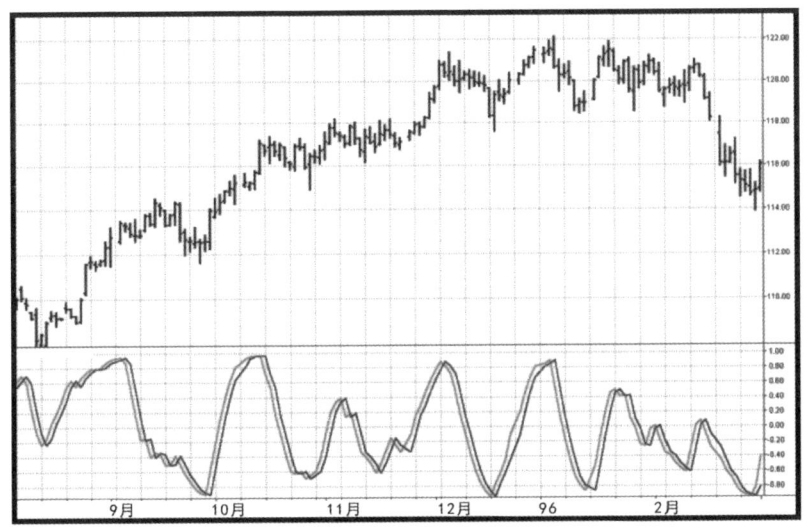

图 8.3 随机 RSI 及时捕捉到了市场的反转点

三个随机化处理后的指标的比较见图 8.10。虽然我比较喜欢随机控制周期指标，因为它的买卖信号纯粹是基于数据的周期分量，但是这三个指标显然非常相似。另一方面，随机 RVI 显然更加规则，具有更少的双人拉锯式信号。无论如何，你已经学会了自己选择工具的方法。当用于某只具体的股票时，如果有必要，交易者可以调整输入参数以对每个指标进行优化。

在第 1 章中我已经指出，正弦波的概率密度函数不是高斯概率密度函数，从正弦波中创建灵敏的指标是困难的，因为当运动已经开始后，指示才会出现。随机化处理后的指标看起来都有些像正弦波。所以，我们可以通过对它们进行费希尔变换而产生尖锐的交易信号。我在图 8.11 和 8.16 所示的指标代码中便进行了这样的处理。我已经把波动幅度的绝对值限制在 0.99 之内，从而避免费希尔变换中出现大值输出。像前面一样，交易信号是由信号线和触发线的交叉给出的。通过把信号线延迟 1 日，我们便得到了触发线。

```
{***********************************************************
              Stochastic Cyber Cycle
***********************************************************}

Inputs: Price((H+L)/2),
        alpha(.07),
        Len(8);

Vars:   Smooth(0),
        Cycle(0),
        MaxCycle(0),
        MinCycle(0);

Smooth = (Price + 2*Price[1] + 2*Price[2]
    + Price[3])/6;
Cycle = (1 - .5*alpha)*(1 - .5*alpha)*(Smooth
    - 2*Smooth[1] + Smooth[2]) + 2*(1 - alpha)*Cycle[1]
    - (1 - alpha)*(1 - alpha)*Cycle[2];
If currentbar < 7 then Cycle = (Price - 2*Price[1]
    + Price[2]) / 4;

MaxCycle = Highest(Cycle, Len);
MinCycle = Lowest(Cycle, Len);
If MaxCycle <> MinCycle then Value1 = (Cycle
    - MinCycle) / (MaxCycle - MinCycle);
Value2 = (4*Value1 + 3*Value1[1] + 2*Value1[2]
    + Value1[3]) / 10;
Value2 = 2*(Value2 - .5);

Plot1(Value2, |Cycle|);
Plot2(.96*(Value2[1] + .02), |Trigger|);
Plot3(0,|Ref|);
```

图 8.4 计算随机控制周期指标的 EasyLanguage 代码

```
/***********************************************************
Title:         Stochastic Cyber Cycle
Coded By:      Chris D. Kryza (Divergence Software, Inc.)
Email:         c.kryza@gte.net
Incept:        06/19/2003
```
(continued)

图 8.5 计算随机控制周期指标的 EFS 代码

```
Version: 1.0.0


========================================================
Fix History:

06/19/2003 -     Initial Release
1.0.0


========================================================
********************************************************/


//External Variables

var nBarCount             = 0;
var nValue2               = 0;

var aPriceArray           = new Array();
var aSmoothArray          = new Array();
var aCycleArray           = new Array();
var aValue1Array          = new Array();


//== PreMain function required by eSignal to set_
   things up
function preMain() {
var x;

  setPriceStudy(false);
  setStudyTitle("StochasticCyberCycle");
  setCursorLabelName("Cycle", 0);
  setCursorLabelName("Trig", 1);
  setDefaultBarFgColor( Color.blue, 0 );
  setDefaultBarFgColor( Color.red, 1 );
  addBand( 0, PS_SOLID, Color.black, 1, -55 );
     //initialize arrays
  for (x=0; x<70; x++) {
     aPriceArray[x]       = 0.0;
     aSmoothArray[x]      = 0.0;
     aCycleArray[x]       = 0.0;
     aValue1Array[x]      = 0.0;
```

图 8.5 (续)

```
        }
}
//== Main processing function
function main( Alpha, OscLength ) {
var x;
var nPrice;
var nMaxCycle;
var nMinCycle;

    //initialize parameters if necessary
    if ( Alpha == null ) {
            Alpha = 0.07;
    }
    if ( OscLength == null ) {
            OscLength = 8;
    }

    // study is initializing
  if (getBarState() == BARSTATE_ALLBARS) {
    return null;
  }

    //on each new bar, save array values
    if ( getBarState() == BARSTATE_NEWBAR ) {

            nBarCount++;

            aPriceArray.pop();
            aPriceArray.unshift( 0 );

            aSmoothArray.pop();
            aSmoothArray.unshift( 0 );

            aCycleArray.pop();
            aCycleArray.unshift( 0 );

            aValue1Array.pop();
            aValue1Array.unshift( 0 );
```

(continued)

图 8.5（续）

第 8 章 指标的随机化和费希尔化

```
            nTrig = nValue2;
    }

    nPrice = ( high()+low() ) / 2;
    aPriceArray[0] = nPrice;

    aSmoothArray[0] = ( aPriceArray[0]
        + 2*aPriceArray[1] + 2*aPriceArray[2]
        + aPriceArray[3] ) / 6;

    if ( nBarCount < 7 ) {
            aCycleArray[0] = ( aPriceArray[0]
                - 2*aPriceArray[1]
                + aPriceArray[2] ) / 4;
    }
     else {
            aCycleArray[0] = ( 1 - 0.5*Alpha ) * ( 1
            - 0.5*Alpha ) * ( aSmoothArray[0]
            - 2*aSmoothArray[1] +
            aSmoothArray[2] ) + 2*( 1-Alpha )
            * aCycleArray[1] - ( 1-Alpha )
            * ( 1- Alpha ) * aCycleArray[2];
    }

    nMaxCycle = Highest( OscLength );
    nMinCycle = Lowest( OscLength );

    if ( nMaxCycle != nMinCycle ) aValue1Array[0]
        = ( aCycleArray[0]-nMinCycle ) / ( nMaxCycle
        - nMinCycle );

    nValue2 = ( 4*aValue1Array[0]
        + 3*aValue1Array[1] + 2*aValue1Array[2]
        + aValue1Array[3] ) / 10;
    nValue2 = 2 * ( nValue2 - 0.5 );

    if (!isNaN( nValue2 ) ) {
            return new Array( nValue2,
                (0.96*(nTrig+0.02)) );
    }
}
```

图 8.5 (续)

```
/************************************************
            SUPPORT FUNCTIONS
*************************************************/

function Highest( nPeriod ) {
var x;
var nTmp = -999999999.0;

        for (x=0; x<nPeriod; x++) {
                nTmp = Math.max( nTmp, aCycleArray[x] );
        }

        return( nTmp );
}

function Lowest( nPeriod ) {
var x;
var nTmp = 999999999.0;

        for (x=0; x<nPeriod; x++) {
                nTmp = Math.min( nTmp, aCycleArray[x] );
        }

        return( nTmp );
}
```

图 8.5（续）

```
{************************************************
            Stochastic CG Oscillator
*************************************************}

Inputs:  Price((H+L)/2),
         Length(8);

Vars:    count(0),
         Num(0),
         Denom(0),
         CG(0),
                                        (continued)
```

图 8.6 计算随机 CG 指标的 EasyLanguage 代码

```
            MaxCG(0),
            MinCG(0);

Num = 0;
Denom = 0;
For count = 0 to Length - 1 begin
        Num = Num + (1 + count)*(Price[count]);
        Denom = Denom + (Price[count]);
End;
If Denom <> 0 then CG = -Num/Denom + (Length + 1) / 2;

MaxCG = Highest(CG, Length);
MinCG = Lowest(CG, Length);
If MaxCG <> MinCG then Value1 = (CG - MinCG) / (MaxCG
   - MinCG);
Value2 = (4*Value1 + 3*Value1[1] + 2*Value1[2]
   + Value1[3]) / 10;
Value2 = 2*(Value2 - .5);

Plot1(Value2, ICGI);
Plot2(.96*(Value2[1] + .02), ITriggerI);
Plot3(0,IRefI);
```

图 8.6（续）

```
/*****************************************************
Title:          Stochastic CG Oscillator
Coded By:   Chris D. Kryza (Divergence Software, Inc.)
Email:      c.kryza@gte.net
Incept:     06/19/2003
Version:    1.0.0



=====================================================
Fix History:

06/19/2003 -    Initial Release
1.0.0
```

图 8.7　计算随机 CG 指标的 EFS 代码

股票和期货的控制论分析

```
============================================================
**********************************************************/


//External Variables
var nPrice                    = 0;
var nCG                       = 0;
var nValue2                   = 0;
var nTrig                     = 0;

var aPriceArray               = new Array();
var aCGArray                  = new Array();
var aValue1Array              = new Array();


//== PreMain function required by eSignal to set_
   things up
function preMain() {
var x;

  setPriceStudy(false);
  setStudyTitle(|StochasticCGOsc|);
  setCursorLabelName(|CG|, 0);
  setCursorLabelName(|Trig|, 1);
  setDefaultBarFgColor( Color.blue, 0 );
  setDefaultBarFgColor( Color.red,  1 );
  addBand( 0, PS_SOLID, Color.black, 1, -55 );

        //initialize arrays
  for (x=0; x<70; x++) {
        aPriceArray[x]        = 0.0;
        aCGArray[x]           = 0.0;
        aValue1Array[x]       = 0.0;
  }

}

//== Main processing function
function main( OscLength ) {
var x;
var nNum;
var nDenom;
```

(continued)

图 8.7（续）

第 8 章　指标的随机化和费希尔化

```
var nMaxCG;
var nMinCG;
var nValue1;

        //initialize parameters if necessary
        if ( OscLength == null ) {
            OscLength = 8;
        }

        // study is initializing
    if (getBarState() == BARSTATE_ALLBARS) {
      return null;
        }

        //on each new bar, save array values
        if ( getBarState() == BARSTATE_NEWBAR ) {
            aPriceArray.pop();
            aPriceArray.unshift( 0 );

            aCGArray.pop();
            aCGArray.unshift( 0 );

            aValue1Array.pop();
            aValue1Array.unshift( 0 );

            nTrig = nValue2;
        }

        nPrice = ( high()+low() ) / 2;
        aPriceArray[0] = nPrice;

        nNum        = 0;
        nDenom      = 0;


        for ( x=0; x<OscLength; x++ ){
            nNum += ( 1.0 + x )
                * ( aPriceArray[x] );
            nDenom += ( aPriceArray[x] );
        }
```

图 8.7（续）

```
            if ( nDenom != 0 ) nCG = -nNum/nDenom
                + ( OscLength+1 )/2;
            aCGArray[0] = nCG;


            nMaxCG = Highest( OscLength );
            nMinCG = Lowest( OscLength );

            nValue1 = 0;
            if ( nMaxCG != nMinCG ) nValue1 = (nCG
                - nMinCG) / (nMaxCG - nMinCG);
            aValue1Array[0] = nValue1;

            nValue2 = ( 4*aValue1Array[0]
                + 3*aValue1Array[1] + 2*aValue1Array[2]
                + aValue1Array[3] ) / 10;
            nValue2 = 2.0 * ( nValue2 - 0.5 );

            //return the calculated values
            if ( !isNaN( nValue2 ) ) {
                    return new Array( nValue2,
                        (0.96*(nTrig+0.02)) );
            }

    }


/************************************************************
              SUPPORT FUNCTIONS
************************************************************/

function Highest( nPeriod ) {
var x;
var nTmp = -999999999.0;

        for (x=0; x<nPeriod; x++) {
                nTmp = Math.max( nTmp, aCGArray[x] );
        }

        return( nTmp );
                                                   (continued)
```

图 8.7（续）

第 8 章 指标的随机化和费希尔化

```
}

function Lowest( nPeriod ) {
var x;
var nTmp = 999999999.0;

        for (x=0; x<nPeriod; x++) {
            nTmp = Math.min( nTmp, aCGArray[x] );
        }

        return( nTmp );
}
```

图 8.7（续）

```
{*****************************************************
             Stochastic Relative Vigor Index (RVI)
*****************************************************}
Inputs: Length(8);

Vars:   Num(0),
        Denom(0),
        count(0),
        RVI(0),
        MaxRVI(0),
        MinRVI(0);

Value1 = ((Close - Open) + 2*(Close[1] - Open[1])
    + 2*(Close[2] - Open[2]) + (Close[3] - Open[3]))/6;
Value2 = ((High - Low) + 2*(High[1] - Low[1])
    + 2*(High[2] - Low[2]) + (High[3] - Low[3]))/6;
Num = 0;
Denom = 0;
For count = 0 to Length - 1 begin
        Num = Num + Value1[count];
        Denom = Denom + Value2[count];
End;
```

图 8.8 计算随机 RVI 指标的 EasyLanguage 代码

```
If Denom <> 0 then RVI = Num / Denom;

MaxRVI = Highest(RVI, Length);
MinRVI = Lowest(RVI, Length);
If MaxRVI <> MinRVI then Value3 = (RVI - MinRVI)
    / (MaxRVI - MinRVI);
Value4 = (4*Value3 + 3*Value3[1] + 2*Value3[2]
    + Value3[3]) / 10;
Value4 = 2*(Value4 - .5);

Plot1(Value4, |RVI|);
Plot2(.96*(Value4[1] + .02), |Trigger|);
Plot3(0,|Ref|);
```

图 8.8（续）

```
/************************************************************
Title:        Stochastic RVI
Coded By:     Chris D. Kryza (Divergence Software, Inc.)
Email:        c.kryza@gte.net
Incept:       06/19/2003
Version:      1.0.0


============================================================
Fix History:

06/19/2003 -   Initial Release
1.0.0



============================================================
************************************************************/


//External Variables
var nValue4                           = 0;
var nTrig                             = 0;
```

(continued)

图 8.9　计算随机 RVI 指标的 EFS 代码

```
var aRVIArray                = new Array();
var aValue1Array             = new Array();
var aValue2Array             = new Array();
var aValue3Array             = new Array();

//== PreMain function required by eSignal to set_
   things up
function preMain() {
var x;

  setPriceStudy(false);
  setStudyTitle("StochasticRVI");
  setCursorLabelName("RVI", 0);
  setCursorLabelName("Trig", 1);
  setDefaultBarFgColor( Color.blue, 0 );
  setDefaultBarFgColor( Color.red, 1 );
  addBand( 0, PS_SOLID, Color.black, 1, -55 );

        //initialize arrays
  for (x=0; x<70; x++) {
        aRVIArray[x]              = 0.0;
        aValue1Array[x]           = 0.0;
        aValue2Array[x]           = 0.0;
        aValue3Array[x]           = 0.0;
  }

}

//== Main processing function
function main( OscLength ) {
var x;
var nNum;
var nDenom;
var nMaxRVI;
var nMinRVI;

        //initialize parameters if necessary
        if ( OscLength == null ) {
            OscLength = 8;
        }
```

图 8.9 (续)

股票和期货的控制论分析

```
           // study is initializing
if (getBarState() == BARSTATE_ALLBARS) {
   return null;
}

      //on each new bar, save array values
      if ( getBarState() == BARSTATE_NEWBAR ) {

            aRVIArray.pop();
            aRVIArray.unshift( 0 );

            aValue1Array.pop();
            aValue1Array.unshift( 0 );

            aValue2Array.pop();
            aValue2Array.unshift( 0 );

            aValue3Array.pop();
            aValue3Array.unshift( 0 );

            nTrig = nValue4;
      }

      aValue1Array[0] = ( ( close()-open() )
         + 2*( close(-1)-open(-1) ) + 2*( close(-2)
         - open(-2) ) + ( close(-3)-open(-3) ) )
         / 6;
      aValue2Array[0] = ( ( high()-low() )
         + 2*( high(-1)-low(-1) ) + 2*( high(-2)
         - low(-2) ) + ( high(-3)-low(-3) ) ) / 6;


      nNum         = 0;
      nDenom       = 0;


      for ( x=0; x<OscLength; x++ ){
            nNum += aValue1Array[x];
            nDenom += aValue2Array[x];
      }

      if ( nDenom != 0 ) aRVIArray[0] = nNum/nDenom;
                                            (continued)
```

图 8.9（续）

```
            nMaxRVI = Highest( OscLength);
            nMinRVI = Lowest( OscLength );

            if ( nMaxRVI != nMinRVI ) aValue3Array[0]
                = ( aRVIArray[0]-nMinRVI )
                / ( nMaxRVI-nMinRVI );

            nValue4 = ( 4*aValue3Array[0]
                + 3*aValue3Array[1] + 2*aValue3Array[2]
                + aValue3Array[3] ) / 10;
            nValue4 = 2.0 * ( nValue4 - 0.5 );

            //return the calculated values
            if ( !isNaN( nValue4 ) ) {
                return new Array( nValue4,
                    (0.96*(nTrig+0.02)) );
            }


}
/**********************************************
            SUPPORT FUNCTIONS
**********************************************/

function Highest( nPeriod ) {
var x;
var nTmp = -999999999.0;

        for (x=0; x<nPeriod; x++) {
            nTmp = Math.max( nTmp, aRVIArray[x] );
        }

        return( nTmp );
}
function Lowest( nPeriod ) {
var x;
var nTmp = 999999999.0;

        for (x=0; x<nPeriod; x++) {
```

图 8.9 (续)

```
                nTmp = Math.min( nTmp, aRVIArray[x] );
        }

        return( nTmp );
}
```

图 8.9（续）

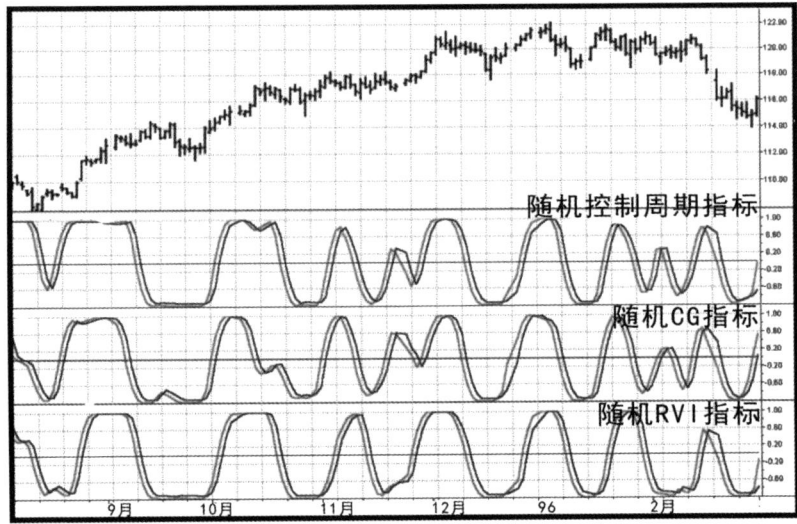

图 8.10 随机化指标的对比

```
{*********************************************************
                    Fisher Cyber Cycle
*********************************************************}
Inputs: Price((H+L)/2),
        alpha(.07),
        Len(8);

Vars:   Smooth(0),
                                                (continued)
```

图 8.11 计算费希尔控制周期指标的 EasyLanguage 代码

```
            Cycle(0),
            MaxCycle(0),
            MinCycle(0),
            Lead(0);

Smooth = (Price + 2*Price[1] + 2*Price[2]
    + Price[3])/6;
Cycle = (1 - .5*alpha)*(1 - .5*alpha)*(Smooth
    - 2*Smooth[1] + Smooth[2]) + 2*(1 - alpha)*Cycle[1]
    - (1 - alpha)*(1 - alpha)*Cycle[2];
If currentbar < 7 then Cycle = (Price - 2*Price[1]
    + Price[2]) / 4;

MaxCycle = Highest(Cycle, Len);
MinCycle = Lowest(Cycle, Len);
If MaxCycle <> MinCycle then Value1 = (Cycle
    - MinCycle) / (MaxCycle - MinCycle);
Value2 = (4*Value1 + 3*Value1[1] + 2*Value1[2]
    + Value1[3]) / 10;

Value3 = .5*Log((1+1.98*(Value2-.5))/(1-1.98
    *(Value2-.5)));

Plot1(Value3, ICycleI);
Plot2(Value3[1], ITriggerI);
Plot3(0,IRefI);
```

图 8.11（续）

```
/**********************************************************
Title:          Fisher Cyber Cycle
Coded By:       Chris D. Kryza (Divergence Software, Inc.)
Email:          c.kryza@gte.net
Incept:         06/19/2003
Version:        1.0.0
```

图 8.12　计算费希尔控制周期指标的 EFS 代码

股票和期货的控制论分析

```
=======================================================
Fix History:
06/19/2003 -    Initial Release
1.0.0

=======================================================
********************************************************/


//External Variables

var nBarCount        = 0;
var nValue3          = 0;

var aPriceArray      = new Array();
var aSmoothArray     = new Array();
var aCycleArray      = new Array();
var aValue1Array     = new Array();


//== PreMain function required by eSignal to set
   things up
function preMain() {
var x;

  setPriceStudy(false);
  setStudyTitle("FisherCyberCycle");
  setCursorLabelName("Cycle", 0);
  setCursorLabelName("Trig", 1);
  setDefaultBarFgColor( Color.blue, 0 );
  setDefaultBarFgColor( Color.red,  1 );
  addBand( 0, PS_SOLID, Color.black, 1, -55 );

        //initialize arrays
  for (x=0; x<70; x++) {
        aPriceArray[x]   = 0.0;
        aSmoothArray[x]  = 0.0;
        aCycleArray[x]   = 0.0;
        aValue1Array[x]  = 0.0;
   }

}
                                              (continued)
```

图 8.12（续）

```
//== Main processing function
function main( Alpha, OscLength ) {
var x;
var nPrice;
var nValue2;
var nMaxCycle;
var nMinCycle;

        //initialize parameters if necessary
        if ( Alpha == null ) {
            Alpha = 0.07;
        }
        if ( OscLength == null ) {
            OscLength = 8;
        }

        // study is initializing
   if (getBarState() == BARSTATE_ALLBARS) {
      return null;
   }

        //on each new bar, save array values
        if ( getBarState() == BARSTATE_NEWBAR ) {

            nBarCount++;

            aPriceArray.pop();
            aPriceArray.unshift( 0 );

            aSmoothArray.pop();
            aSmoothArray.unshift( 0 );

            aCycleArray.pop();
            aCycleArray.unshift( 0 );

            aValue1Array.pop();
            aValue1Array.unshift( 0 );

            nTrig = nValue3;
        }
```

图 8.12（续）

```
nPrice = ( high()+low() ) / 2;
aPriceArray[0] = nPrice;

aSmoothArray[0] = ( aPriceArray[0]
    + 2*aPriceArray[1] + 2*aPriceArray[2]
    + aPriceArray[3] ) / 6;

if ( nBarCount < 7 ) {
    aCycleArray[0] = ( aPriceArray[0]
        - 2*aPriceArray[1]
        + aPriceArray[2] ) / 4;
}
else {
    aCycleArray[0] = ( 1 - 0.5*Alpha ) * ( 1
        - 0.5*Alpha ) * ( aSmoothArray[0]
        - 2*aSmoothArray[1] +
        aSmoothArray[2] ) + 2*( 1-Alpha )
        * aCycleArray[1] - ( 1-Alpha )
        * ( 1-Alpha ) * aCycleArray[2];
}

nMaxCycle = Highest( OscLength );
nMinCycle = Lowest( OscLength );

if ( nMaxCycle != nMinCycle ) aValue1Array[0]
    = ( aCycleArray[0]-nMinCycle )
    / ( nMaxCycle - nMinCycle );

nValue2 = ( 4*aValue1Array[0]
    + 3*aValue1Array[1] + 2*aValue1Array[2]
    + aValue1Array[3] ) / 10;
nValue3 = 0.5 * Math.log( ( 1 + 1.98
    * ( nValue2-0.5 ) ) / ( 1 - 1.98
    * ( nValue2-0.5 ) ) );

//return the calculated values
if (!isNaN( nValue3 ) ) {
    return new Array( nValue3, nTrig );
}

}
```

(continued)

图 8.12（续）

```
/*********************************************************
                  SUPPORT FUNCTIONS
*********************************************************/

function Highest( nPeriod ) {
var x;
var nTmp = -999999999.0;

        for (x=0; x<nPeriod; x++) {
                nTmp = Math.max( nTmp, aCycleArray[x] );
        }

         return( nTmp );
}
function Lowest( nPeriod ) {
var x;
var nTmp = 999999999.0;

        for (x=0; x<nPeriod; x++) {
                nTmp = Math.min( nTmp, aCycleArray[x] );
        }

         return( nTmp );
}
```

图 8.12（续）

```
{***********************************************************
                       Fisher CG
************************************************************}
Inputs: Price((H+L)/2),
        Length(8);

Vars:   count(0),
        Num(0),
        Denom(0),
        CG(0),
        MaxCG(0),
        MinCG(0),
        Lead(0);

Num = 0;
Denom = 0;
For count = 0 to Length - 1 begin
        Num = Num + (1 + count)*(Price[count]);
        Denom = Denom + (Price[count]);
End;
If Denom <> 0 then CG = -Num/Denom + (Length + 1) / 2;

MaxCG = Highest(CG, Length);
MinCG = Lowest(CG, Length);
If MaxCG <> MinCG then Value1 = (CG - MinCG) /
   (MaxCG - MinCG);
Value2 = (4*Value1 + 3*Value1[1] + 2*Value1[2] +
   Value1[3]) / 10;

Value3 = .5*Log((1+1.98*(Value2-.5))/(1-1.98
   *(Value2-.5)));

Plot1(Value3, "CG");
Plot2(Value3[1], "Trigger");
Plot3(0,"Ref");
```

图 8.13 计算费希尔随机 CG 的 EasyLanguage 代码

```
/***********************************************
  Title:       Fisher Stochastic CG Oscillator
  Coded By:    Chris D. Kryza (Divergence Software, Inc.)
  Email:       c.kryza@gte.net
  Incept:      06/19/2003
  Version:     1.0.0


  ================================================
  Fix History:

  06/19/2003 -  Initial Release
  1.0.0


  ================================================
************************************************/


//External Variables
var nPrice                    = 0;
var nCG                       = 0;
var nValue3                   = 0;
var nTrig                     = 0;

var aPriceArray               = new Array();
var aCGArray                  = new Array();
var aValue1Array              = new Array();

//== PreMain function required by eSignal to set_
   things up
function preMain() {
var x;

  setPriceStudy(false);
  setStudyTitle("FisherStochasticCGOsc");
  setCursorLabelName("CG", 0);
  setCursorLabelName("Trig", 1);
  setDefaultBarFgColor( Color.blue, 0 );
  setDefaultBarFgColor( Color.red, 1 );
  addBand( 0, PS_SOLID, Color.black, 1, -55 );
```

图 8.14 计算费希尔随机 CG 的 EFS 代码

```
            //initialize arrays
    for (x=0; x<70; x++) {
        aPriceArray[x]      = 0.0;
        aCGArray[x]         = 0.0;
        aValue1Array[x]     = 0.0;
    }
}

//== Main processing function
function main( OscLength ) {
var x;
var nNum;
var nDenom;
var nMaxCG;
var nMinCG;
var nValue1;

        //initialize parameters if necessary
        if ( OscLength == null ) {
            OscLength = 8;
        }

        // study is initializing
    if (getBarState() == BARSTATE_ALLBARS) {
        return null;
    }

        //on each new bar, save array values
        if ( getBarState() == BARSTATE_NEWBAR ) {
            aPriceArray.pop();
            aPriceArray.unshift( 0 );

            aCGArray.pop();
            aCGArray.unshift( 0 );

            aValue1Array.pop();
            aValue1Array.unshift( 0 );
```

(continued)

图 8.14（续）

```
            nTrig = nValue3;
    }

    nPrice = ( high()+low() ) / 2;
    aPriceArray[0] = nPrice;

    nNum         = 0;
    nDenom       = 0;


    for ( x=0; x<OscLength; x++ ){
        nNum += ( 1.0 + x )
            * ( aPriceArray[x] );
        nDenom += ( aPriceArray[x] );
    }
    if ( nDenom != 0 ) nCG = -nNum/nDenom
        + ( OscLength+1 )/2;
    aCGArray[0] = nCG;

    nMaxCG = Highest( OscLength );
    nMinCG = Lowest( OscLength );

    if ( nMaxCG != nMinCG ) aValue1Array[0]
        = (nCG - nMinCG) / (nMaxCG - nMinCG);

    nValue2 = ( 4*aValue1Array[0]
        + 3*aValue1Array[1] + 2*aValue1Array[2]
        + aValue1Array[3] ) / 10;
    nValue3 = 0.5 * Math.log( ( 1 + 1.98
        * ( nValue2-0.5 ) ) / ( 1 - 1.98
        * ( nValue2-0.5 ) ) );

    //return the calculated values
    if ( !isNaN( nValue3 ) ) {
        return new Array( nValue3, nTrig );
    }

}
```

图 8.14 (续)

```
/*****************************************************
                SUPPORT FUNCTIONS
*****************************************************/

function Highest( nPeriod ) {
var x;
var nTmp = -999999999.0;

        for (x=0; x<nPeriod; x++) {
                nTmp = Math.max( nTmp, aCGArray[x] );
        }

        return( nTmp );
}
function Lowest( nPeriod ) {
var x;
var nTmp = 999999999.0;

        for (x=0; x<nPeriod; x++) {
                nTmp = Math.min( nTmp, aCGArray[x] );
        }

        return( nTmp );
}
```

图 8.14（续）

```
{*****************************************************
                    Fisher RVI
*****************************************************}

Inputs: Length(8);

Vars:   Num(0),
        Denom(0),
        count(0),
                                              (continued)
```

图 8.15　计算费希尔随机 RVI 的 EasyLanguage 代码

```
            RVI(0),
            Lead(0),
            MaxRVI(0),
            MinRVI(0);

Value1 = ((Close - Open) + 2*(Close[1] - Open[1])
    + 2*(Close[2] - Open[2]) + (Close[3] - Open[3]))/6;
Value2 = ((High - Low) + 2*(High[1] - Low[1])
    + 2*(High[2] - Low[2]) + (High[3] - Low[3]))/6;
Num = 0;
Denom = 0;
For count = 0 to Length - 1 begin
        Num = Num + Value1[count];
        Denom = Denom + Value2[count];
End;
If Denom <> 0 then RVI = Num / Denom;

MaxRVI = Highest(RVI, Length);
MinRVI = Lowest(RVI, Length);
If MaxRVI <> MinRVI then Value3 = (RVI - MinRVI)
    / (MaxRVI - MinRVI);
Value4 = (4*Value3 + 3*Value3[1] + 2*Value3[2]
    + Value3[3]) / 10;

Value5 = .5*Log((1+1.98*(Value4 - .5))/(1-1.98*(Value4
    - .5)));

Plot1(Value5, |RVI|);
Plot2(Value5[1], |Trigger|);
Plot3(0,|Ref|);
```

图 8.15（续）

```
/***********************************************************
   Title:       FisherStochastic RVI
   Coded By:    Chris D. Kryza (Divergence Software, Inc.)
   Email:       c.kryza@gte.net
   Incept:      06/19/2003
   Version:     1.0.0


   ==========================================================
   Fix History:

   06/19/2003 -  Initial Release
   1.0.0


   ==========================================================
***********************************************************/


//External Variables
var nValue5                    = 0;
var nTrig                      = 0;

var aRVIArray                  = new Array();
var aValue1Array               = new Array();
var aValue2Array               = new Array();
var aValue3Array               = new Array();

//== PreMain function required by eSignal to set_
   things up
function preMain() {
var x;

  setPriceStudy(false);
  setStudyTitle("FisherStochasticRVI");
  setCursorLabelName("RVI", 0);
  setCursorLabelName("Trig", 1);
  setDefaultBarFgColor( Color.blue, 0 );
  setDefaultBarFgColor( Color.red, 1 );
  addBand( 0, PS_SOLID, Color.black, 1, -55 );

       //initialize arrays
  for (x=0; x<70; x++) {
```
(continued)

图 8.16 计算费希尔随机 RVI 的 EFS 代码

```
            aRVIArray[x]            = 0.0;
            aValue1Array[x]         = 0.0;
            aValue2Array[x]         = 0.0;
            aValue3Array[x]         = 0.0;
    }
}

//== Main processing function
function main( OscLength ) {
var x;
var nNum;
var nDenom;
var nValue4;
var nMaxRVI;
var nMinRVI;

        //initialize parameters if necessary
        if ( OscLength == null ) {
            OscLength = 8;
        }

        // study is initializing
    if (getBarState() == BARSTATE_ALLBARS) {
        return null;
    }

        //on each new bar, save array values
        if ( getBarState() == BARSTATE_NEWBAR ) {

            aRVIArray.pop();
            aRVIArray.unshift( 0 );

            aValue1Array.pop();
            aValue1Array.unshift( 0 );

            aValue2Array.pop();
            aValue2Array.unshift( 0 );

            aValue3Array.pop();
            aValue3Array.unshift( 0 );
```

图 8.16（续）

```
            nTrig = nValue5;
    }

    aValue1Array[0] = ( ( close()-open() )
        + 2*( close(-1)-open(-1) )
        + 2*( close(-2)-open(-2) )
        + ( close(-3)-open(-3) ) ) / 6;
    aValue2Array[0] = ( ( high()-low() )
        + 2*( high(-1)-low(-1) )
        + 2*( high(-2)-low(-2) )
        + ( high(-3)-low(-3) ) ) / 6;


    nNum          = 0;
    nDenom        = 0;


    for ( x=0; x<OscLength; x++ ){
        nNum += aValue1Array[x];
        nDenom += aValue2Array[x];
    }

    if ( nDenom != 0 ) aRVIArray[0] = nNum/nDenom;
    nMaxRVI = Highest( OscLength );
    nMinRVI = Lowest( OscLength );

    if ( nMaxRVI != nMinRVI ) aValue3Array[0]
        = ( aRVIArray[0]-nMinRVI )
        / ( nMaxRVI-nMinRVI );

    nValue4 = ( 4*aValue3Array[0]
        + 3*aValue3Array[1] + 2*aValue3Array[2]
        + aValue3Array[3] ) / 10;
    nValue5 = 0.5 * Math.log( ( 1 + 1.98
        * ( nValue4-0.5 ) ) / ( 1 - 1.98
        * ( nValue4-0.5 ) ) );

    //return the calculated values
    if ( !isNaN( nValue5 ) ) {
        return new Array( nValue5, nTrig );
    }
}
```

(continued)

图 8.16（续）

```
/*****************************************************
            SUPPORT FUNCTIONS
*****************************************************/

function Highest( nPeriod ) {
var x;
var nTmp = -999999999.0;

        for (x=0; x<nPeriod; x++) {
                nTmp = Math.max( nTmp, aRVIArray[x] );
        }

        return( nTmp );
}
function Lowest( nPeriod ) {
var x;
var nTmp = 999999999.0;

        for (x=0; x<nPeriod; x++) {
                nTmp = Math.min( nTmp, aRVIArray[x] );
        }

        return( nTmp );
}
```

图 8.16（续）

三个费希尔化的指标比较见图 8.17。通过忽略绝对幅度小于 2 时出现的交叉，在任何情况下，费希尔变换都为我们提供了一种过滤双人拉锯式信号的方法。看起来费希尔 RVI 是一个超级振荡指标，因为它都几乎毫无例外地先于其他指标几日给出交易信号。这使它成为一个真正的优秀指标，因为其他两个都不如它及时。这三个指标都可加入你的技术分析工具箱。

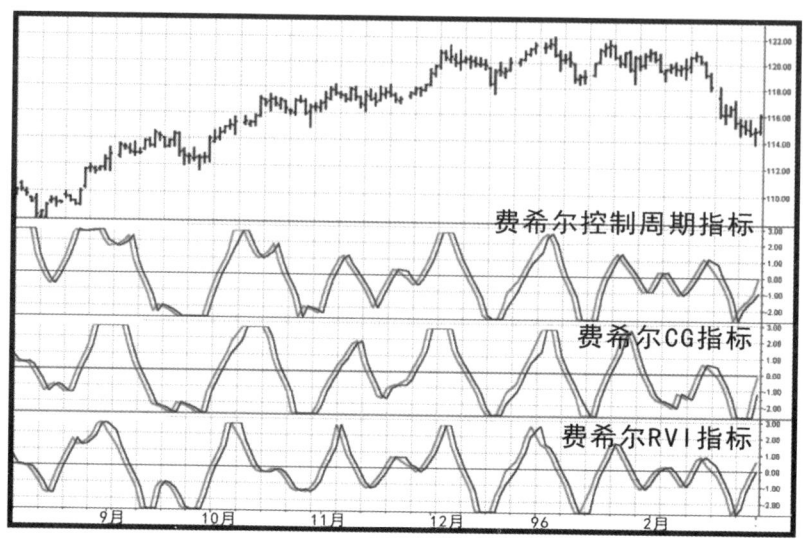

图8.17 费希尔化后的指标给出尖锐的交易信号

需要牢记的要点

- 通过对现有指标进行随机化处理,我们可以得到新的、更容易阅读的振荡指标。
- 随机RVI是一个非常平滑、一致性非常好的振荡指标。
- 对限制了幅度的振荡指标进行费希尔变换,通过忽略幅度小于2时出现的交叉,提供了一种滤除双人拉锯式信号的方法。
- 费希尔RSI提供了及时而准确的信号。

第 9 章　测量循环周期

"看起来像要下雨。"汤姆出人意料地说。

市场中显然存在循环。最马虎的观察者也会在任意图表上发现循环，现在不清楚的是如何辨识那些循环，以及如何利用它们交易。当韦尔斯·韦尔德（Welles Wilder）首次介绍相对强弱指数（RSI）时，我奇怪于它为什么选择 14 日作为计算的基础。当时经过分析后我认为，如果我知道正确的市场行情，那么我就可以使 RSI 这样的指标去适应那些行情。循环便是答案，我知道循环是可以测量的。一旦我测量出了循环周期，那么就可以设计一大堆自适应指标。

对市场循环周期的测量并不容易。市场数据的信噪比（signal-to-noise ratio）一般非常低，因此，即使使用优秀的测量技术，测量难度也非常大。另外，这些测量在理论上要同时解决参数值的三重无限问题（triple infinity）。我们一般需要的三个参数是频率、幅度和相位。一些工程上使用的标准测量工具，比如快速傅立叶变换（FFT），并不适合测量市场循环，因为 FFT 不能在满足稳定性约束的情况下，同时产生具有恰当分辨率的结果。所以，我引入了最大熵谱分析（MESA）来测量市场循环。这种方法最初在石油勘探中被用于解释地震仪的信息，只用非常少的信息量便可产生高分辨率的输出结果。较短的数据长度提高了接近静态数据（静态数据是指在数据长度上数据的频率和幅度都不发生变化。）的概率。我注意到在多年的数据上循环是瞬息变化的，它们的周期可能持续延长和缩短。它们的幅度也是变化的，所以信噪比也是不断变化的。虽然它们都是与周期性分量一起变化的，但是对于正在使用的数据集来说，不变的特性是通常每次只有一个可用于交易的循环。我喜欢使用术语主循环（dominant cycle）来表示价格数据中的那个周期性分量。假设数据之中只有一个循环，极大地降低了测量工作的难度。

假设数据中只存在一个循环，那么我们便可使用鉴频器（frequency discriminator）来进行测量。鉴频器实际上测量的是连续数据样本之间的微分相位（differential phase）。因为每个周期有360°，所以360除以微分相位之后便得到所测的周期长度。举例说明，如果微分相位是20°，那么所测周期长度将是360/20 = 18日。也就是说，一个18日循环就是以每个样本20°的速率改变相位，于是在18个样本之后便达到360°（一个周期）。相当简单！显然，从理论上讲只要两个样本便可测量出循环周期。

为了测量相位，我们需要用相量而不是我们熟悉的传统波形来描述循环。循环波形和相量之间的关系见图9.1。我们可以把相量看作尾部固定在原点，然后逆时针旋转的箭头，这个箭头的投影便会勾画出正弦波循环。随着相量的旋转，首先达到最大峰值幅度（peak amplitude），然后穿过零点，接下来达到最小循环幅度，随后又返回零点，如此循环不止。这个相量转动完整的一周便是一个循环周期。

这个相量可以被分为两部分，分别为同相分量（InPhase component）和正交分量（Quadrature component），见图9.2。通过对任意给定样本的这两个部分的比值求反正切（arctangent），我们很容易便可求出相位角。

第9章 测量循环周期

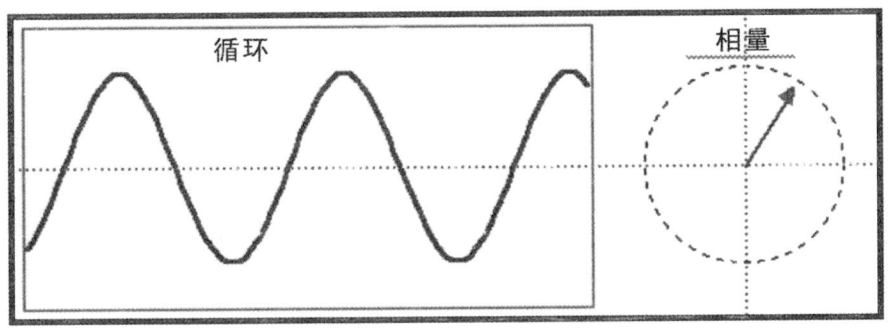

图9.1 用相量表示一个循环

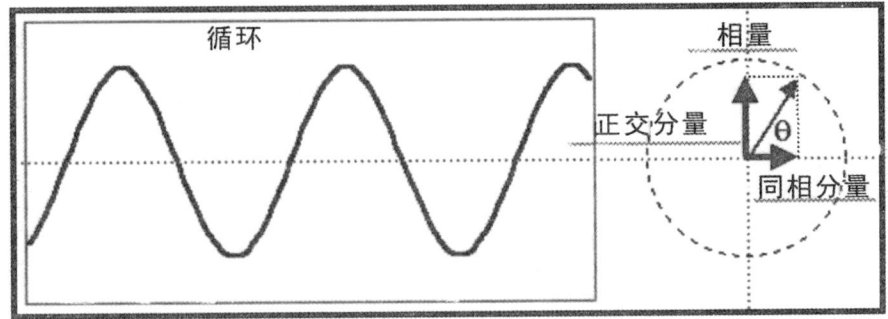

图9.2 相位角是正交分量和同相分量的比值的反正切值

关键在于把分析的波形（我们熟悉的价格周期性分量的表现形式）分解为同相分量和正交分量。这可以通过希耳伯特变换（Hilbert transform）[①]来实现。希耳伯特变换是一个理论上的无穷级数；为了用于交易，我已经把这个级数缩短为四项。在EasyLanguage代码中计算正交分量的公式如下：

$$Q = 0.0962 * \text{Price} + 0.5769 * \text{Price}[2] - 0.5769 * \text{Price}[4] - 0.0962 * \text{Price}[6] \tag{9.1}$$

正交分量的滞后是半个滤波器长度，或者说3日。所以同相分量就是延迟3日的价格，即：

---

① 《火箭技术的交易应用》，第6章。

$$I = \text{Price}[3] \qquad (9.2)$$

为了测试周期测量过程的速度,我创建了单个周期的 20 日正弦波。然后我使用希耳伯特变换计算相位角,并且使用一个鉴频器来测量循环周期。这次试验的结果见图 9.3。这些结果给人的印象非常深刻。循环周期的精确测量在循环开始的 4 个样本内便完成了。这 4 个样本的滞后就是希耳伯特变换的滞后再加上一个样本的滞后,原因是计算周期需要求出样本之间的相位差。

在因看到这些结果而变得太兴奋之前,请回想一下这只是一个纯粹的单频率理论波形,具有一个无穷大的信噪比。另外,由于循环波动是在零线附近,所以波形已经被去趋势(detrended)。对于真实数据,我们必须做去趋势处理,以便提取周期性分量,同时还要处理信号上面叠加的噪声。换句话说,我们需要像图 4.2 所示的那样计算市场价格的周期性分量,然后才可以计算循环周期。

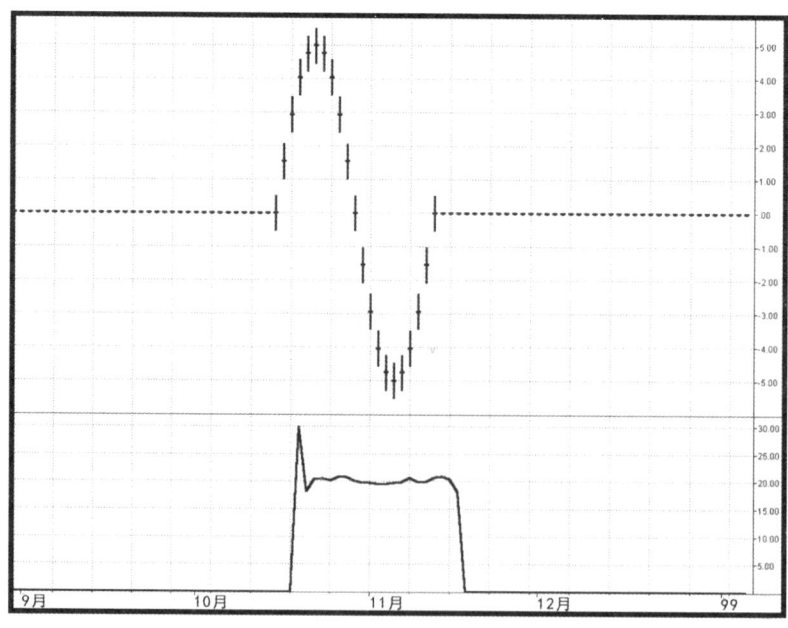

图 9.3　希耳伯特变换使我们可以对循环周期实现快速测量

计算循环周期的 EasyLanguage 代码和 EFS 代码分别见图 9.4 和 9.5。这些计算的说明参照图 9.4。在定义了输入并且声明了变量之后，前三行代码恢复了周期性分量，就像图 4.2 一样。我们使用周期性分量计算希耳伯特变换的正交分量（Q1）和同相分量（I1）。缩短无穷级数来计算正交分量的代价是，对于较长的循环周期来说，正交分量的幅度被衰减了。计算 Q1 的最后一项是直线幅度校正。由于在代码中此时还不知道周期，而且周期是逐个样本变化相对缓慢的函数，所以使用 1 日前计算的周期作为补偿可以得到令人满意的结果。我发现这种反馈补偿是最健全的方法。

还有另一种幅度补偿方案可以使用。在纯周期信号的情况下，我们可以把同相分量记作 cos（θ），而把正交分量记作 sin（θ）。那么，正交分量中的幅度衰减补偿可以从简单的三角恒等式中得出：

$$\sin^2(\theta) = 1 - \cos^2(\theta)$$

然后对幅度进行规格化。虽然这是一个伟大的理论，并且在理论波形上有效，但是因为实际价格数据中存在噪声，所以我未能得到满意的补偿效果。所以我在代码中使用反馈幅度补偿。

```
Inputs:         Price((H+L)/2),
                alpha(.07);

Vars:           Smooth(0),
                Cycle(0),
                Q1(0),
                I1(0),
                DeltaPhase(0),
                MedianDelta(0),
                DC(0),
                InstPeriod(0),
                Period(0),
                I2(0),
                Q2(0);

Smooth = (Price + 2*Price[1] + 2*Price[2]
    + Price[3])/6;
Cycle = (1 - .5*alpha)*(1 - .5*alpha)*(Smooth
    - 2*Smooth[1] + Smooth[2]) + 2*(1 - alpha)*Cycle[1]
    - (1 - alpha)*(1 - alpha)*Cycle[2];
If currentbar < 7 then Cycle = (Price - 2*Price[1]
    + Price[2]) / 4;

Q1 = (.0962*Cycle + .5769*Cycle[2] - .5769*Cycle[4]
    - .0962*Cycle[6])*(.5 + .08*InstPeriod[1]);
I1 = Cycle[3];

If Q1 <> 0 and Q1[1] <> 0 then DeltaPhase = (I1/Q1
    - I1[1]/Q1[1]) / (1 + I1*I1[1]/(Q1*Q1[1]));
If DeltaPhase < 0.1 then DeltaPhase = 0.1;
If DeltaPhase > 1.1 then DeltaPhase = 1.1;
MedianDelta = Median(DeltaPhase, 5);

If MedianDelta = 0 then DC = 15 else DC
    = 6.28318 / MedianDelta + .5;

InstPeriod = .33*DC + .67*InstPeriod[1];
Period = .15*InstPeriod + .85*Period[1];


Plot1(Period, IPeriodI);
```

图 9.4 计算控制周期指标的 EasyLanguage 代码

第 9 章 测量循环周期

```
/*********************************************************
Title:      Cycle Period
Coded By:   Chris D. Kryza (Divergence Software, Inc.)
Email:      c.kryza@gte.net
Incept:     06/19/2003
Version:    1.0.0


=========================================================
Fix History:

06/19/2003 -   Initial Release
1.0.0


=========================================================
*********************************************************/


//External Variables

var nBarCount            = 0;

var aPriceArray          = new Array();
var aSmoothArray         = new Array();
var aCycleArray          = new Array();
var aDeltaPhase          = new Array();
var aPeriod              = new Array();
var aInstPeriod          = new Array();
var aQ1                  = new Array();
var aI1                  = new Array();


//== PreMain function required by eSignal to set_
    things up
function preMain() {
var x;

   setPriceStudy(false);
   setStudyTitle(ICycle PeriodI);
   setCursorLabelName(IPeriodI, 0);
   setDefaultBarFgColor( Color.blue, 0 );
```

图 9.5 计算控制周期指标的 EFS 代码

```
        //initialize arrays
    for (x=0; x<10; x++) {
        aPriceArray[x]      = 0.0;
        aSmoothArray[x]     = 0.0;
        aCycleArray[x]      = 0.0;
        aQ1[x]              = 0.0;
        aI1[x]              = 0.0;
        aDeltaPhase[x]      = 0.0;
        aPeriod[x]          = 0.0;
        aInstPeriod[x]      = 0.0;
    }

}

//== Main processing function
function main( Alpha ) {
var x;
var nDC;
var nMedianDelta;

        //initialize parameters if necessary
        if ( Alpha == null ) {
                Alpha = 0.07;
        }

        // study is initializing
    if ( getBarState() == BARSTATE_ALLBARS ) {
       return null;
    }

        //on each new bar, save array values
        if ( getBarState() == BARSTATE_NEWBAR ) {

                nBarCount++;

                aPriceArray.pop();
                aPriceArray.unshift( 0 );

                aSmoothArray.pop();
                aSmoothArray.unshift( 0 );

                                                        (continued)
```

图 9.5（续）

```
                aCycleArray.pop();
                aCycleArray.unshift( 0 );

                aQ1.pop();
                aQ1.unshift( 0 );

                aI1.pop();
                aI1.unshift( 0 );

                aDeltaPhase.pop();
                aDeltaPhase.unshift( 0 );

                aInstPeriod.pop();
                aInstPeriod.unshift( 0 );

                aPeriod.pop();
                aPeriod.unshift( 0 );


}

aPriceArray[0] = ( high()+low() ) / 2;

aSmoothArray[0] = ( aPriceArray[0]
    + 2*aPriceArray[1] + 2*aPriceArray[2]
    + aPriceArray[3] ) / 6;

if ( nBarCount < 7 ) {
        aCycleArray[0] = ( aPriceArray[0]
            - 2*aPriceArray[1]
            + aPriceArray[2] ) / 4;
}
else {
        aCycleArray[0] = ( 1 - 0.5*Alpha )
            * ( 1 - 0.5*Alpha )
            * ( aSmoothArray[0]
            - 2*aSmoothArray[1]
            + aSmoothArray[2] ) + 2*( 1-Alpha )
            * aCycleArray[1] - ( 1-Alpha )
            * ( 1-Alpha ) * aCycleArray[2];
}
```

图 9.5（续）

```
            aQ1[0] = ( 0.0962*aCycleArray[0]
                + 0.5769*aCycleArray[2]
                - 0.5769*aCycleArray[4]
                - 0.0962*aCycleArray[6] ) * ( 0.5 + 0.08
                * aInstPeriod[1] );
            aI1[0] = aCycleArray[3];

            if ( aQ1[0] != 0 && aQ1[1] != 0 ) {
                    aDeltaPhase[0] = (aI1[0]/aQ1[0]
                        - aI1[1]/aQ1[1]) / (1
                        + aI1[0]*aI1[1]/(aQ1[0]*aQ1[1]));
            }
            if ( aDeltaPhase[0] < 0.1 ) aDeltaPhase[0]
                = 0.1;
            if ( aDeltaPhase[0] > 1.1 ) aDeltaPhase[0]
                = 1.1;
            //Need a 5 bar Median filter of DeltaPhase here_
                (MedianDelta)
            nMedianDelta = Median( 5, aDeltaPhase );

            if ( nMedianDelta == 0 ) {
                    nDC = 15;
            }
            else {
                    nDC = 6.28318 / nMedianDelta + 0.5;
            }

            aInstPeriod[0] = 0.33 * nDC + 0.67
                * aInstPeriod[1];
            aPeriod[0] = 0.15*aInstPeriod[0]
                + 0.85*aPeriod[1];

            return( aPeriod[0] );


}



function Median( nBars, aArray ) {
var aTmp = new Array();
                                                    (continued)
```

图 9.5（续）

```
var nTmp;
var result;
var x;

    //transfer elements to temp array
    x = 0;
    while( x < nBars ) {
        aTmp[x] = aArray[x++];
    }
    //sort array in asc order
    aTmp.sort( SortAsc );


    //if odd # of elements, just take middle
    if ( nBars % 2 != 0 ) {
        result = aTmp[ (nBars+1) / 2 ]
        aTmp = null;
        return( result );
    }
    //if even # elements, take average of two_
       middle elements
    else {
        nTmp = nBars/2;
        result = (aTmp[nTmp] + aTmp[nTmp+1])/2;
        aTmp = null;
        return ( result );
    }
}


function SortAsc( arg1, arg2 ) {
    if (arg1<arg2) {
        return( -1 )
    }
    else {
        return( 1 );
    }
}
```

图 9.5（续）

在计算 DeltaPhase 时，我们先用一条条件 IF 语句消除被 0 除的可能性。我需要对剩余代码做一些解释。当前棒线的相位角是 arctan（I1/Q1），前 1 条棒线的相位角是 arctan（I1［1］/Q1［1］）。利用三角恒等式，很容易便可计算出微分相位：

$$\arctan(A) - \arctan(B) = \arctan\left(\frac{A-B}{1+AB}\right) \quad (9.3)$$

6 日周期是我们需要测量的最短周期。一个 6 日循环的相移是每日 60°，或者说每日 1.047 弧度。由于微分相位的最大值大约是 1 弧度，所以一个合理的近似是以弧度为单位表示的角度约等于那个角的反正切值。我们在计算微分相位的代码中使用了这种近似。

在计算出 DeltaPhase 后，我们必须添加一些限制条件。首先，DeltaPhase 必须总为正，因为时间不可能倒退。如果我们得到一个负的 DeltaPhase 计算结果，那么可能是因为存在噪声，也可能是因为两个绝对相位测量结果不在相量的同一个象限内。（反正切值在第一和第三象限为正，在第二和第四象限为负。）当 DeltaPhase 为负时，替换前一个计算结果便可符合要求。反之，如果 DeltaPhase 小于 0.1 弧度，那么我就把它限制为 0.1 弧度。这是因为 DeltaPhase 小于 0.1 意味着周期大于 63 日（2 * π/0.1）。另一个限制条件是不计算小于 6 日的周期。通过把 DeltaPhase 限制为 1.1 弧度，便可满足我们的限制条件。

循环周期的实际计算或许是代码中最容易理解的部分。简而言之，计算思路就是用 DeltaPhase 除以 2π，因为 2π 代表着用弧度表示的一个完整的循环。实际上，DeltaPhase 中叠加了大量的噪声，每天都存在大量的变化。如果直接使用 DeltaPhase，需要对它进行大量的平滑，以便恢复一个合理的主周期。有一种比较有效的平滑方式。对于波动强烈的数据来说，最好的一种滤波器是中值滤波器。因此，我利用一个中值滤波器过滤 5 个样本上的 DeltaPhase，得出变量 MedianDelta。然后用 MedianDelta 除以 2π，计算出主周期。在测量理论上的正弦波周期时，我发现在周期测量中有一个约等于 0.5 的恒定误差，于是我增加一个补偿项来消除那个恒定误差。我用一个 $\alpha = 0.33$ 的指数移动平均对主周期进行平滑，由于在 Q1 的计算中存在反馈项，所以响应速度相对较快。我把这个变量叫作瞬时周期（InstPeriod）。然后我又用一个 $\alpha = 0.15$ 的指数移动平均对 InstPeriod 进行平滑。选择这个值，以完成一个从 0 开始的 20 日信号的一个循环中整个循环长度的测量。

为了检验周期测量的质量，我进行了一系列严格的测试。首先我检验了这种方法的启动瞬态特性，所用方法类似于图 9.3 中单周期测量所用的方法。最后结果见图 9.6 下部的子图。在这种情况下，我继续使用第一个 20 日循环之后的 20 日循环。InstPeriod 从开始到达到 20 日的测量值，共用了 8 日。平滑滤波器 1.5 日的滞后，加上希耳伯特变换 4 日的滞后，再加上中值滤波器 2.5 日的滞后，恰好是 8 日的滞后。周期输出的平滑是由指数移动平均完成的。我本应该少用一些平滑计算。然而，真实数据中循环周期一般变化相对缓慢，而且在不怎么考虑滞后时，较大量的平滑是可取的。这些结果应该结合市场行情来观察。举例说明，一个快速傅立叶变换（FFT）大约要用 16 个周期的数据才能得出比较准确的测量结果。是的，没错——FFT 需要 16 个完整周期的数据才可得到相同的结果。即使最大熵谱分析（MESA）也需要一个周期的较大部分才能得出首次测量结果。

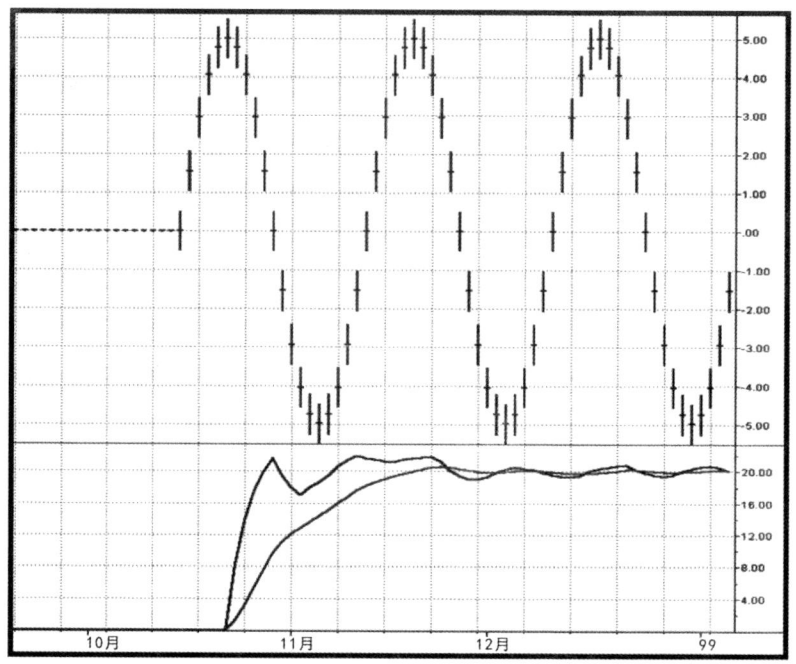

图 9.6　单频率 20 日循环的周期测量

对于任何测量算法，一项关键测试是看输入数据在较宽范围上变化时，该算法是否能够进行正确地测量。为此，我制作了一个理论上的正弦波，其周期从 6 日逐渐增加到 40 日。在图 9.7 中我们可以看到这个波形，下部的测量结果表明我们的测量是非常准确的。

另一个瞬态和准确性测试是在信号周期从 30 日到 15 日，然后又返回 30 日的变化过程中，看这种测量算法测量的速度有多快。在图 9.8 中，测试用数据包含两个周期的 30 日循环，4 个周期的 15 日循环，和另外两个周期的 30 日循环。这是一项严格的测试，需要这种测量算法在不同周期的循环之间快速变换。这项测试表明，在 15 个样本内无论向哪个方向切换，这种测量方法得出的结果都在实际周期的合理范围内。

第9章 测量循环周期

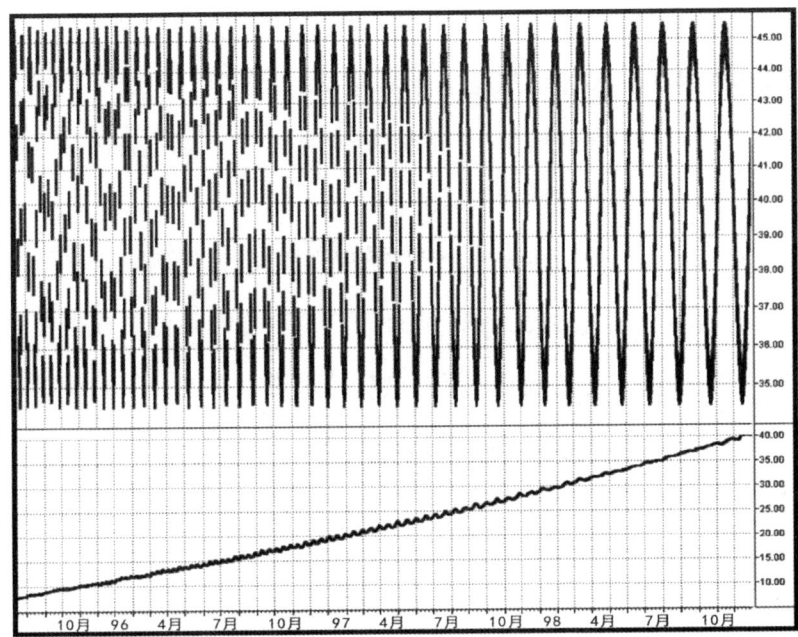

图9.7 周期从6日逐渐增加到40日的线性调频脉冲波形（Chirped Waveform）的周期测量结果

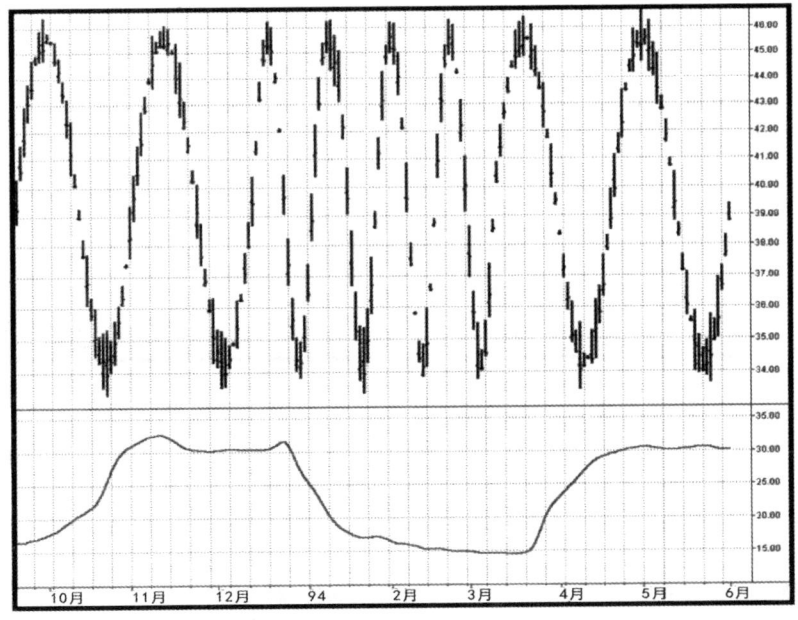

图9.8 周期从30日变化为15日，又返回30日的循环周期的测量

此处我们得到的基本信息是这种周期测量方法有一个大约 8 日的滞后，如图 9.6 所示，在最坏的情况下，滞后最大为 15 日。当这种测量方法用于交易时，我们应该认识到这些滞后的存在。

图 9.9 所示为这种循环周期测量方法对实际数据的测量示例。这种测量方法比普通测量方法灵敏得多。通过计算主要连续最低点或主要连续最高点之间的棒线数，并且与那一点的测量结果进行对比，我们可以对测量准确性做出评价。每两个水平单位之间有 5 条棒线，从而方便你的计数。请你记住，在对周期波形的测量中存在大约 8 日的滞后。

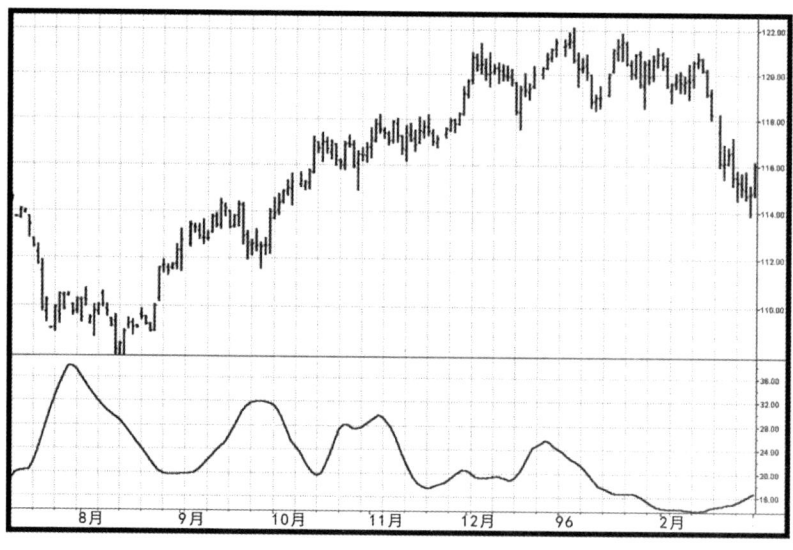

图 9.9 真实数据的周期测量

需要牢记的要点

- 通过使用希耳伯特变换，我们只要 4 条棒线便可测量循环周期。
- 我们必须首先从数据中提取周期性分量，然后才可测量主循环的周期。

- 用鉴频器测量主周期，就是把棒线间的微分相位求和直到达到 360°——一个完整的循环。
- 我们用一个 5 日中值滤波器产生求和用的微分相位。
- 通过使用对中值微分相位求和的方法测量周期，使我们只需要 5 个样本便可完成测量。
- 测量主周期的滞后大约是 8 日。
- 本章讲解的主循环周期测量技术是目前反应最灵敏的技术。

第10章 自适应周期指标

"恐龙未能幸存。"汤姆顺应时势地说。

在第9章中我们已经对循环周期进行了测量,一种较为直接的应用就是记下最新的最高点,然后向前数出半个主循环周期长度以确定下个买入机会。幸运的是,我们可以利用指标分析把这种应用做得更加巧妙。如果用固定长度计算的指标有效性适中,那么当对它们的计算长度根据测得主周期而做相应调整时,它们的表现就相当优秀了。

我在第4章至第6章设计了几个振荡型指标。现在我将利用主循环周期的测量结果对它们的计算长度进行调整,使之适应最新的市场行情,逐一分析它们的性能是否有所提高。对于每个指标,我都要对它的自适应版本和静态版本进行对比。不仅如此,我还对三个自适应指标进行了横向比较,有助于你判断哪一个比较适合自己。为了一致性的目的,我在本书中使用相同的价格图表,因为你可以在你自己的电脑上使用自己的数据对这些指标进行测试,所以我没有把那些令人厌烦的细节全部列出来。

自适应控制周期振荡指标

最简单的周期指标是控制周期振荡指标,它是从第4章中的价格序列中通过滤除趋势分量得出的。这个滤波器是在第 2 章导出的。它使用的系数 $\alpha = 0.07$。计算自适应版本控制周期指标的 EasyLanguage 代码和 EFS 代码分别见图 10.1 和 10.2。这里主周期的计算与第 9 章完全相同。我们使用一个固定的 alpha（即 α）值来做主循环周期测量；然后使用测得主周期计算系数 α_1。一般认为指数移动平均的系数 α 与简单移动平均的长度满足等式 $\alpha = 2/(Length + 1)$。在这种情况下，我使用主循环周期作为 α_1 的计算长度。这使得控制周期指标会随着测得主循环周期而变化。通过把自适应循环延迟 1 日，我们得到一条触发线，一起包含在该指标中。自适应控制周期指标和触发信号的交叉代表着该指标辨识出的买卖机会。

图 10.3 显示出自适应控制周期指标与静态控制周期指标的比较。通过这个比较我们可以看出，自适应指标一般会把周期性波动重点显示出来，并且常常是比静态指标提前 1 日产生买卖信号。

CG 振荡指标是我们在第 5 章得出的，随着取样窗口逐日移动，它求的是固定长度数据样本的重心。自适应 CG 振荡指标把测得的主周期长度的一半作为自适应 CG 振荡指标的计算长度。计算自适应 CG 振荡指标的 EasyLanguage 代码和 EFS 代码分别见图 10.4 和 10.5。这里主周期的计算与第 9 章完全相同。在计算主周期长度时我们使用的是一个定值的 α。变量 IntPeriod 是测得主周期的 4 日加权移动平均的整数部分。由于加权系数要除以它们的总和的两倍，所以 IntPeriod 是主循环周期的一半的整数值。在后面的代码中对分子和分母求和需要一个整数值。由于求和长度随着测得主循环周期的长度而变化，所以 CG 指标是自适应性的。

图 10.6 显示出自适应 CG 振荡指标和静态 CG 振荡指标的比较。在这一组数据中的比较没有显示出 CG 指标在变为自适应后有任何明显的变化。

自适应相对活力指数

相对活力指数（RVI）这个指标，我们是在第 6 章导出的，它求的是收盘价与开盘价之差和最高价与最低价之差的比值。这个比值是在一个固定时间段上计算的。自适应 RVI 振荡指标把测得的主周期长度的一半作为自适应 RVI 振荡指标的计算长度。计算自适应 RVI 的 EasyLanguage 代码和 EFS 代码分别见图 10.7 和 10.8。这里主周期的计算与第 9 章完全相同。在计算主周期长度时我们使用的是一个定值的 α。变量 Length 是测得主周期的 4 日加权移动平均的整数部分。由于加权系数要除以它们的总和的两倍，所以 Length 是主循环周期的一半的整数值。在后面的代码中对分子和分母求和需要一个整数值。由于求和长度随着测得主循环周期的长度而变化，所以 RVI 指标是自适应性的。

```
{*********************************************************
                    Adaptive Cycle
*********************************************************}
Inputs: Price((H+L)/2),
        alpha(.07);

Vars:   Smooth(0),
        Cycle(0),
        Q1(0),
        I1(0),
        DeltaPhase(0),
        MedianDelta(0),
        DC(0),
        InstPeriod(0),
        Period(0),
        Length(0),
        Num(0),
        Denom(0),
        alpha1(0),
        AdaptCycle(0);

Smooth = (Price + 2*Price[1] + 2*Price[2]
    + Price[3])/6;
Cycle = (1 - .5*alpha)*(1 - .5*alpha)*(Smooth
    - 2*Smooth[1] + Smooth[2]) + 2*(1 - alpha)*Cycle[1]
    - (1 - alpha)*(1 - alpha)*Cycle[2];
If currentbar < 7 then Cycle = (Price - 2*Price[1]
    + Price[2]) / 4;

Q1 = (.0962*Cycle + .5769*Cycle[2] - .5769*Cycle[4]
    - .0962*Cycle[6])*(.5 + .08*InstPeriod[1]);
I1 = Cycle[3];

If Q1 <> 0 and Q1[1] <> 0 then DeltaPhase = (I1/Q1
    - I1[1]/Q1[1]) / (1 + I1*I1[1]/(Q1*Q1[1]));
If DeltaPhase < 0.1 then DeltaPhase = 0.1;
If DeltaPhase > 1.1 then DeltaPhase = 1.1;
MedianDelta = Median(DeltaPhase, 5);

If MedianDelta = 0 then DC = 15 else DC = 6.28318
    / MedianDelta + .5;

InstPeriod = .33*DC + .67*InstPeriod[1];

                                           (continued)
```

图 10.1　计算自适应控制周期指标的 EasyLanguage 代码

第 10 章 自适应周期指标

```
Period = .15*InstPeriod + .85*Period[1];

alpha1 = 2 / (Period + 1);
AdaptCycle = (1 - .5*alpha1)*(1 - .5*alpha1)*(Smooth
    - 2*Smooth[1] + Smooth[2]) + 2*(1
    - alpha1)*AdaptCycle[1] - (1 - alpha1)*(1
    - alpha1)*AdaptCycle[2];
If currentbar < 7 then AdaptCycle = (Price
    - 2*Price[1] + Price[2]) / 4;

Plot1(AdaptCycle, IAdaptCycleI);
Plot2(AdaptCycle[1], ITriggerI);
```

图 10.1（续）

```
/************************************************************
Title:          Adaptive Cyber Cycle Indicator
Coded By:   Chris D. Kryza (Divergence Software, Inc.)
Email:      c.kryza@gte.net
Incept:     07/09/2003
Version:    1.0.0


========================================================
Fix History:

07/09/2003 -    Initial Release
1.0.0


========================================================
************************************************************/


//External Variables

var nBarCount           = 0;

var aPriceArray         = new Array();
var aSmoothArray        = new Array();
```

图 10.2　计算自适应控制周期指标的 EFS 代码

```
var aCycleArray              = new Array();
var aDeltaPhase              = new Array();
var aPeriod                  = new Array();
var aInstPeriod              = new Array();
var aQ1                      = new Array();
var aI1                      = new Array();
var aACycleArray             = new Array();

//== PreMain function required by eSignal to set_
   things up
function preMain() {
var x;

   setPriceStudy(false);
   setStudyTitle(IAdaptive CyberCycleI);
   setCursorLabelName(ICycleI, 0);
   setCursorLabelName(ITrigI, 1);
   setDefaultBarFgColor( Color.blue, 0 );
   setDefaultBarFgColor( Color.red,  1 );

       //initialize arrays
   for (x=0; x<10; x++) {
       aPriceArray[x]        = 0.0;
       aSmoothArray[x]       = 0.0;
       aCycleArray[x]        = 0.0;
       aQ1[x]                = 0.0;
       aI1[x]                = 0.0;
       aDeltaPhase[x]        = 0.0;
       aPeriod[x]            = 0.0;
       aInstPeriod[x]        = 0.0;
       aACycleArray[x]       = 0.0;
   }

}

//== Main processing function
function main( Alpha ) {
var x;
var Alpha1;
var nDC;
var nMedianDelta;

       //initialize parameters if necessary
                                              (continued)
```

图 10.2（续）

```
        if ( Alpha == null ) {
            Alpha = 0.07;
        }

        // study is initializing
    if (getBarState() == BARSTATE_ALLBARS) {
        return null;
    }

        //on each new bar, save array values
        if ( getBarState() == BARSTATE_NEWBAR ) {

            nBarCount++;

            aPriceArray.pop();
            aPriceArray.unshift( 0 );

            aSmoothArray.pop();
            aSmoothArray.unshift( 0 );

            aCycleArray.pop();
            aCycleArray.unshift( 0 );

            aQ1.pop();
            aQ1.unshift( 0 );

            aI1.pop();
            aI1.unshift( 0 );

            aDeltaPhase.pop();
            aDeltaPhase.unshift( 0 );

            aInstPeriod.pop();
            aInstPeriod.unshift( 0 );

            aPeriod.pop();
            aPeriod.unshift( 0 );

            aACycleArray.pop();
            aACycleArray.unshift( 0 );
```

图 10.2（续）

```
                }
        aPriceArray[0] = ( high()+low() ) / 2;

        aSmoothArray[0] = ( aPriceArray[0]
            + 2*aPriceArray[1] + 2*aPriceArray[2]
            + aPriceArray[3] ) / 6;

        if ( nBarCount < 7 ) {
                aCycleArray[0] = ( aPriceArray[0]
                    - 2*aPriceArray[1] + aPriceArray[2] )
                    / 4;
        }
        else {
                aCycleArray[0] = ( 1 - 0.5*Alpha )
                    * ( 1 - 0.5*Alpha )
                    * ( aSmoothArray[0]
                    - 2*aSmoothArray[1]
                    + aSmoothArray[2] ) + 2*( 1-Alpha )
                    * aCycleArray[1] - ( 1-Alpha )
                    * ( 1-Alpha ) * aCycleArray[2];
        }

        aQ1[0] = ( 0.0962*aCycleArray[0]
            + 0.5769*aCycleArray[2]
            - 0.5769*aCycleArray[4]
            - 0.0962*aCycleArray[6] ) * ( 0.5 + 0.08
            * aInstPeriod[1] );
        aI1[0] = aCycleArray[3];

        if ( aQ1[0] != 0 && aQ1[1] != 0 ) {
                aDeltaPhase[0] = (aI1[0]/aQ1[0]
                    - aI1[1]/aQ1[1]) / (1
                    + aI1[0]*aI1[1]/(aQ1[0]*aQ1[1]));
        }
        if ( aDeltaPhase[0] < 0.1 ) aDeltaPhase[0]
            = 0.1;
        if ( aDeltaPhase[0] > 1.1 ) aDeltaPhase[0]
            = 1.1;

        nMedianDelta = Median( 5, aDeltaPhase );
                                                (continued)
```

图 10.2（续）

```
if ( nMedianDelta == 0 ) {
     nDC = 15;
}
else {
     nDC = 6.28318 / nMedianDelta + 0.5;
}

aInstPeriod[0] = 0.33 * nDC + 0.67
   * aInstPeriod[1];
aPeriod[0] = 0.15*aInstPeriod[0]
   + 0.85*aPeriod[1];


Alpha1 = 2 / ( aPeriod[0] + 1 );


if ( nBarCount < 7 ) {
     aACycleArray[0] = (aPriceArray[0]
        - 2*aPriceArray[1]
        + aPriceArray[2])/4;
}
else {
     aACycleArray[0] = ( 1 - 0.5*Alpha1 )
        * ( 1 - 0.5*Alpha1 )
        * ( aSmoothArray[0]
        - 2*aSmoothArray[1] +
       aSmoothArray[2] ) + 2*( 1
          - Alpha1 ) * aACycleArray[1]
          - ( 1-Alpha1 ) * ( 1-Alpha1 )
          * aACycleArray[2];
}


//return the calculated values
if (!isNaN( aACycleArray[0] ) ) {
     return new Array( aACycleArray[0],_
        aACycleArray[1] );
}

}
```

图 10.2 (续)

```
function Median( nBars, aArray ) {
var aTmp = new Array();
var nTmp;
var result;
var x;

        //transfer elements to temp array
        x = 0;
        while( x < nBars ) {
                aTmp[x] = aArray[x++];
        }
        //sort array in asc order
        aTmp.sort( SortAsc );


        //if odd # of elements, just take middle
        if ( nBars % 2 != 0 ) {
                result = aTmp[ (nBars+1) / 2 ]
                aTmp = null;
                return( result );
        }
        //if even # elements, take average of two middle
            elements
        else {
                nTmp = nBars/2;
                result = (aTmp[nTmp] + aTmp[nTmp+1])/2;
                aTmp = null;
                return ( result );
        }
}

function SortAsc( arg1, arg2 ) {
    if (arg1<arg2) {
      return( -1 )
    }
    else {
      return( 1 );
    }
}
```

图 10.2 (续)

第10章 自适应周期指标

图10.3 对于周期性价格变化，自适应控制周期指标比静态控制周期指标更灵敏

```
{********************************************************
                    Adaptive CG
********************************************************}
Inputs: Price((H+L)/2),
        alpha(.07);

Vars:   Smooth(0),
        Cycle(0),
        Q1(0),
        I1(0),
        DeltaPhase(0),
        MedianDelta(0),
        DC(0),
        InstPeriod(0),
        Period(0),
        count(0),
        Num(0),
        Denom(0),
        CG(0),
        IntPeriod(0);
```

图10.4 计算自适应CG指标的EasyLanguage代码

```
Smooth = (Price + 2*Price[1] + 2*Price[2]
    + Price[3])/6;
Cycle = (1 - .5*alpha)*(1 - .5*alpha)*(Smooth
    - 2*Smooth[1] + Smooth[2]) + 2*(1 - alpha)*Cycle[1]
    - (1 - alpha)*(1 - alpha)*Cycle[2];
If currentbar < 7 then Cycle = (Price - 2*Price[1]
    + Price[2]) / 4;

Q1 = (.0962*Cycle + .5769*Cycle[2] - .5769*Cycle[4]
    - .0962*Cycle[6])*(.5 + .08*InstPeriod[1]);
I1 = Cycle[3];

If Q1 <> 0 and Q1[1] <> 0 then DeltaPhase = (I1/Q1
    - I1[1]/Q1[1]) / (1 + I1*I1[1]/(Q1*Q1[1]));
If DeltaPhase < 0.1 then DeltaPhase = 0.1;
If DeltaPhase > 1.1 then DeltaPhase = 1.1;
MedianDelta = Median(DeltaPhase, 5);

If MedianDelta = 0 then DC = 15 else DC = 6.28318
    / MedianDelta + .5;

InstPeriod = .33*DC + .67*InstPeriod[1];
Value1 = .15*InstPeriod + .85*Value1[1];
IntPeriod = intportion(Value1 / 2);

Num = 0;
Denom = 0;
For count = 0 to IntPeriod - 1 begin
        Num = Num + (1 + count)*(Price[count]);
        Denom = Denom + (Price[count]);
End;
If Denom <> 0 then CG = -Num/Denom + (IntPeriod + 1)
    / 2;

Plot1(CG, ICGI);
Plot2(CG[1], ITriggerI);
```

图 10.4（续）

```
/***********************************************************
Title:         Adaptive CG Oscillator
Coded By:  Chris D. Kryza (Divergence Software, Inc.)
Email:     c.kryza@gte.net
Incept:    07/09/2003
Version:   1.0.0


===========================================================
Fix History:

07/09/2003 -   Initial Release
1.0.0

===========================================================
***********************************************************/


//External Variables

var nBarCount              = 0;

var aPriceArray            = new Array();
var aSmoothArray           = new Array();
var aCycleArray            = new Array();
var aDeltaPhase            = new Array();
var aPeriod                = new Array();
var aInstPeriod            = new Array();
var aQ1                    = new Array();
var aI1                    = new Array();
var aCGArray               = new Array();



//== PreMain function required by eSignal to set_
   things up
function preMain() {
var x;

  setPriceStudy(false);
  setStudyTitle("Adaptive CG");
  setCursorLabelName("CG", 0);
```

图 10.5 计算自适应 CG 指标的 EFS 代码

```
setCursorLabelName(|Trig|, 1);
setDefaultBarFgColor( Color.blue, 0 );
setDefaultBarFgColor( Color.red, 1 );

    //initialize arrays
for (x=0; x<70; x++) {
    aPriceArray[x]      = 0.0;
    aSmoothArray[x]     = 0.0;
    aCycleArray[x]      = 0.0;
    aQ1[x]              = 0.0;
    aI1[x]              = 0.0;
    aDeltaPhase[x]      = 0.0;
    aPeriod[x]          = 0.0;
    aInstPeriod[x]      = 0.0;
    aCGArray[x]         = 0.0;
}

}

//== Main processing function
function main( Alpha ) {
var x;
var nCG = 0;
var nDC;
var nIntPeriod;
var nNum;
var nDenom;
var nMedianDelta;

    //initialize parameters if necessary
    if ( Alpha == null ) {
        Alpha = 0.07;
    }

    // study is initializing
    if (getBarState() == BARSTATE_ALLBARS) {
        return null;
    }

    //on each new bar, save array values
    if ( getBarState() == BARSTATE_NEWBAR ) {
                                            (continued)
```

图 10.5 (续)

```
            nBarCount++;

            aPriceArray.pop();
            aPriceArray.unshift( 0 );

            aSmoothArray.pop();
            aSmoothArray.unshift( 0 );

            aCycleArray.pop();
            aCycleArray.unshift( 0 );

            aQ1.pop();
            aQ1.unshift( 0 );

            aI1.pop();
            aI1.unshift( 0 );

            aDeltaPhase.pop();
            aDeltaPhase.unshift( 0 );

            aInstPeriod.pop();
            aInstPeriod.unshift( 0 );

            aPeriod.pop();
            aPeriod.unshift( 0 );

            aCGArray.pop();
            aCGArray.unshift( 0 );


    }

    aPriceArray[0] = ( high()+low() ) / 2;

    aSmoothArray[0] = ( aPriceArray[0]
        + 2*aPriceArray[1] + 2*aPriceArray[2]
        + aPriceArray[3] ) / 6;

    if ( nBarCount < 7 ) {
            aCycleArray[0] = ( aPriceArray[0]
                - 2*aPriceArray[1]
                + aPriceArray[2] ) / 4;
```

图 10.5（续）

```
      }
      else {
          aCycleArray[0] = ( 1 - 0.5*Alpha ) * ( 1
              - 0.5*Alpha ) * ( aSmoothArray[0]
              - 2*aSmoothArray[1]
              + aSmoothArray[2] ) + 2*( 1-Alpha )
              * aCycleArray[1] - ( 1-Alpha ) * ( 1-
              Alpha ) * aCycleArray[2];
      }

      aQ1[0] = ( 0.0962*aCycleArray[0]
          + 0.5769*aCycleArray[2]
          - 0.5769*aCycleArray[4]
          - 0.0962*aCycleArray[6] ) * ( 0.5 + 0.08
          * aInstPeriod[1] );
      aI1[0] = aCycleArray[3];

      if ( aQ1[0] != 0 && aQ1[1] != 0 ) {
          aDeltaPhase[0] = (aI1[0]/aQ1[0]
              - aI1[1]/aQ1[1]) / (1
              + aI1[0]*aI1[1]/(aQ1[0]*aQ1[1]));
      }
      if ( aDeltaPhase[0] < 0.1 ) aDeltaPhase[0]
          = 0.1;
      if ( aDeltaPhase[0] > 1.1 ) aDeltaPhase[0]
          = 1.1;

      nMedianDelta = Median( 5, aDeltaPhase );

      if ( nMedianDelta == 0 ) {
          nDC = 15;
      }
      else {
          nDC = 6.28318 / nMedianDelta + 0.5;
      }

      aInstPeriod[0] = 0.33 * nDC + 0.67
          * aInstPeriod[1];
      aPeriod[0] = 0.15*aInstPeriod[0]
          + 0.85*aPeriod[1];

                                        (continued)
```

图 10.5（续）

```
            nIntPeriod = Math.floor( ( 4*aPeriod[0]
                + 3*aPeriod[1] +
                2*aPeriod[3] + aPeriod[4] ) / 20 );

            nNum           = 0;
            nDenom         = 0;


            for ( x=0; x<nIntPeriod; x++ ){
                nNum += ( 1.0 + x )
                    * ( aPriceArray[x]   );
                nDenom += ( aPriceArray[x] );
            }


            if ( nDenom != 0 ) nCG = -nNum/nDenom
                + ( nIntPeriod+1 )/2;
            aCGArray[0] = nCG;


            //return the calculated values
            if (!isNaN( aCGArray[0] ) ) {
                return new Array( aCGArray[0],
                    aCGArray[1] );
            }

}


function Median( nBars, aArray ) {
var aTmp = new Array();
var nTmp;
var result;
var x;

            //transfer elements to temp array
            x = 0;
            while( x < nBars ) {
                aTmp[x] = aArray[x++];
```

图 10.5（续）

```
        }
        //sort array in asc order
        aTmp.sort( SortAsc );


        //if odd # of elements, just take middle
        if ( nBars % 2 != 0 ) {
              result = aTmp[ (nBars+1) / 2 ]
              aTmp = null;
              return( result );
        }
        //if even # elements, take average of two middle_
            elements
        else {
              nTmp = nBars/2;
              result = (aTmp[nTmp] + aTmp[nTmp+1])/2;
              aTmp = null;
              return ( result );
        }
}


function SortAsc( arg1, arg2 ) {
        if (arg1<arg2) {
            return( -1 )
        }
        else {
            return( 1 );
        }
}
```

图 10.5（续）

第 10 章 自适应周期指标

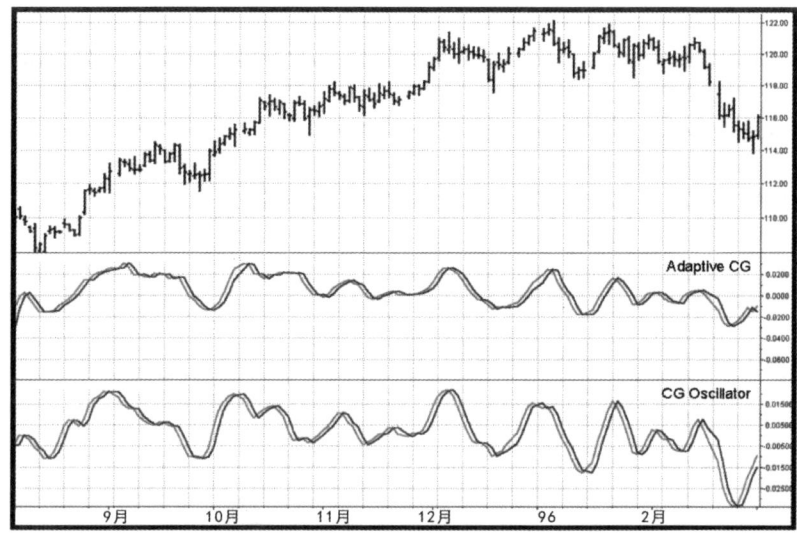

图 10.6 自适应 CG 振荡指标与静态 CG 振荡指标的对比

```
{*********************************************************
                    Adaptive RVI
*********************************************************}
Inputs: Price((H+L)/2),
        alpha(.07);

Vars:   Smooth(0),
        Cycle(0),
        Q1(0),
        I1(0),
        DeltaPhase(0),
        MedianDelta(0),
        DC(0),
        InstPeriod(0),
        Period(0),
        count(0),
        Length(0),
        Num(0),
        Denom(0),
        RVI(0),
        MaxRVI(0),
```

图 10.7 计算自适应 RVI 的 EasyLanguage 代码

```
         MinRVI(0);
Smooth = (Price + 2*Price[1] + 2*Price[2]
    + Price[3])/6;
Cycle = (1 - .5*alpha)*(1 - .5*alpha)*(Smooth
    - 2*Smooth[1] + Smooth[2]) + 2*(1 - alpha)*Cycle[1]
    - (1 - alpha)*(1 - alpha)*Cycle[2];
If currentbar < 7 then Cycle = (Price - 2*Price[1]
    + Price[2]) / 4;

Q1 = (.0962*Cycle + .5769*Cycle[2] - .5769*Cycle[4]
    - .0962*Cycle[6])*(.5 + .08*InstPeriod[1]);
I1 = Cycle[3];

If Q1 <> 0 and Q1[1] <> 0 then DeltaPhase = (I1/Q1
    - I1[1]/Q1[1]) / (1 + I1*I1[1]/(Q1*Q1[1]));
If DeltaPhase < 0.1 then DeltaPhase = 0.1;
If DeltaPhase > 1.1 then DeltaPhase = 1.1;
MedianDelta = Median(DeltaPhase, 5);

If MedianDelta = 0 then DC = 15 else DC = 6.28318
    / MedianDelta + .5;

InstPeriod = .33*DC + .67*InstPeriod[1];
Period = .15*InstPeriod + .85*Period[1];
Length = intportion((4*Period + 3*Period[1]
    + 2*Period[3] + Period[4]) / 20);

Value1 = ((Close - Open) + 2*(Close[1] - Open[1])
    + 2*(Close[2] - Open[2]) + (Close[3] - Open[3]))/6;
Value2 = ((High - Low) + 2*(High[1] - Low[1])
    + 2*(High[2] - Low[2]) + (High[3] - Low[3]))/6;
Num = 0;
Denom = 0;
For count = 0 to Length - 1 begin
        Num = Num + Value1[count];
        Denom = Denom + Value2[count];
End;
If Denom <> 0 then RVI = Num / Denom;

Plot1(RVI, |RVI|);
Plot2(RVI[1], |Trigger|);
```

图 10.7（续）

```
/**********************************************************
  Title:         Adaptive RVI
  Coded By:   Chris D. Kryza (Divergence Software, Inc.)
  Email:      c.kryza@gte.net
  Incept:     07/09/2003
  Version:    1.0.0


  ==========================================================
  Fix History:

  07/09/2003 -   Initial Release
  1.0.0


  ==========================================================
**********************************************************/


//External Variables

var nBarCount             = 0;

var aPriceArray           = new Array();
var aSmoothArray          = new Array();
var aCycleArray           = new Array();
var aDeltaPhase           = new Array();
var aPeriod               = new Array();
var aInstPeriod           = new Array();
var aQ1                   = new Array();
var aI1                   = new Array();
var aRVIArray             = new Array();
var aV1Array              = new Array();
var aV2Array              = new Array();


//== PreMain function required by eSignal to set_
   things up
function preMain() {
var x;

   setPriceStudy(false);
   setStudyTitle("Adaptive RVI");
```

图 10.8　计算自适应 RVI 的 EFS 代码

```
    setCursorLabelName(|RVI|, 0);
    setCursorLabelName(|Trig|, 1);
    setDefaultBarFgColor( Color.blue, 0 );
    setDefaultBarFgColor( Color.red, 1 );

        //initialize arrays
    for (x=0; x<70; x++) {
        aPriceArray[x]         = 0.0;
        aSmoothArray[x]        = 0.0;
        aCycleArray[x]         = 0.0;
        aQ1[x]                 = 0.0;
        aI1[x]                 = 0.0;
        aDeltaPhase[x]         = 0.0;
        aPeriod[x]             = 0.0;
        aInstPeriod[x]         = 0.0;
        aRVIArray[x]           = 0.0;
        aV1Array[x]            = 0.0;
        aV2Array[x]            = 0.0;
    }

}

//== Main processing function
function main( Alpha ) {
var x;
var nRVI = 0;
var nDC;
var nLength;
var nNum;
var nDenom;
var nMedianDelta;

        //initialize parameters if necessary
        if ( Alpha == null ) {
            Alpha = 0.07;
        }

        // study is initializing
    if (getBarState() == BARSTATE_ALLBARS) {
      return null;
    }
```

(continued)

图 10.8（续）

```
//on each new bar, save array values
if ( getBarState() == BARSTATE_NEWBAR ) {

    nBarCount++;

    aPriceArray.pop();
    aPriceArray.unshift( 0 );

    aSmoothArray.pop();
    aSmoothArray.unshift( 0 );

    aCycleArray.pop();
    aCycleArray.unshift( 0 );

    aQ1.pop();
    aQ1.unshift( 0 );

    aI1.pop();
    aI1.unshift( 0 );

    aDeltaPhase.pop();
    aDeltaPhase.unshift( 0 );

    aInstPeriod.pop();
    aInstPeriod.unshift( 0 );

    aPeriod.pop();
    aPeriod.unshift( 0 );

    aRVIArray.pop();
    aRVIArray.unshift( 0 );

    aV1Array.pop();
    aV1Array.unshift( 0 );

    aV2Array.pop();
    aV2Array.unshift( 0 );

}

aPriceArray[0] = ( high()+low() ) / 2;
```

图 10.8 (续)

```
aSmoothArray[0] = ( aPriceArray[0]
    + 2*aPriceArray[1] + 2*aPriceArray[2]
    + aPriceArray[3] ) / 6;

if ( nBarCount < 7 ) {
      aCycleArray[0] = ( aPriceArray[0]
          - 2*aPriceArray[1] + aPriceArray[2] )
          / 4;
}
else {
      aCycleArray[0] = ( 1 - 0.5*Alpha ) * ( 1
          - 0.5*Alpha ) * ( aSmoothArray[0]
          - 2*aSmoothArray[1]
          + aSmoothArray[2] ) + 2*( 1-Alpha )
          * aCycleArray[1] - ( 1-Alpha ) * ( 1-
          Alpha ) * aCycleArray[2];
}

aQ1[0] = ( 0.0962*aCycleArray[0]
    + 0.5769*aCycleArray[2]
    - 0.5769*aCycleArray[4]
    - 0.0962*aCycleArray[6] ) * ( 0.5 + 0.08
    * aInstPeriod[1] );
aI1[0] = aCycleArray[3];

if ( aQ1[0] != 0 && aQ1[1] != 0 ) {
      aDeltaPhase[0] = (aI1[0]/aQ1[0]
          - aI1[1]/aQ1[1])
          / (1 + aI1[0]*aI1[1]/(aQ1[0]*aQ1[1]));
}
if ( aDeltaPhase[0] < 0.1 ) aDeltaPhase[0]
    = 0.1;
if ( aDeltaPhase[0] > 1.1 ) aDeltaPhase[0]
    = 1.1;

nMedianDelta = Median( 5, aDeltaPhase );

nPhaseSum              = 0;
nOldPhaseSum           = 0;
nDC                    = 0;

if ( nMedianDelta == 0 ) {
```

(continued)

图 10.8（续）

```
            nDC = 15;
    }
    else {
            nDC = 6.28318 / nMedianDelta + 0.5;
    }

    aInstPeriod[0] = 0.33 * nDC + 0.67
       * aInstPeriod[1];
    aPeriod[0] = 0.15*aInstPeriod[0]
       + 0.85*aPeriod[1];

    nLength = Math.floor( ( 4*aPeriod[0]
       + 3*aPeriod[1] +
              2*aPeriod[3] + aPeriod[4] ) / 20 );

    aV1Array[0] = ( ( close()-open() )
       + 2*( close(-1)-open(-1) )
       + 2*( close(-2)-open(-2) )
       + ( close(-3)-open(-3) ) ) / 6;
    aV2Array[0] = ( ( high()-low() )
       + 2*( high(-1)-low(-1) )
       + 2*( high(-2)-low(-2) )
       + ( high(-3)-low(-3) ) ) / 6;

    nNum          = 0;
    nDenom        = 0;

    for ( x=0; x<nLength; x++ ){
           nNum += aV1Array[x];
           nDenom += aV2Array[x];
    }


    if ( nDenom != 0 ) nRVI = nNum/nDenom;
    aRVIArray[0] = nRVI;


    //return the calculated values
    if (!isNaN( aRVIArray[0] ) ) {
            return new Array( aRVIArray[0],_
                aRVIArray[1] );
    }
```

图 10.8（续）

```
}
function Median( nBars, aArray ) {
var aTmp = new Array();
var nTmp;
var result;
var x;

        //transfer elements to temp array
        x = 0;
        while( x < nBars ) {
                aTmp[x] = aArray[x++];
        }
        //sort array in asc order
        aTmp.sort( SortAsc );


        //if odd # of elements, just take middle
        if ( nBars % 2 != 0 ) {
                result = aTmp[ (nBars+1) / 2 ]
                aTmp = null;
                return( result );
        }
        //if even # elements, take average of two middle
            elements
        else {
                nTmp = nBars/2;
                result = (aTmp[nTmp] + aTmp[nTmp+1])/2;
                aTmp = null;
                return ( result );
        }
}

function SortAsc( arg1, arg2 ) {
     if (arg1<arg2) {
        return( -1 )
     }
     else {
          return( 1 );
     }
}
```

图 10.8（续）

第 10 章　自适应周期指标

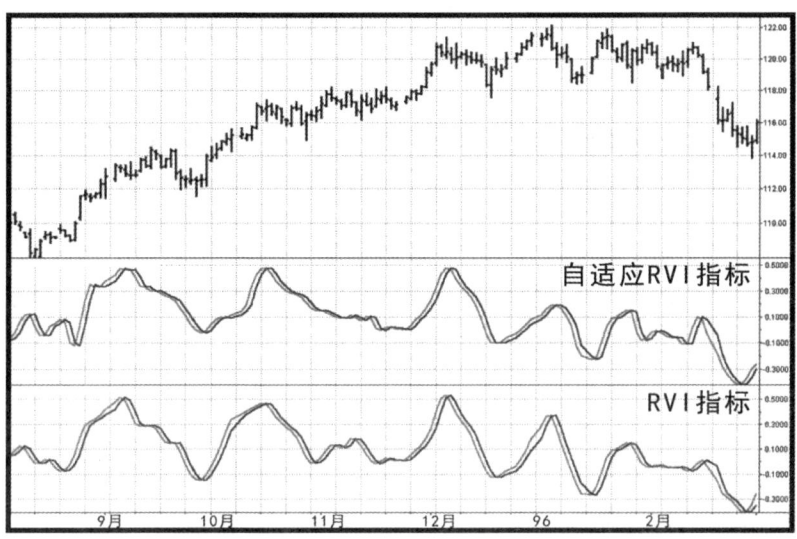

图 10.9　对于周期较短的市场循环，自适应 RVI 指标比静态 RVI 指标反应灵敏

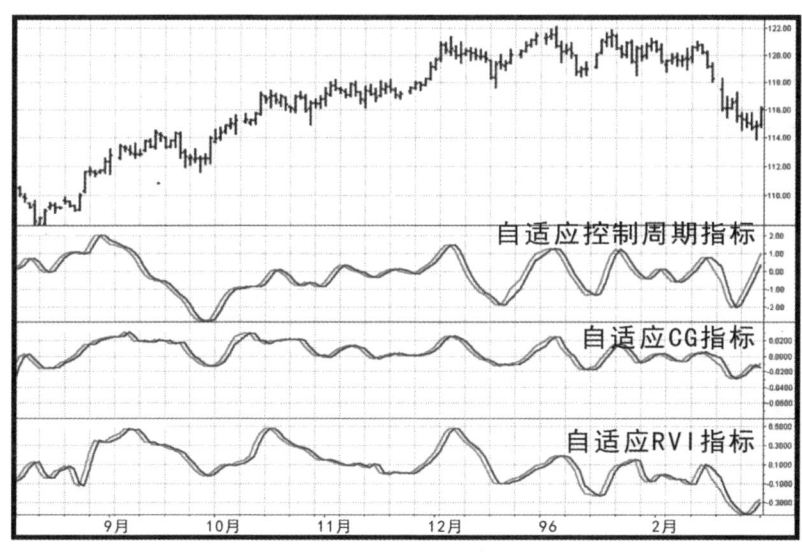

图 10.10　自适应指标的对比

图 10.9 所示为自适应 RVI 指标和静态 RVI 指标的比较。同其他自适

应指标一样，与它们的静态版本相比，较短循环周期的作用被加强了。

图 10.10 显示出三种自适应指标的相互比较。同它们的静态版本一样，三个自适应指标都显示出大致相同的性能。或许我们可以得出一个结论，一旦我们从数据中正确提取了周期性分量，那么大多数振荡型指标将具有大致相同的性能。可能某个指标在一组数据中优于另一个。总之，现在你的工具箱中又增加了三个独立的指标可供选用。至于选择哪一个，就是个人爱好的问题了。

需要牢记的要点

● 自适应指标都用测得的主周期作为它们的自适应标准。

● 自适应控制周期指标在计算其 $\alpha1$ 滤波器参数时使用的是整个主循环周期。

● 自适应 CG 振荡指标使用半个主循环周期的整数部分计算重心滤波器。

● 自适应 RVI 振荡指标使用半个主循环周期的整数部分计算活力比。

● 三个自适应指标都展示出相似的性能。

第 11 章　正弦波指标

"我能够预测未来。"汤姆有预见性地说。

因果滤波器永远不可能预测未来。事实上，所有因果滤波器都具有滞后性。在第9章中，我们设计优秀的自适应指标的目的是尽可能多地消除滞后，而不是做出预测。而对于正弦波指标，我们试着设计一种非因果滤波器，从而预测市场循环的反转点。当与其他振荡指标相比时，对周期性反转点的预示是正弦波指标的一个主要优点。比如 RSI 和随机指标，它们都必须等待价格的确认。

在第9章，已经对如何测量市场数据中的主循环周期进行了讲解。但是，那种测量并未告诉我们处于那个循环中的什么位置。为了定位在循环中的位置，我们必须测量主循环的相位。知道了主循环的相位之后，我们可以求出该相位的正弦值，从而设计一个人为的振荡型指标。也就是说，市场数据的周期性分量被人为合成为一个纯正弦波。在测量相位的过程中，产生的任何滞后都可以通过数学方法消除。此外，只要把测得相位加上 45°，便可产生一个人为的相位领先，这就是非因果因子。这种相位领先的结论建立在这样一个假设之上：测得周期在过去存在（至少短暂存在），并且将向未来延续（至少是短暂延续）。使相位领先45°，然后求出领先相位角的正弦值，将产生一个振荡指标波形，它领先于原来的正弦波1/8个周期。所以，这两个正弦波将领先于尖峰和低谷反转点1/16个周期而交叉。如果主循环周期为16日，那么该指标将提前1日给出主循环反转的信号。如果主循环周期为48日，那么领先的时间将增加至3日。而如果主循环周期为8日，那么理论上的领先时间只有半日。

我的简化市场模型包含一个趋势和一个循环。在真实市场中当然还存在其他分量，但我们在这个简化模型中把它们忽略掉了。我把幅度最高的循环叫作主循环（Dominant Cycle）。经验证明，假设市场存在单个主循环是一种有效的近似。在知道了主循环的周期之后，我们就可以测量主循环的相位。但是，如果市场以纯趋势运动，那么就没有循环可言。在这种情况下，相位停止领先。如果相位不再领先，那么正弦波指标的两个正弦波波形便不会出现交叉。如果两个正弦波波形不交叉，那么正弦波指标将不会产生周期性买卖信号。于是，正弦波指标可以避免产生错误的双人拉锯式信号，与其他传统的振荡指标相比，这是一个比较明显的优点。实际上，主周期的相位并非真的停止了；该相位只是变得越来越弱，与市场在循环模式中产生的恒变化率相比，该相位的波形明显不同。该相位在0°和360°之间变化。如果循环周期变化，那么正弦波指标偶尔会出现一个交叉，以便修正当前循环周期测量的相位角。在这些情况下，正弦波指标在交叉点附近并不显示为正弦波。所以，这些偶尔出现的虚假交叉信号很容易辨别。

我们通过绘制测得相位角的正弦值得到了正弦波指标。这个振荡指标在-1和+1之间来回振荡。通过把相位角提前45°后再求正弦值，我们加强了这个振荡指标的实用性。在图11.1中，通过相量域图和时域图我们可以看出绘制这两条线的效果。增加45°后使相位明显地从一个45°斜角向竖直位置提前。这种相位提前意味着 LeadSine 波形将先于 Sine 波形到达峰值。LeadSine 线和 Sine 线的交叉将在周期反转点之前的 22.5°，或者说 1/16 周期处出现。如果市场循环为 16 日或更短，那么这就是一种立即进入或退出交易的信号。如果市场有一个较长的循环，那么在你"扣动扳机"之前便有一段固定的预估时间。

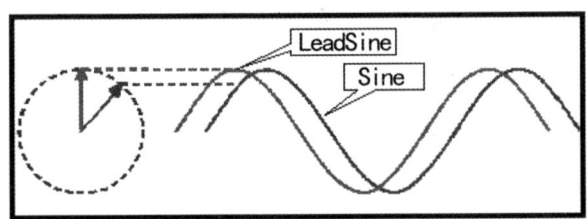

图 11.1　正弦波指标的相量域和时域观察

与随机指标和 RSI 等传统振荡指标相比，正弦波指标有两个主要优势：

1. 正弦波指标预测市场在循环模式中的周期性反转点，而不是等待确认。

2. 当市场处于趋势模式时，主循环的相位不会提前。所以，当市场在趋势模式下运动时，正弦波指标一般不会给出虚假的双人拉锯式信号。

另外一个优势是，预估信号是通过数学方法把相位提前，是经过严密计算得出的，其中并未包含动量因素。所以，正弦波指标的信号并不比原始信号包含更多噪声。

测量主循环相位，然后合成为正弦波的 EasyLanguage 代码和 EFS 代码分别见图 11.2 和 11.3。代码的开头部分测量主循环周期，同第 9 章中所用代码完全一样。测得周期必须用一个指数移动平均（α = 0.15）进一步平滑,因为在计算相位时没有进行平滑。变量 DCPeriod 是主循环周期平滑后的整数部分,我们用它在所选时间段上求和,而且只有整型变量才可达到这个目的。否则,舍入误差将导致不可靠的结果。将市场价格数据的周期性分量分别与主循环周期的正弦和余弦相乘,然后在一个完整的周期上对这两个乘积分别求和。这些和便是大家熟知的数据的实部(real part)和虚部(imaginary part)。大家都知道,它们的比值的反正切便是周期性分量的相位。反正切函数值可以趋于无穷大,因此我在代码中对变量 ImagPart 小于 0.001 时的取值做了限制,以防止计算错误。根据计算变量所在的象限,反正切函数还很容易出现模糊性的结果。在 EasyLanguage 中,解决这种问题的最简便方法是,如果变量使变量 ImagPart 为负,那么就把 DCPhase 旋转 90°,再加上 180°。在把这部分代码转换为其他语言时,对于正弦函数的处理应该加以注意。首先,大多数计算机语言以弧度为单位表示角,而非以角度为单位。其次,此处我所用的消除模糊结果的方案并非通用于所有语言。Sine 线就是画出主循环的相伴角的正弦值,LeadSine 线就是把相位角加上 45°后再画出它的正弦值,从而获得所需的相位提前特性。

我们在理论分析波形和实际数据上绘制正弦波指标,以展示它们的性能。图 11.4 所示为一个理论上假想的 20 日周期的正弦波分析波形。注意在每个尖峰和低谷,LeadSine 是如何领先于价格波形而与 Sine 线交叉的。LeadSine 线总是在周期性反转点之前与 Sine 线交叉,提前给出周期性反转点出现的信号。信号提前的时间长度与循环周期的长度有关,周期越短,提前的时间越短。

```
{***********************************************************
                    Sinewave Indicator
***********************************************************}

Inputs: Price((H+L)/2),
        alpha(.07);

Vars:   Smooth(0),
        Cycle(0),
        I1(0),
        Q1(0),
        I2(0),
        Q2(0),
        DeltaPhase(0),
        MedianDelta(0),
        MaxAmp(0),
        AmpFix(0),
        Re(0),
        Im(0),
        DC(0),
        alpha1(0),
        InstPeriod(0),
        DCPeriod(0),
        count(0),
        SmoothCycle(0),
        RealPart(0),
        ImagPart(0),
        DCPhase(0);

Smooth = (Price + 2*Price[1] + 2*Price[2]
    + Price[3])/6;
Cycle = (1 - .5*alpha)*(1 - .5*alpha)*(Smooth
    - 2*Smooth[1] + Smooth[2]) + 2*(1 - alpha)*Cycle[1]
    - (1 - alpha)*(1 - alpha)*Cycle[2];
If currentbar < 7 then Cycle = (Price - 2*Price[1]
    + Price[2]) / 4;
{Cycle = Price;}
Q1 = (.0962*Cycle + .5769*Cycle[2] - .5769*Cycle[4]
    - .0962*Cycle[6])*(.5 + .08*InstPeriod[1]);
I1 = Cycle[3];

If Q1 <> 0 and Q1[1] <> 0 then DeltaPhase = (I1/Q1
    - I1[1]/Q1[1]) / (1 + I1*I1[1]/(Q1*Q1[1]));
```

图 11.2 计算正弦波指标的 EasyLanguage 代码

```
If DeltaPhase < 0.1 then DeltaPhase = 0.1;
If DeltaPhase > 1.1 then DeltaPhase = 1.1;
MedianDelta = Median(DeltaPhase, 5);

If MedianDelta = 0 then DC = 15 else DC = 6.28318 /
    MedianDelta + .5;

InstPeriod = .33*DC + .67*InstPeriod[1];
Value1 = .15*InstPeriod + .85*Value1[1];

{Compute Dominant Cycle Phase}
DCPeriod = IntPortion(Value1);
RealPart = 0;
ImagPart = 0;
For count = 0 To DCPeriod - 1 begin
        RealPart = RealPart + Sine(360 * count
            / DCPeriod) * (Cycle[count]);
        ImagPart = ImagPart + Cosine(360 * count
            / DCPeriod) * (Cycle[count]);
End;
If AbsValue(ImagPart) > 0.001 then DCPhase
    = Arctangent(RealPart / ImagPart);
If AbsValue(ImagPart) <= 0.001 then DCPhase = 90
    * Sign(RealPart);

DCPhase = DCPhase + 90;
If ImagPart < 0 then DCPhase = DCPhase + 180;
If DCPhase > 315 then DCPhase = DCPhase - 360;

Plot1(Sine(DCPhase), ISineI);
Plot2(Sine(DCPhase + 45), ILeadSineI);
```

图 11.2（续）

在图 11.5 中，正弦波指标被绘制在标准数据的下方。在图表左侧的 8 月份和 9 月份，市场以趋势方式运动。我们从正弦波指标未出现交叉的波动中可以得出这一结论。换句话说，正弦波指标指示，我们应该使用某种趋势跟随系统。随后出现三个明显的周期性反转点，直至 11 月份的趋势出现。在趋势运动中，主周期的相位不再旋转，指标中没有明显的周期性交叉。正弦波指标然后连续出现 6 个标准的反转点，直至图表右侧的 2 月底，市场又返回趋势状态。

```
/***********************************************************
    Title:        Sine Wave Indicator
    Coded By:     Chris D. Kryza (Divergence Software, Inc.)
    Email:        c.kryza@gte.net
    Incept:       07/09/2003
    Version:      1.0.0



    ========================================================
    Fix History:

    07/09/2003 -   Initial Release
    1.0.0

    ========================================================
***********************************************************/


//External Variables

var nBarCount              = 0;

var aPriceArray            = new Array();
var aSmoothArray           = new Array();
var aCycleArray            = new Array();
var aDeltaPhase            = new Array();
var aPeriod                = new Array();
var aInstPeriod            = new Array();
var aQ1                    = new Array();
var aI1                    = new Array();
var aV1Array               = new Array();

//== PreMain function required by eSignal to set_
   things up
function preMain() {
var x;

  setPriceStudy(false);
  setStudyTitle("Sine Wave");
  setCursorLabelName("Sine", 0);
  setCursorLabelName("LeadSine", 1);
  setDefaultBarFgColor( Color.blue, 0 );
```

图 11.3 计算正弦波指标的 EFS 代码

```
    setDefaultBarFgColor( Color.red,  1 );

        //initialize arrays
    for (x=0; x<70; x++) {
        aPriceArray[x]      = 0.0;
        aSmoothArray[x]     = 0.0;
        aCycleArray[x]      = 0.0;
        aQ1[x]              = 0.0;
        aI1[x]              = 0.0;
        aDeltaPhase[x]      = 0.0;
        aPeriod[x]          = 0.0;
        aInstPeriod[x]      = 0.0;
        aV1Array[x]         = 0.0;
    }

}

//== Main processing function
function main( Alpha ) {
var x;
var nDC;
var nDCPeriod;
var nRealPart;
var nImagPart;
var nDCPhase = 0.0;
var nMedianDelta;

        //initialize parameters if necessary
        if ( Alpha == null ) {
                Alpha = 0.07;
        }

        // study is initializing
    if (getBarState() == BARSTATE_ALLBARS) {
      return null;
    }

        //on each new bar, save array values
        if ( getBarState() == BARSTATE_NEWBAR ) {

                nBarCount++;
```

(continued)

图 11.3（续）

```
        aPriceArray.pop();
        aPriceArray.unshift( 0 );

        aSmoothArray.pop();
        aSmoothArray.unshift( 0 );

        aCycleArray.pop();
        aCycleArray.unshift( 0 );

        aQ1.pop();
        aQ1.unshift( 0 );

        aI1.pop();
        aI1.unshift( 0 );

        aDeltaPhase.pop();
        aDeltaPhase.unshift( 0 );

        aInstPeriod.pop();
        aInstPeriod.unshift( 0 );

        aPeriod.pop();
        aPeriod.unshift( 0 );

        aV1Array.pop();
        aV1Array.unshift( 0 );
    }

    aPriceArray[0] = ( high()+low() ) / 2;

    aSmoothArray[0] = ( aPriceArray[0]
        + 2*aPriceArray[1] + 2*aPriceArray[2]
        + aPriceArray[3] ) / 6;

    if ( nBarCount < 7 ) {
            aCycleArray[0] = ( aPriceArray[0]
                - 2*aPriceArray[1] + aPriceArray[2] )
                / 4;
    }
    else {
```

图 11.3（续）

```
            aCycleArray[0] = ( 1 - 0.5*Alpha )
                * ( 1 - 0.5*Alpha )
                * ( aSmoothArray[0] - 2
                *aSmoothArray[1] + aSmoothArray[2] )
                + 2*( 1-Alpha ) * aCycleArray[1]
                - ( 1-Alpha ) * ( 1-Alpha )
                * aCycleArray[2];
    }

    aQ1[0] = ( 0.0962*aCycleArray[0]
        + 0.5769*aCycleArray[2]
        - 0.5769*aCycleArray[4]
        - 0.0962*aCycleArray[6] ) * ( 0.5 + 0.08
        * aInstPeriod[1] );
    aI1[0] = aCycleArray[3];

    if ( aQ1[0] != 0 && aQ1[1] != 0 ) {
        aDeltaPhase[0] = (aI1[0]/aQ1[0]
            - aI1[1]/aQ1[1])
            / (1 + aI1[0]*aI1[1]/(aQ1[0]*aQ1[1]));
    }
    if ( aDeltaPhase[0] < 0.1 ) aDeltaPhase[0]
        = 0.1;
    if ( aDeltaPhase[0] > 1.1 ) aDeltaPhase[0]
        = 1.1;

    nMedianDelta = Median( 5, aDeltaPhase );

    if ( nMedianDelta == 0 ) {
        nDC = 15;
    }
    else {
        nDC = 6.28318 / nMedianDelta + 0.5;
    }

    aInstPeriod[0] = 0.33 * nDC + 0.67
        * aInstPeriod[1];
    aPeriod[0] = 0.15*aInstPeriod[0]
        + 0.85*aPeriod[1];

    aV1Array[0] = 0.15*aPeriod[0]
        + 0.85*aV1Array[1];

                                        (continued)
```

图 11.3 (续)

```
//compute dominant cycle phase
nDCPeriod = Math.floor( aV1Array[0] );
nRealPart = 0.0;
nImagPart = 0.0;

for ( x=0; x<nDCPeriod; x++ ) {
        nRealPart += Math.sin( DegToRad_
            ( 360*x/nDCPeriod ) )
            * ( aCycleArray[x] );
        nImagPart += Math.cos( DegToRad_
            ( 360*x/nDCPeriod ) )
            * ( aCycleArray[x] );
}

if ( Math.abs( nImagPart ) > 0.001 ) nDCPhase
    = RadToDeg( Math.atan_
    ( nRealPart/nImagPart ) );

if ( Math.abs( nImagPart ) <= 0.001 ) nDCPhase
    = 90 * ( nRealPart<0 ? -1 : 1 );

nDCPhase += 90;
if ( nImagPart < 0 ) nDCPhase += 180;


//return the calculated values
if (!isNaN( nDCPhase ) ) {
        return new Array( Math.sin( DegToRad_
            ( nDCPhase) ), Math.sin( DegToRad_
            ( nDCPhase+45 ) ) );
}

}


//== Convert Degrees to Radians
function DegToRad( nValue ) {
var nTmp;
    nTmp = nValue * ( Math.PI / 180 );
    return( nTmp );
}
```

图 11.3 (续)

```
//== Convert Radians to Degrees
function RadToDeg( nValue ) {
var nTmp;

        nTmp = nValue * ( 180 / Math.PI );

        return( nTmp );

}

function Median( nBars, aArray ) {
var aTmp = new Array();
var nTmp;
var result;
var x;

        //transfer elements to temp array
        x = 0;
        while( x < nBars ) {
                aTmp[x] = aArray[x++];
        }
        //sort array in asc order
        aTmp.sort( SortAsc );


        //if odd # of elements, just take middle
        if ( nBars % 2 != 0 ) {
                result = aTmp[ (nBars+1) / 2 ]
                aTmp = null;
                return( result );
        }
        //if even # elements, take average of two_
            middle elements
        else {
                nTmp = nBars/2;
                result = (aTmp[nTmp] + aTmp[nTmp+1])/2;
                aTmp = null;
                return ( result );
        }
}
```

(continued)

图 11.3 (续)

第 11 章 正弦波指标

```
function SortAsc( arg1, arg2 ) {
      if (arg1<arg2) {
        return( -1 )
      }
      else {
         return( 1 );
      }
}
```

图 11.3（续）

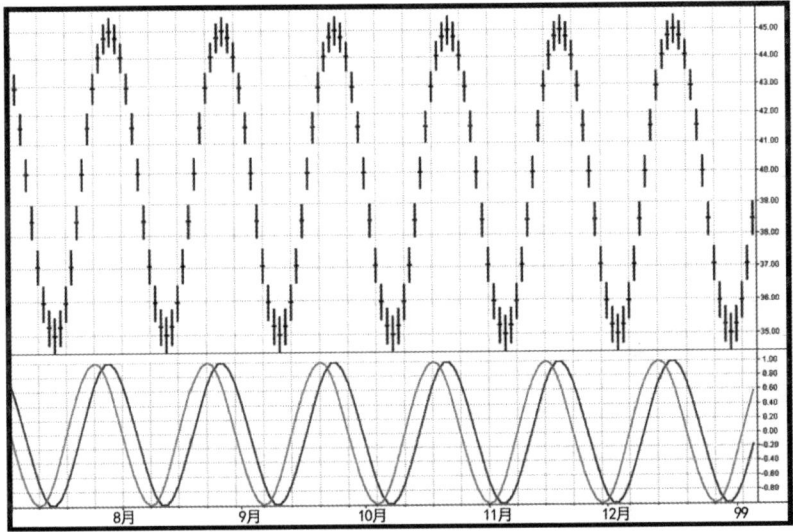

图 11.4　正弦波指标总是提前给出反转点警示信号

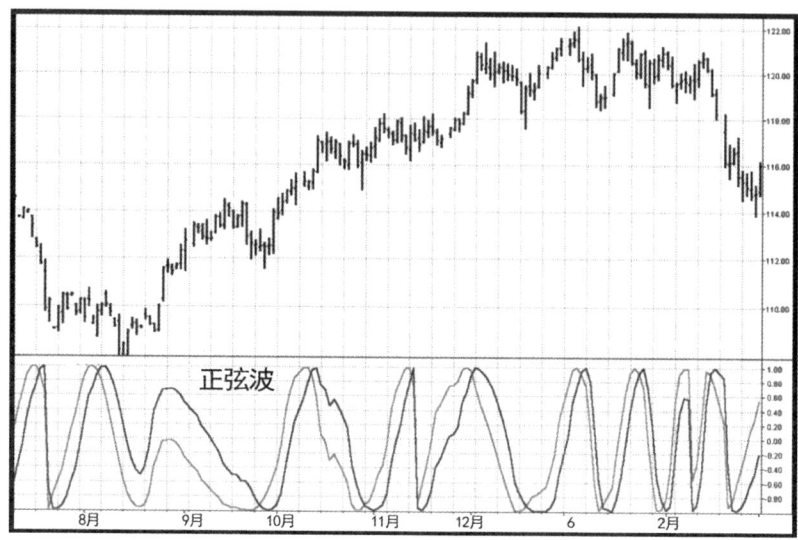

图 11.5 正弦波指标给出正确的循环信号

需要牢记的要点

- 正弦波指标是一种非因果预测滤波器，其基础理论是，在短暂的过去存在的主循环，将在短暂的将来继续存在。
- 当市场处于循环模式中时，主循环的相位按照恒定速率变化。
- 当市场处于趋势模式中时，主循环的相位变得很弱，甚至出现负的变化率。
- 正弦波指标包括主循环相位的正弦线和主循环相位提前45°的正弦线。
- 正弦波指标领先于主循环反转点1/16个循环周期给出入场和出场信号。
- 当市场处于趋势模式中时，正弦波指标极少会给出虚假的双人拉锯式信号。

第 12 章 适应趋势

"我没有办法了。"汤姆轻率地说。

至此,我所讲解的工具已经足够让你制定一些严肃的交易策略了。本章将给出一个这种策略的开头。你可以把这种策略作为一个开始,然后添加你自己的规则,从而提高胜算率。

在之前的章节中,我推导并改进了几个振荡型指标,目的是使它们与市场数据的周期性分量一起运动,并且具有尽可能小的滞后。大多数分析趋势跟随技术不使用振荡指标;它们使用移动平均线或类似指标。本章我将向你展示如何把周期测量用作趋势指标和交易系统。

一个循环中任意给定点的斜率与下个循环中的同一个点的斜率完全相同。无论你选择的点是位于尖峰处、低谷处,还是其间的任意位置;在理想循环中相同点之间的斜率差是 0。如果连续样本之间存在幅度差异,要么就是循环周期改变了,要么就是市场进入了趋势模式。由于循环周期在逐个循环中变化非常缓慢,所以一个周期中的动量就可以作为趋势的指示。

我们的交易策略是先测量主循环周期,然后使用测得周期计算出一个循环的动量。众所周知,动量函数充满噪声,所以我使用将在下章讲解的三极超级平滑滤波器对动量进行平滑。就是那么简单。计算平滑自适应动量的 EasyLanguage 代码和 EFS 代码分别见图 12.1 和 12.2。

```
{***********************************************************
            Smoothed Adaptive Momentum
************************************************************}
Inputs: Price((H+L)/2),
        alpha(.07),
        Cutoff(8);

Vars:   Smooth(0),
        Cycle(0),
        Q1(0),
        I1(0),
        DeltaPhase(0),
        MedianDelta(0),
        DC(0),
        InstPeriod(0),
        Period(0),
        Num(0),
        Denom(0),
        a1(0),
        b1(0),
        c1(0),
        coef1(0),
        coef2(0),
        coef3(0),
        coef4(0),
        Filt3(0);

Smooth = (Price + 2*Price[1] + 2*Price[2]
    + Price[3])/6;
Cycle = (1 - .5*alpha)*(1 - .5*alpha)*(Smooth
    - 2*Smooth[1] + Smooth[2]) + 2*(1 - alpha)*Cycle[1]
    - (1 - alpha)*(1 - alpha)*Cycle[2];
If currentbar < 7 then Cycle = (Price - 2*Price[1]
    + Price[2]) / 4;

Q1 = (.0962*Cycle + .5769*Cycle[2] - .5769*Cycle[4]
    - .0962*Cycle[6])*(.5 + .08*InstPeriod[1]);
I1 = Cycle[3];

If Q1 <> 0 and Q1[1] <> 0 then DeltaPhase = (I1/Q1
    - I1[1]/Q1[1]) / (1 + I1*I1[1]/(Q1*Q1[1]));
```

图 12.1 计算平滑自适应动量的 EasyLanguage 代码

```
If DeltaPhase < 0.1 then DeltaPhase = 0.1;
If DeltaPhase > 1.1 then DeltaPhase = 1.1;
MedianDelta = Median(DeltaPhase, 5);

If MedianDelta = 0 then DC = 15 else DC = 6.28318
    / MedianDelta + .5;

InstPeriod = .33*DC + .67*InstPeriod[1];
Period = .15*InstPeriod + .85*Period[1];

Value1 = Price - Price[IntPortion(Period - 1)];

a1 = expvalue(-3.14159 / Cutoff);
b1 = 2*a1*Cosine(1.738*180 / Cutoff);
c1 = a1*a1;
coef2 = b1 + c1;
coef3 = -(c1 + b1*c1);
coef4 = c1*c1;
coef1 = 1 - coef2 - coef3 - coef4;

Filt3 = coef1*Value1 + coef2*Filt3[1] + coef3*Filt3[2]
    + coef4*Filt3[3];
If CurrentBar < 4 then Filt3 = Value1;

Plot1(Filt3, IFilt3I);
Plot2(0, IRefI);
```

图 12.1（续）

```
/***********************************************************
Title:        Smoothed Adaptive Momentum Indicator
Coded By:     Chris D. Kryza (Divergence Software, Inc.)
Email:        c.kryza@gte.net
Incept:       07/09/2003
Version:      1.0.0
```
(continued)

图 12.2　计算平滑自适应动量的 EFS 代码

```
================================================================
Fix History:

07/09/2003 -    Initial Release
1.0.0

================================================================
***************************************************************/


//External Variables

var nBarCount            = 0;

var aPriceArray          = new Array();
var aSmoothArray         = new Array();
var aCycleArray          = new Array();
var aDeltaPhase          = new Array();
var aPeriod              = new Array();
var aInstPeriod          = new Array();
var aQ1                  = new Array();
var aI1                  = new Array();
var aFiltArray           = new Array();


//== PreMain function required by eSignal to set_
   things up
function preMain() {
var x;

  setPriceStudy(false);
  setStudyTitle("Smoothed Adaptive Momentum");
  setCursorLabelName("Filt3", 0);
  setDefaultBarFgColor( Color.blue, 0 );
  addBand( 0.0, PS_SOLID, 1, Color.black, -10 );

       //initialize arrays
  for (x=0; x<150; x++) {
       aPriceArray[x]     = 0.0;
       aSmoothArray[x]    = 0.0;
       aCycleArray[x]     = 0.0;
       aQ1[x]             = 0.0;
```

图 12.2（续）

```
            aI1[x]              = 0.0;
            aDeltaPhase[x]      = 0.0;
            aPeriod[x]          = 0.0;
            aInstPeriod[x]      = 0.0;
            aFiltArray[x]       = 0.0;
    }

}

//== Main processing function
function main( Alpha, Cutoff ) {
var x;
var nValue1;
var nDC;
var nOffset;
var nCoef1;
var nCoef2;
var nCoef3;
var nCoef4;
var nA1;
var nB1;
var nC1;
var nMedianDelta;

        //initialize parameters if necessary
        if ( Alpha == null ) {
              Alpha = 0.07;
        }
        if ( Cutoff == null ) {
              Cutoff = 8;
        }


        // study is initializing
   if (getBarState() == BARSTATE_ALLBARS) {
     return null;
   }

        //on each new bar, save array values
        if ( getBarState() == BARSTATE_NEWBAR ) {

                nBarCount++;
```
(continued)

图 12.2（续）

```
            aPriceArray.pop();
            aPriceArray.unshift( 0 );

            aSmoothArray.pop();
            aSmoothArray.unshift( 0 );

            aCycleArray.pop();
            aCycleArray.unshift( 0 );

            aQ1.pop();
            aQ1.unshift( 0 );

            aI1.pop();
            aI1.unshift( 0 );

            aDeltaPhase.pop();
            aDeltaPhase.unshift( 0 );

            aInstPeriod.pop();
            aInstPeriod.unshift( 0 );

            aPeriod.pop();
            aPeriod.unshift( 0 );

            aFiltArray.pop();
            aFiltArray.unshift( 0 );
    }

    aPriceArray[0] = ( high()+low() ) / 2;

    aSmoothArray[0] = ( aPriceArray[0]
        + 2*aPriceArray[1] + 2*aPriceArray[2]
        + aPriceArray[3] ) / 6;

    if ( nBarCount < 7 ) {
            aCycleArray[0] = ( aPriceArray[0]
                - 2*aPriceArray[1] + aPriceArray[2] )
                / 4;
    }
    else {
```

图 12.2（续）

第 12 章 适应趋势

```
            aCycleArray[0] = ( 1 - 0.5*Alpha )
                * ( 1 - 0.5*Alpha )
                * ( aSmoothArray[0]
                - 2*aSmoothArray[1]
                + aSmoothArray[2] ) + 2*( 1-Alpha )
                * aCycleArray[1] - ( 1-Alpha )
                * ( 1-Alpha ) * aCycleArray[2];
    }

    aQ1[0] = ( 0.0962*aCycleArray[0]
        + 0.5769*aCycleArray[2]
        - 0.5769*aCycleArray[4]
        - 0.0962*aCycleArray[6] ) * ( 0.5 + 0.08
        * aInstPeriod[1] );
    aI1[0] = aCycleArray[3];

    if ( aQ1[0] != 0 && aQ1[1] != 0 ) {
            aDeltaPhase[0] = (aI1[0]/aQ1[0]
                - aI1[1]/aQ1[1]) / (1 + aI1[0]
                *aI1[1]/(aQ1[0]*aQ1[1]));
    }
    if ( aDeltaPhase[0] < 0.1 ) aDeltaPhase[0]
        = 0.1;
    if ( aDeltaPhase[0] > 1.1 ) aDeltaPhase[0]
        = 1.1;

    nMedianDelta = Median( 5, aDeltaPhase );

    if ( nMedianDelta == 0 ) {
            nDC = 15;
    }
    else {
            nDC = 6.28318 / nMedianDelta + 0.5;
    }

    aInstPeriod[0] = 0.33 * nDC + 0.67
        * aInstPeriod[1];
    aPeriod[0] = 0.15*aInstPeriod[0]
        + 0.85*aPeriod[1];


    nOffset = Math.floor( aPeriod[0] )-1;
```
(continued)

图 12.2（续）

```
                if ( nOffset < 0 ) nOffset = 0;

                nValue1 = aPriceArray[0]
                    - aPriceArray[ nOffset ];

                nA1 = Math.exp( -3.14159 / Cutoff );
                nB1 = 2*nA1 * Math.cos( DegToRad( 1.738 * 180
                    / Cutoff ) );
                nC1 = nA1 * nA1;

                nCoef2 = nB1 + nC1;
                nCoef3 = -( nC1 + nB1 * nC1 );
                nCoef4 = nC1 * nC1;
                nCoef1 = 1 - nCoef2 - nCoef3 - nCoef4;

                if ( nBarCount < 4 ) {
                        aFiltArray[0] = nValue1;
                }
                else {
                        aFiltArray[0] = nCoef1*nValue1
                            + nCoef2*aFiltArray[1]
                            + nCoef3*aFiltArray[2]
                            + nCoef4*aFiltArray[3];
                }


                //return the calculated values
                if (!isNaN( aFiltArray[0] ) ) {
                        return( aFiltArray[0] );
                }


}

//== Convert Degrees to Radians
function DegToRad( nValue ) {
var nTmp;

        nTmp = nValue * ( Math.PI / 180 );
        return( nTmp );
```

图 12.2 (续)

```
}

//== Convert Radians to Degrees
function RadToDeg( nValue ) {
var nTmp;

        nTmp = nValue * ( 180 / Math.PI );

        return( nTmp );

}

function Median( nBars, aArray ) {
var aTmp = new Array();
var nTmp;
var result;
var x;

        //transfer elements to temp array
        x = 0;
        while( x < nBars ) {
                aTmp[x] = aArray[x++];
        }
        //sort array in asc order
        aTmp.sort( SortAsc );


        //if odd # of elements, just take middle
        if ( nBars % 2 != 0 ) {
                result = aTmp[ (nBars+1) / 2 ]
                aTmp = null;
                return( result );
        }
        //if even # elements, take average of two middle
            elements
        else {
                nTmp = nBars/2;
                result = (aTmp[nTmp] + aTmp[nTmp+1])/2;
                aTmp = null;
                return ( result );
        }
}
```

(continued)

图 12.2 (续)

```
function SortAsc( arg1, arg2 ) {
      if (arg1<arg2) {
        return( -1 )
      }
      else {
         return( 1 );
      }
}
```

图 12.2（续）

从图 12.3 中我们可以看出，当该指标向上穿越零线时市场开始进入上升趋势，而当该指标向下穿越零线时市场开始进入下降趋势。

我把平滑自适应动量指标转换为一个自动交易策略，交易规则是每当该指标向上穿越零线时买多，而每当该指标向下穿越零线时卖空。同时，我还添加了一条资金管理止损规则。这个简单而优秀的趋势跟随自动交易策略产生的结果见表 12.1。平滑自适应动量策略的 EasyLanguage 代码和 EFS 代码分别见图 12.4 和 12.5。

图 12.3　把平滑自适应动量用作一个趋势指标

第 12 章 适应趋势

表 12.1 使用平滑自适应动量交易策略的交易结果示例

Future 期货	Net Profit 净利润	Number of Trades 交易总数	Percent Profitable 获利百分比	Profit Factor 获利因子	Max DD 最大资金回撤
EC (4/81-3/03)	$112,112	196	40.3%	2.03	($8,137)
JY (9/81-3/03)	$160,950	277	39.7%	2.01	($13,450)
SF (6/76-3/03)	$157,337	523	38.8%	1.64	($13,587)

```
{*****************************************************
             Smoothed Adaptive Momentum
 *****************************************************}
Inputs: Price((H+L)/2),
        alpha(.07),
        Cutoff(8);

Vars:   Smooth(0),
        Cycle(0),
        Q1(0),
        I1(0),
        DeltaPhase(0),
        MedianDelta(0),
        DC(0),
        InstPeriod(0),
        Period(0),
        Num(0),
        Denom(0),
        a1(0),
        b1(0),
        c1(0),
        coef1(0),
        coef2(0),
        coef3(0),
        coef4(0),
        Filt3(0);

Smooth = (Price + 2*Price[1] + 2*Price[2]
    + Price[3])/6;
Cycle = (1 - .5*alpha)*(1 - .5*alpha)*(Smooth
    - 2*Smooth[1] + Smooth[2]) + 2*(1 - alpha)*Cycle[1]
    - (1 - alpha)*(1 - alpha)*Cycle[2];
                                              (continued)
```

图 12.4 平滑自适应动量策略的 EasyLanguage 代码

```
If currentbar < 7 then Cycle = (Price - 2*Price[1]
    + Price[2]) / 4;

Q1 = (.0962*Cycle + .5769*Cycle[2] - .5769*Cycle[4]
    - .0962*Cycle[6])*(.5 + .08*InstPeriod[1]);
I1 = Cycle[3];

If Q1 <> 0 and Q1[1] <> 0 then DeltaPhase = (I1/Q1
    - I1[1]/Q1[1]) / (1 + I1*I1[1]/(Q1*Q1[1]));
If DeltaPhase < 0.1 then DeltaPhase = 0.1;
If DeltaPhase > 1.1 then DeltaPhase = 1.1;
MedianDelta = Median(DeltaPhase, 5);

If MedianDelta = 0 then DC = 15 else DC = 6.28318
    / MedianDelta + .5;

InstPeriod = .33*DC + .67*InstPeriod[1];
Period = .15*InstPeriod + .85*Period[1];

Value1 = Price - Price[IntPortion(Period - 1)];

a1 = expvalue(-3.14159 / Cutoff);
b1 = 2*a1*Cosine(1.738*180 / Cutoff);
c1 = a1*a1;
coef2 = b1 + c1;
coef3 = -(c1 + b1*c1);
coef4 = c1*c1;
coef1 = 1 - coef2 - coef3 -coef4;

Filt3 = coef1*Value1 + coef2*Filt3[1] + coef3*Filt3[2]
    + coef4*Filt3[3];
If CurrentBar < 4 then Filt3 = Value1;

If Filt3 Crosses Over 0 then Buy Next Bar on Open;
If Filt3 Crosses Under 0 then Sell Short Next Bar
    on Open;
```

图 12.4（续）

```
/**********************************************************
Title:          Smoothed Adaptive Momentum Trading
                Strategy
Coded By:   Chris D. Kryza (Divergence Software, Inc.)
Email:      c.kryza@gte.net
Incept:     07/09/2003
Version:    1.0.0


==========================================================
Fix History:

07/09/2003 -    Initial Release
1.0.0


==========================================================
**********************************************************/


//External Variables

var nBarCount               = 0;

var aPriceArray             = new Array();
var aSmoothArray            = new Array();
var aCycleArray             = new Array();
var aDeltaPhase             = new Array();
var aPeriod                 = new Array();
var aInstPeriod             = new Array();
var aQ1                     = new Array();
var aI1                     = new Array();
var aFiltArray              = new Array();


var nStatus                 = 0;
var nEntryPrice             = 0;
var nStop                   = 0;
var nPVal                   = 0;
var nSVal                   = 0;

var grID                    = 0;
```

(continued)

图 12.5 平滑自适应动量策略的 EFS 代码

```
//== PreMain function required by eSignal to set_
   things up
function preMain() {
var x;

  setPriceStudy( true );
  setStudyTitle(|Smoothed Adaptive Momentum
    Strategy|);
  setShowCursorLabel( false );

      //initialize arrays
  for (x=0; x<150; x++) {
      aPriceArray[x]      = 0.0;
      aSmoothArray[x]     = 0.0;
      aCycleArray[x]      = 0.0;
      aQ1[x]              = 0.0;
      aI1[x]              = 0.0;
      aDeltaPhase[x]      = 0.0;
      aPeriod[x]          = 0.0;
      aInstPeriod[x]      = 0.0;
      aFiltArray[x]       = 0.0;
  }

}

//== Main processing function
function main( Alpha, Cutoff, StopAmt, PointValue ) {
var x;
var nValue1;
var nDC;
var nOffset;
var nCoef1;
var nCoef2;
var nCoef3;
var nCoef4;
var nA1;
var nB1;
var nC1;
var nMedianDelta;

      //initialize parameters if necessary
      if ( Alpha == null ) {
```

图 12.5（续）

```
            Alpha = 0.07;
    }
    if ( Cutoff == null ) {
            Cutoff = 8;
    }
    if ( StopAmt == null ) {
            StopAmt = 1000.0;
    }
    if ( PointValue == null ) {
            PointValue = 50;
    }

    nSVal = StopAmt;
    nPVal = PointValue;

    // study is initializing
if (getBarState() == BARSTATE_ALLBARS) {
  return null;
}

    //on each new bar, save array values
    if ( getBarState() == BARSTATE_NEWBAR ) {

            nBarCount++;

            aPriceArray.pop();
            aPriceArray.unshift( 0 );

            aSmoothArray.pop();
            aSmoothArray.unshift( 0 );

            aCycleArray.pop();
            aCycleArray.unshift( 0 );

            aQ1.pop();
            aQ1.unshift( 0 );

            aI1.pop();
            aI1.unshift( 0 );

            aDeltaPhase.pop();
            aDeltaPhase.unshift( 0 );
                                                    (continued)
```

图 12.5（续）

```
            aInstPeriod.pop();
            aInstPeriod.unshift( 0 );

            aPeriod.pop();
            aPeriod.unshift( 0 );

            aFiltArray.pop();
            aFiltArray.unshift( 0 );

        }

        aPriceArray[0] = ( high()+low() ) / 2;

        aSmoothArray[0] = ( aPriceArray[0]
            + 2*aPriceArray[1] + 2*aPriceArray[2]
            + aPriceArray[3] ) / 6;

        if ( nBarCount < 7 ) {
            aCycleArray[0] = ( aPriceArray[0]
                - 2*aPriceArray[1] + aPriceArray[2] )
                / 4;
        }
        else {
            aCycleArray[0] = ( 1 - 0.5*Alpha )
                * ( 1 - 0.5*Alpha )
                * ( aSmoothArray[0]
                - 2*aSmoothArray[1]
                + aSmoothArray[2] ) + 2*( 1-Alpha )
                * aCycleArray[1] - ( 1-Alpha )
                * ( 1-Alpha ) * aCycleArray[2];
        }

        aQ1[0] = ( 0.0962*aCycleArray[0]
            + 0.5769*aCycleArray[2]
            - 0.5769*aCycleArray[4]
            - 0.0962*aCycleArray[6] ) * ( 0.5 + 0.08
            * aInstPeriod[1] );
        aI1[0] = aCycleArray[3];

        if ( aQ1[0] != 0 && aQ1[1] != 0 ) {
            aDeltaPhase[0] = (aI1[0]/aQ1[0]
```

图 12.5（续）

```
                    - aI1[1]/aQ1[1]) / (1
                    + aI1[0]*aI1[1]/(aQ1[0]*aQ1[1]));
        }
        if ( aDeltaPhase[0] < 0.1 ) aDeltaPhase[0]
            = 0.1;
        if ( aDeltaPhase[0] > 1.1 ) aDeltaPhase[0]
            = 1.1;

        nMedianDelta = Median( 5, aDeltaPhase );

        if ( nMedianDelta == 0 ) {
            nDC = 15;
        }
        else {
            nDC = 6.28318 / nMedianDelta + 0.5;
        }

        aInstPeriod[0] = 0.33 * nDC + 0.67
            * aInstPeriod[1];
        aPeriod[0] = 0.15*aInstPeriod[0]
            + 0.85*aPeriod[1];

        nOffset = Math.floor( aPeriod[0] )-1;
        if ( nOffset < 0 ) nOffset = 0;

        nValue1 = aPriceArray[0]
            - aPriceArray[ nOffset ];

        nA1 = Math.exp( -3.14159 / Cutoff );
        nB1 = 2*nA1 * Math.cos( DegToRad( 1.738 * 180
            / Cutoff ) );
        nC1 = nA1 * nA1;

        nCoef2 = nB1 + nC1;
        nCoef3 = -( nC1 + nB1 * nC1 );
        nCoef4 = nC1 * nC1;
        nCoef1 = 1 - nCoef2 - nCoef3 - nCoef4;

        if ( nBarCount < 4 ) {
            aFiltArray[0] = nValue1;
        }
        else {
```
(continued)

图 12.5（续）

```
                aFiltArray[0] = nCoef1*nValue1
                    + nCoef2*aFiltArray[1]
                    + nCoef3*aFiltArray[2]
                    + nCoef4*aFiltArray[3];
        }

        // if currently flat, look for a trade entry
        if ( nStatus == 0 ) {

                if ( nStatus <= 0 && aFiltArray[0]
                    > 0 && aFiltArray[1] <= 0 ) {
                        goLong();
                }
                else if ( nStatus >= 0 && aFiltArray[0]
                    < 0 && aFiltArray[1] >= 0 ) {
                        goShort();
                }

        }
        else {

                // in a long trade
                if ( nStatus == 1 ) {

                        // if stop hit, sell long
                        if ( low() <= nStop ) {
                                if ( open() <= nStop ) {
                                        closeLong( open() );
                                }
                                else {
                                        closeLong( nStop );
                                }
                        }
                        // check for reversal signal
                        else if ( aFiltArray[0]
                            < 0 && aFiltArray[1] >= 0 ) {
                                goShort();
                        }
                }
                // in a short trade
                else if ( nStatus == -1 ) {
```

图 12.5（续）

```
                    // if stop hit, cover short
                    if ( high() >= nStop ) {
                        if ( open() >= nStop ) {
                            closeShort( open() );
                        }
                        else {
                            closeShort( nStop );
                        }
                    }
                    // check for reversal signal
                    else if ( aFiltArray[0]
                        > 0 && aFiltArray[1] <= 0 ) {
                            goLong();
                    }
                }
            }
        }


//== gID function assigns unique identifier to
    graphic/text routines
function gID() {
  grID ++;
  return( grID );
}

//== Convert Degrees to Radians
function DegToRad( nValue ) {
var nTmp;

        nTmp = nValue * ( Math.PI / 180 );
        return( nTmp );
}

//== Convert Radians to Degrees
function RadToDeg( nValue ) {
var nTmp;
```

(continued)

图 12.5（续）

```
            nTmp = nValue * ( 180 / Math.PI );

        return( nTmp );

}

function Median( nBars, aArray ) {
var aTmp = new Array();
var nTmp;
var result;
var x;

        //transfer elements to temp array
        x = 0;
        while( x < nBars ) {
                aTmp[x] = aArray[x++];
        }
        //sort array in asc order
        aTmp.sort( SortAsc );

        //if odd # of elements, just take middle
        if ( nBars % 2 != 0 ) {
                result = aTmp[ (nBars+1) / 2 ]
                aTmp = null;
                return( result );
        }
        //if even # elements, take average of two middle
            elements
        else {
                nTmp = nBars/2;
                result = (aTmp[nTmp] + aTmp[nTmp+1])/2;
                aTmp = null;
                return ( result );
        }
}

function SortAsc( arg1, arg2 ) {
    if (arg1<arg2) {
      return( -1 )
    }
```

图 12.5 (续)

```
        else {
          return( 1 );
        }
}

//enter a short trade
function goShort() {
        drawShapeRelative(1, high(1), Shape.
            DOWNARROW, "",
            Color.maroon, Shape.ONTOP|Shape.BOTTOM,_
                gID());
        Strategy.doShort("Short", Strategy.MARKET,
            Strategy.NEXTBAR, Strategy.DEFAULT );
        nEntryPrice         = open(1);
        nStop               = ( nEntryPrice + nSVal
                                / nPVal );
        nStatus             = -1;
}

//close a short trade
function closeShort( nPrice ) {
        drawShapeRelative(0, low(), Shape.UPARROW, "",
            Color.blue, Shape.ONTOP|Shape.BOTTOM, gID());
        Strategy.doCover("Short Stopped Out",
        Strategy.STOP, Strategy.THISBAR, Strategy.ALL,
            nPrice );
        nStatus             = 0;
}


//enter a long trade
function goLong() {
        drawShapeRelative(1, low(1), Shape.UPARROW, "",
            Color.lime, Shape.ONTOP|Shape.TOP, gID());
        Strategy.doLong("Long", Strategy.MARKET,_
            Strategy.NEXTBAR, Strategy.DEFAULT );
        nEntryPrice         = open(1);
        nStop               = ( nEntryPrice - nSVal
                                / nPVal );
        nStatus             = 1;
}
```

(continued)

图 12.5（续）

```
//close a long trade
function closeLong( nPrice ) {
    drawShapeRelative(0, high(),  Shape._
        DOWNARROW, ||,
    Color.blue, Shape.ONTOP|Shape.TOP, gID());
    Strategy.doSell(|Long Stopped Out|,_
        Strategy.STOP, Strategy.THISBAR,_
        Strategy.ALL, nPrice);
    nStatus              = 0;
}
```

图 12.5（续）

需要牢记的要点

● 主循环的测量的确非常重要。

● 我们通过求一个完整主循环的动量来测量趋势分量。

第 13 章 超级平滑器

"那使它变化平稳。"汤姆平静地说。

克里斯·萨彻韦尔博士（Dr. Chris Satchwell）为交易者们引入了一种叫作调整（regularization）的平滑方法。[①] 他开始先使用如下式所示的指数移动平均：

$$F = \alpha * G + (1 - \alpha) * F[1] \qquad (13.1)$$

其中 F［1］是前一个样本的 F 值，这是一种 EasyLanguage 标记。如果把等式 13.1 整理到等式的一边并进行平方，如式 13.2 所示，然后对 F 求微分，那么它的最小值与等式 13.1 一致。这表明指数移动平均可以通过最小化一个连带函数（associated function）得出。在式 13.2 中，D 表示求微分。

$$D[F - \alpha * G - (1-\alpha) * F[1]]^2 / D(F) = 0 \qquad (13.2)$$

误差函数的最小二乘（least-squares）部分可以从等式 13.2 的分子变

[①] 克里斯·萨彻韦尔（Chris Satchwell）博士：《正则化》，《股票和期货杂志》（*Stocks & Commodities Magazine*）2003 年 7 月，第 38 页。

量中得出，我们可以引入曲率（curvature）的惩罚项（penalty term）来实现调整。惩罚项来自有限差分（finite differences）数学，其中等式 13.3 的第二部分是基于 F 对时间的二次导数。

$$E = [F-\alpha*G-(1-\alpha)*F[1]]^2 + \lambda*(F-2*F[1]+F[2])^2 \quad (13.3)$$

对式 13.3 求 F 的微分，并且令其等于 0，则得到下式：

$$2*[F-\alpha*G-(1-\alpha)*F[1]] + 2*\lambda*(F-2*F[1]+F[2]) = 0 \quad (13.4)$$

对等式 13.4 重新整理一下，我们得到更加简洁的下式

$$F = [\alpha*G+(1-\alpha+2*\lambda)*F[1] - \lambda*F[2]]/(1+\lambda) \quad (13.5)$$

对于调整常数 λ 的值没有明确的限制。但是，只要经过少量试验便可证明，如果调整常数太大的话，将得出不合理的结果。例如，图 13.1 所示为 $\alpha = 0.33$ 和 $\lambda = 10$ 时的调整滤波器的传递响应。在这个例子中，当频率为每日 0.03 循环（一个循环周期为 33 日）时，该滤波器的增益大于 6dB。那就意味着输入波形中的 33 日周期分量将被放大而不是被平滑。

理想情况下，我们希望通过滤波器的频率分量根本不被放大，而我们想滤除的频率分量被滤波器衰减。如果 α 和 λ 满足下式的关系，那么便可近似实现调整滤波器的理想目标。

$$\lambda = \text{expvalue}(0.16/\alpha) \quad (13.6)$$

举例说明，如果 $\alpha = 0.33$，那么 λ 的理想值应该是 1.624。该滤波器在使用这对参数时的传递响应如图 13.2 所示。

第 13 章 超级平滑器

从频率为 0 至 0.05 循环/日的频率响应几乎是平的。从那一点开始,较高频率的分量的衰减越来越大。

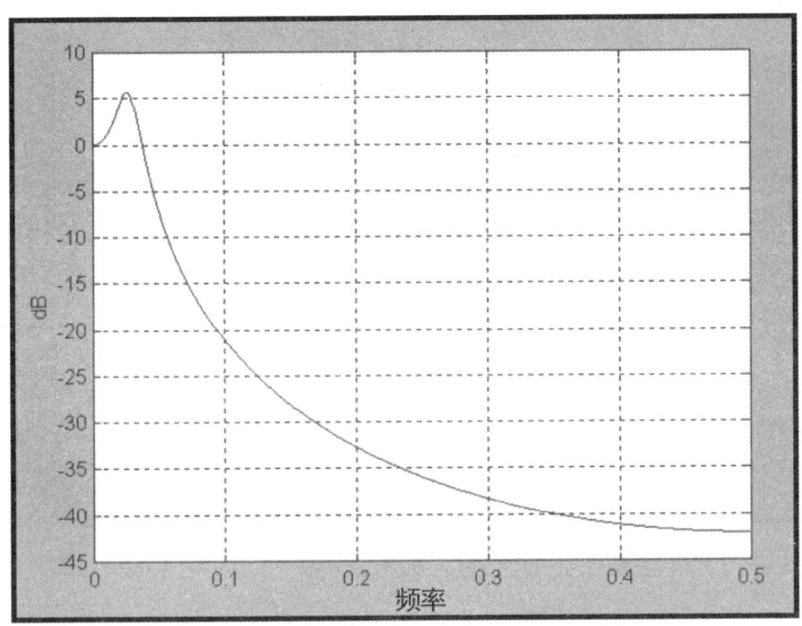

图 13.1 调整滤波器的传递响应 ($\alpha = 0.33$,$\lambda = 10$)

调整滤波器的一个迷人特性是,它的零频滞后主要决定于参数 α,而与 λ 值无关。对于 λ 的理想值,调整滤波器滞后响应的一个例子见图 13.3。在指数移动平均中,零频滞后和 α 的关系是:

$$\alpha = \frac{1}{\text{滞后} + 1} \qquad (13.7)$$

所以,如果零频滞后为 2,那么 $\alpha = 0.33$,反之亦然。

回想一下在第 2 章中我们曾经介绍过指数移动平均的传递响应,如 13.8 式:

$$H(z) = \frac{\text{输出}}{\text{输入}} = \frac{\alpha}{1-(1-\alpha)*Z^{-1}} \qquad (13.8)$$

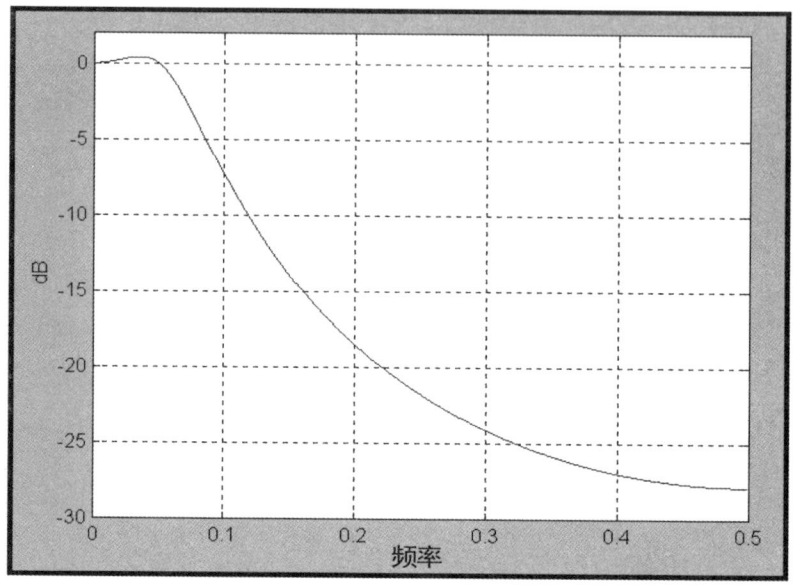

图 13.2　调整滤波器的传递响应（$\alpha = 0.33$，$\lambda = 1.624$）

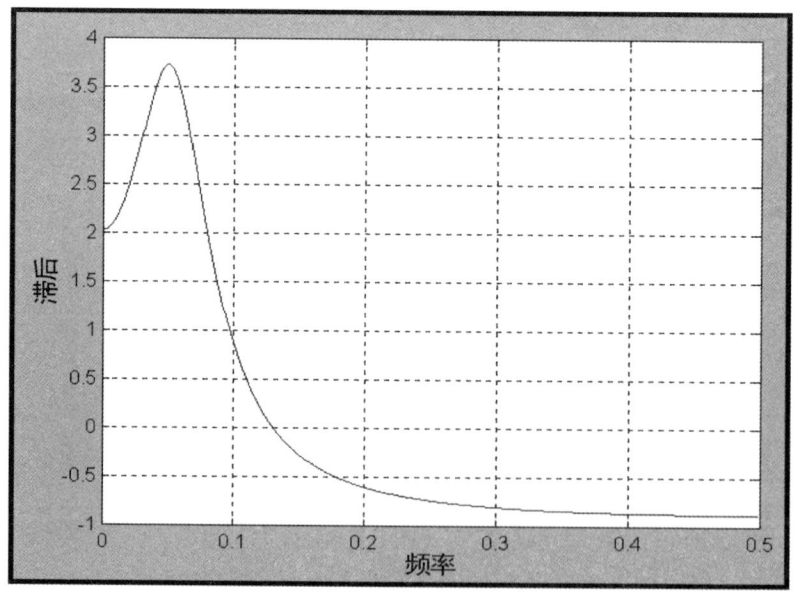

图 13.3　调整滤波器的滞后响应（$\alpha = 0.33$，$\lambda = 1.624$）

如果延迟因子 Z^{-1} 等于 $1/(1-\alpha)$，那么分母将趋于 0，于是传递响应趋于无穷大。这被称为传递响应的极点。不必担心：由于 α 必须小于单位 1，并且延迟只能是正数值，所以永远不会满足极点条件——它不过是传递响应的一个描述符。在这种情况下，分母是 Z^{-1} 的一次多项式。

调整滤波器的传递响应写作：

$$H(z) = \frac{\text{输出}}{\text{输入}} = \frac{\dfrac{\alpha}{1+\lambda}}{1 - \dfrac{(1-\alpha+2\lambda)}{1+\lambda}Z^{-1} + \dfrac{\lambda}{1+\lambda}Z^{-2}} \quad (13.9)$$

从式 13.9 中我们可以看出，现在的传递响应的分母是一个二次多项式。从基本的代数理论中我们知道，一个 N 次多项式可以分解因式求出 N 个根。多项式的根就是那些使多项式为 0 的变量值。所以，一个 N 次多项式将在滤波器的传递响应中产生 N 个极点。一个滤波器的极点越多，它相对于频率的衰减曲线就越陡峭。我们把传递响应看作一顶马戏团的帐篷；那么我们的滤波就像是在帐篷上转动一个弹珠，但却不接触帐篷支柱。帐篷里面的支柱越多，你就可以让弹子转得越快。与指数移动平均相比，调整滤波器至少多一个极点，所以它具有优异的平滑能力。

调整滤波器平坦的传递响应及其多次求导的计算过程，使我们想起巴特沃斯滤波器（Butterworth filters）。巴特沃斯滤波器是模拟滤波器（与数字滤波器相对），它在通频带内的频率响应曲线是最大限度平坦的，因为在 0 频处 N 阶巴特沃斯滤波器的头 N 次导数为 0。

几年以前我把巴特沃斯滤波器转换为它的数字近似型。传递响应以单个变量——截止频率（cutoff frequency）为特征。在截止频率处输入衰减为 3dB。低于截止频率的输入频率分量被传递到输出；高于截止频率的输入频率分量则根据滤波器的特性而被阻止。由于交易者感觉使用周期（频率的倒数）比较方便，所以我们用截止周期（cutoff period）来表征巴特沃斯数字滤波器。

下面是一个两极巴特沃斯数字滤波器的等式，采用了 EasyLanguage 标记：

$$a = \text{ExpValue}(-1.414 * 3.14159/\text{Cutoff})$$
$$b = 2 * a * \text{Cosine}(1.414 * 180/\text{Cutoff})$$
$$\text{Butter} = [(1-b+a*a)/4] * (\text{Price}+2*\text{Price}[1]+\text{Price}[2])$$
$$+ b * \text{Butter}[1] + a * a * \text{Butter}[2]$$

(13.10)

计算两极巴特沃斯数字滤波器的 EasyLanguage 代码和 EFS 代码分别见图 13.4 和 13.5。

对于有些读者来说，把这个滤波器作为给定截止周期的一个函数可能更方便一些。表 13.1 给出了这个例子。在以前的书中[1]，我也已经给出了高斯滤波器的表格。

与调整滤波器不同，我们可以增加巴特沃斯滤波器的阶数来增加滤波器响应曲线的陡峭程度。对于交易者来说，这并不是一个很好的选择，因为增加滤波器中的极点数也意味着滤波器的滞后同时增加。对于一个选定的截止周期，一个三极滤波器恰好达到我们可以容忍的滞后上限。EasyLanguage 格式的三极巴特沃斯滤波器为：

---

[1] 《火箭技术的交易应用》，第 15 章。

第 13 章 超级平滑器

```
{***********************************************
        Butter=coef1*(Price + 2*Price[1]+Price[2])
***********************************************}

Inputs: Price((H+L)/2),
        Period(15);

Vars:   a1(0),
        b1(0),
        coef1(0),
        coef2(0),
        coef3(0),
        Butter(0);

a1 = expvalue(-1.414*3.14159 / Period);
b1 = 2*a1*Cosine(1.414*180 / Period);
coef2 = b1;
coef3 = -a1*a1;
coef1 = (1 - b1 + a1*a1) / 4;

Butter = coef1*(Price + 2*Price[1] + Price[3])
    + coef2*Butter[1] + coef3*Butter[2];
If CurrentBar < 3 then Butter = Price;

Plot1(Butter, IButterI);
```

图 13.4 计算两极巴特沃斯滤波器的 EasyLanguage 代码

$$a = ExpValue(-3.14159 | Cutoff)$$

$$b = 2 * a * Cosine(1.738 * 180 | Cutoff)$$

$$c = a * a$$

$$\begin{aligned} Butter = & [(1-b+c)*(1-c)/8]*(Price+3*Price[1] \\ & +3*Price[2]+Price[3]) \\ & +(b+c)*Butter[1]-(c+b*c) \\ & *Butter[2]+c*c*Butter[3] \end{aligned} \qquad (13.11)$$

计算三极巴特沃斯数字滤波器的 EasyLanguage 代码和 EFS 代码分别见图 13.6 和 13.7。

表 13.2 列出了三极巴特沃斯滤波器作为它们的截止频率的函数的系数。对于那些只希望快速得到这些系数值，而不是去计算它们的那些读者，该表提供了很大的便利。

```
/*************************************************
Title:   2 Pole Butterworth Filter
Coded By: Chris D. Kryza (Divergence Software, Inc.)
Email:   c.kryza@gte.net
Incept:  07/09/2003
Version: 1.0.0


=================================================
Fix History:

07/09/2003 -   Initial Release
1.0.0


=================================================
*************************************************/


//External Variables
var nPrice              = 0;
var nBarCount           = 0;

var aPriceArray         = new Array();
var aButterArray        = new Array();


//== PreMain function required by eSignal to set
    things up
function preMain() {
var x;

  setPriceStudy(true);
  setStudyTitle("2-Pole Butterworth");
  setCursorLabelName("Butter", 0);
  setDefaultBarFgColor( Color.blue, 0 );

      //initialize arrays
  for (x=0; x<10; x++) {
      aPriceArray[x]            = 0.0;
      aButterArray[x]           = 0.0;
  }
```

(continued)

图 13.5 计算两极巴特沃斯滤波器的 EFS 代码

```
}
//== Main processing function
function main( Period ) {
var x;
var nA1;
var nB1;
var nCoef1;
var nCoef2;
var nCoef3;

    //initialize parameters if necessary
    if ( Period == null ) {
         Period = 15;
    }

    // study is initializing
 if (getBarState() == BARSTATE_ALLBARS) {
   return null;
 }

    //on each new bar, save array values
    if ( getBarState() == BARSTATE_NEWBAR ) {

         nBarCount++;

         aPriceArray.pop();
         aPriceArray.unshift( 0 );

         aButterArray.pop();
         aButterArray.unshift( 0 );

    }

    nPrice = ( high()+low() ) / 2;
    aPriceArray[0] = nPrice;


    nA1 = Math.exp( -1.414 * 3.14159 / Period );
    nB1 = 2*nA1 * Math.cos( DegToRad( 1.414 * 180
       / Period ) );
```

图 13.5 (续)

```
            nCoef2 = nB1;
            nCoef3 = -nA1 * nA1;
            nCoef1 = ( 1 - nB1 + nA1 * nA1 ) / 4;

            if ( nBarCount < 3 ) {
                    aButterArray[0] = aPriceArray[0];
            }
            else {
                    aButterArray[0] = nCoef1*( aPriceArray[0]
                        + 2*aPriceArray[1] + aPriceArray[2] )
                        + nCoef2*aButterArray[1]
                        + nCoef3*aButterArray[2];
            }


            //return the calculated values
            if ( !isNaN( aButterArray[0] ) ) {
                    return( aButterArray[0] );
            }



}


//== Convert Degrees to Radians
function DegToRad( nValue ) {
var nTmp;

            nTmp = nValue * ( Math.PI / 180 );
            return( nTmp );
}
```

图 13.5（续）

表 13.1　两极巴特沃斯滤波器的系数

Y = A[0] * X[0]+A[1] * X[1]+A[2] * X[2]+B[1] * Y[1]+B[2] * Y[2];

Cutoff Period 截止周期	A[0]	A[1]	A[2]	B[1]	B[2]
2	0.285784	0.571568	0.285784	-0.13137	-0.011770
4	0.203973	0.407946	0.203973	0.292597	-0.108489
6	0.130825	0.261650	0.130825	0.704171	-0.227470
8	0.088501	0.177002	0.088501	0.975372	-0.329377
10	0.063284	0.126567	0.063284	1.158161	-0.411296
12	0.047322	0.094643	0.047322	1.287652	-0.476938
14	0.036654	0.073308	0.036654	1.383531	-0.530147
16	0.029198	0.058397	0.029198	1.457120	-0.573914
18	0.023793	0.047586	0.023793	1.515266	-0.610438
20	0.019754	0.039507	0.019754	1.562309	-0.641324
22	0.016658	0.033317	0.016658	1.601119	-0.667753
24	0.014235	0.028470	0.014235	1.633667	-0.690607
26	0.012303	0.024607	0.012303	1.661342	-0.710555
28	0.010739	0.021477	0.010739	1.685157	-0.728112
30	0.009454	0.018908	0.009454	1.705862	-0.743678
32	0.008386	0.016773	0.008386	1.724025	-0.757571
34	0.007490	0.014980	0.007490	1.740086	-0.770045
36	0.006729	0.013459	0.006729	1.754388	-0.781305
38	0.006079	0.012158	0.006079	1.767204	-0.791520
40	0.005518	0.011037	0.005518	1.778753	-0.800827

第 13 章 超级平滑器

```
{**********************************************************
              Three Pole Butterworth Filter
***********************************************************}

Inputs: Price((H+L)/2),
        Period(15);

Vars:   a1(0),
        b1(0),
        c1(0),
        coef1(0),
        coef2(0),
        coef3(0),
        coef4(0),
        Butter(0);

a1 = expvalue(-3.14159 / Period);
b1 = 2*a1*Cosine(1.738*180 / Period);
c1 = a1*a1;
coef2 = b1 + c1;
coef3 = -(c1 + b1*c1);
coef4 = c1*c1;
coef1 = (1 - b1 +c1)*(1 - c1) / 8;

Butter = coef1*(Price + 3*Price[1] + 3*Price[2]
    + Price[3]) + coef2*Butter[1] + coef3*Butter[2]
    + coef4*Butter[3];
If CurrentBar < 4 then Butter = Price;

Plot1(Butter, IButterI);
```

图 13.6 计算三极巴特沃斯滤波器的 EasyLanguage 代码

```
/************************************************************
Title:    3 Pole Butterworth Filter
Coded By: Chris D. Kryza (Divergence Software, Inc.)
Email:    c.kryza@gte.net
Incept:   07/09/2003
Version:  1.0.0


============================================================
Fix History:

07/09/2003 -   Initial Release
1.0.0


============================================================
************************************************************/


//External Variables
var nPrice              = 0;
var nBarCount           = 0;

var aPriceArray         = new Array();
var aButterArray        = new Array();
```

(continued)

图 13.7 计算三极巴特沃斯滤波器的 EFS 代码

```
//== PreMain function required by eSignal to set
   things up
function preMain() {
var x;

  setPriceStudy(true);
  setStudyTitle("3-Pole Butterworth");
  setCursorLabelName("Butter", 0);
  setDefaultBarFgColor( Color.blue, 0 );

      //initialize arrays
  for (x=0; x<10; x++) {
       aPriceArray[x]            = 0.0;
       aButterArray[x]           = 0.0;
  }

}

//== Main processing function
function main( Period ) {
var x;
var nCoef1;
var nCoef2;
var nCoef3;
var nCoef4;
var nA1;
var nB1;
var nC1;

      //initialize parameters if necessary
      if ( Period == null ) {
           Period = 15;
      }

      // study is initializing
  if (getBarState() == BARSTATE_ALLBARS) {
    return null;
  }
      //on each new bar, save array values
      if ( getBarState() == BARSTATE_NEWBAR ) {
```

图 13.7 (续)

```
            nBarCount++;

            aPriceArray.pop();
            aPriceArray.unshift( 0 );

            aButterArray.pop();
            aButterArray.unshift( 0 );
    }

    nPrice = ( high()+low() ) / 2;
    aPriceArray[0] = nPrice;


    nA1 = Math.exp( -3.14159 / Period );
    nB1 = 2*nA1 * Math.cos( DegToRad( 1.738 * 180
        / Period ) );
    nC1 = nA1 * nA1;

    nCoef2 = nB1 + nC1;
    nCoef3 = -( nC1 + nB1 * nC1 );
    nCoef4 = nC1 * nC1;
    nCoef1 = ( 1 - nB1 + nC1 ) * ( 1 - nC1 ) / 8;

    if ( nBarCount < 4 ) {
            aButterArray[0] = aPriceArray[0];
    }
    else {
            aButterArray[0] = nCoef1
                * ( aPriceArray[0]
                + 3*aPriceArray[1] + 3*aPriceArray[2]
                + aPriceArray[3] )
                + nCoef2*aButterArray[1]
                + nCoef3*aButterArray[2]
                + nCoef4*aButterArray[3];
    }



    //return the calculated values
    if ( !isNaN( aButterArray[0] ) ) {
            return( aButterArray[0] );
                                               (continued)
```

图 13.7（续）

```
        }

}

//== Convert Degrees to Radians
function DegToRad( nValue ) {
var nTmp;

        nTmp = nValue * ( Math.PI / 180 );
        return( nTmp );
}
```

图 13.7（续）

表 13.2 三极巴特沃斯滤波器的系数

$$Y = A[0]*X[0]+A[1]*X[1]+A[2]*X[2]+A[3]*X[3]+B[1]*Y[1]+B[2]*Y[2]+B[3]*Y[3];$$

Cutoff Period 截止周期	A[0]	A[1]	A[2]	A[3]	B[1]	B[2]	B[3]
2	0.170149	0.510448	0.510448	0.170149	−0.336246	−0.026816	0.001867
4	0.100733	0.302200	0.302200	0.100733	0.398405	−0.247486	0.043214
6	0.050373	0.151118	0.151118	0.050373	1.080990	−0.607116	0.123145
8	0.027610	0.082830	0.082830	0.027610	1.505892	−0.934652	0.207880
10	0.016541	0.049622	0.049622	0.016541	1.783327	−1.200263	0.284610
12	0.010629	0.031887	0.031887	0.010629	1.976163	−1.412114	0.350920
14	0.007213	0.021640	0.021640	0.007213	2.117205	−1.582459	0.407548
16	0.005111	0.015334	0.015334	0.005111	2.224560	−1.721388	0.455938
18	0.003750	0.011250	0.011250	0.003750	2.308883	−1.836396	0.497514
20	0.002831	0.008492	0.008492	0.002831	2.376806	−1.932941	0.533488

表13.2（续）

22	0.002188	0.006565	0.006565	0.002188	2.432658	-2.015013	0.564848
24	0.001726	0.005179	0.005179	0.001726	2.479376	-2.085571	0.592385
26	0.001385	0.004156	0.004156	0.001385	2.519020	-2.146834	0.616731
28	0.001128	0.003385	0.003385	0.001128	2.553078	-2.200500	0.638395
30	0.000931	0.002794	0.002794	0.000931	2.582648	-2.247883	0.657784
32	0.000778	0.002333	0.002333	0.000778	2.608560	-2.290012	0.675232
34	0.000656	0.001967	0.001967	0.000656	2.631451	-2.327708	0.691011
36	0.000558	0.001674	0.001674	0.000558	2.651819	-2.361631	0.705347
38	0.000479	0.001437	0.001437	0.000479	2.670059	-2.392315	0.718425
40	0.000414	0.001242	0.001242	0.000414	2.686486	-2.420202	0.730403

多极平滑滤波器

巴特沃斯滤波器的传递响应的分子和分母都是多项式。例如，两极巴特沃斯滤波器的传递响应是：

$$H(z) = \frac{输出}{输入} = \frac{A[0] + A[1] + A[2]Z^{-2}}{1 + B[1]Z^{-1} + B[2]Z^{-2}} \qquad (13.12)$$

分子和分母都是多项式。分子中的多项式的意义是，它代表滤波器的有限脉冲响应（FIR）部分。这一部分就像是一个简单移动平均。分母构成了滤波器计算的重复部分，是滤波器的无限脉冲响应（IIR）部分。滤波器的FIR部分使滤波器的频率响应曲线变得更加陡峭，但同时会增加响应的滞后。在认识到巴特沃斯滤波器的各个部分是可分的之后，我把分子中的多项式删掉，便构成了多极超级平滑滤波器。由于当 $Z^{-1} = -1$ 时的传递响应必须是单位1，所以我用固定系数 $C[0] = 1 - B[1] + B[2]$ 替换该多项式。两极超级平滑器的 EasyLanguage 代码和 EFS 代码分别见图 13.8 和 13.9。该滤波器的系数见表 13.3。

两极超级平滑器的传递响应见图 13.10。注意，它与图 13.2 所示的调整滤波器的传递响应几乎完全一样。二者的区别就是超级平滑器的特性是由单个参数决定的，通带响应的平坦性得到了保证。

像巴特沃斯滤波器一样，超级平滑滤波器的阶数可以无限增加，从而增加滤波器频率响应曲线的陡峭程度。计算三极超级平滑滤波器的 EasyLanguage 代码和 EFS 代码分别见图 13.11 和 13.12。

表 13.4 列出了三极超级平滑滤波器作为它们的截止频率的函数的系数。对于那些只希望快速得到这些系数值，而不是去计算它们的读者，该表提供了这种便利。

从图 13.13 中我们可以看出，三极超级平滑滤波器在阻频带内比图 13.2 和 13.10 所示的两极滤波器具有更大的衰减。三种情况下的通频带是完全相同的。

```
{*********************************************************
                    Two Pole Super Smoother
*********************************************************}

Inputs: Price((H+L)/2),
        Period(15);

Vars:   a1(0),
        b1(0),
        coef1(0),
        coef2(0),
        coef3(0),
        Filt2(0);

a1 = expvalue(-1.414*3.14159 / Period);
b1 = 2*a1*Cosine(1.414*180 / Period);
coef2 = b1;
coef3 = -a1*a1;
coef1 = 1 - coef2 | coef3;

Filt2 = coef1*Price + coef2*Filt2[1] + coef3*Filt2[2];
If CurrentBar < 3 then Filt2 = Price;

Plot1(Filt2, |Filt2|);
```

图 13.8　计算两极超级平滑滤波器的 EasyLanguage 代码

```
/*********************************************************
Title:   Two Pole Super Smoother
Coded By:    Chris D. Kryza (Divergence Software, Inc.)
Email:   c.kryza@gte.net
Incept:  07/09/2003
Version: 1.0.0



==========================================================
Fix History:

07/09/2003 -    Initial Release
1.0.0
```

图 13.9　计算两极超级平滑滤波器的 EFS 代码

```
===========================================================
***********************************************************/

//External Variables
var nPrice                  = 0;
var nBarCount               = 0;

var aPriceArray             = new Array();
var aFiltArray              = new Array();


//== PreMain function required by eSignal to set_
   things up
function preMain() {
var x;

  setPriceStudy(true);
  setStudyTitle("2-Pole Super Smoother");
  setCursorLabelName("Filt2", 0);
  setDefaultBarFgColor( Color.blue, 0 );

        //initialize arrays
  for (x=0; x<10; x++) {
        aPriceArray[x]      = 0.0;
        aFiltArray[x]       = 0.0;
  }

}

//== Main processing function
function main( Period ) {
var x;
var nA1;
var nB1;
var nCoef1;
var nCoef2;
var nCoef3;

        //initialize parameters if necessary
        if ( Period == null ) {
              Period = 15;
```
(continued)

图 13.9（续）

```
        }

    // study is initializing
if (getBarState() == BARSTATE_ALLBARS) {
  return null;
}

    //on each new bar, save array values
    if ( getBarState() == BARSTATE_NEWBAR ) {

            nBarCount++;

            aPriceArray.pop();
            aPriceArray.unshift( 0 );

            aFiltArray.pop();
            aFiltArray.unshift( 0 );

    }

    nPrice = ( high()+low() ) / 2;
    aPriceArray[0] = nPrice;


    nA1 = Math.exp( -1.414 * 3.14159 / Period );
    nB1 = 2*nA1 * Math.cos( DegToRad( 1.414 * 180_
        / Period ) );

    nCoef2 = nB1;
    nCoef3 = -nA1 * nA1;
    nCoef1 = 1 - nCoef2 - nCoef3;

    if ( nBarCount < 3 ) {
            aFiltArray[0] = aPriceArray[0];
    }
    else {
            aFiltArray[0] = nCoef1*aPriceArray[0]_
                + nCoef2*aFiltArray[1]
                + nCoef3*aFiltArray[2];
    }
    //return the calculated values
    if ( !isNaN( aFiltArray[0] ) ) {
            return( aFiltArray[0] );
```

图 13.9（续）

```
            }

    }

//== Convert Degrees to Radians
function DegToRad( nValue ) {
var nTmp;

        nTmp = nValue * ( Math.PI / 180 );
        return( nTmp );
}
```

图 13.9（续）

表 13.3 两极超级平滑滤波器的系数

Y = C [0] * X [0] + B [1] * Y [1] + B [2] * Y [2];

Cutoff Period 截止频率	C [0]	B [1]	B [2]
2	1.143136	−0.13137	−0.01177
4	0.815892	0.292597	−0.10849
6	0.523299	0.704171	−0.22747
8	0.354005	0.975372	−0.32938
10	0.253135	1.158161	−0.4113
12	0.189286	1.287652	−0.47694
14	0.146616	1.383531	−0.53015
16	0.116794	1.45712	−0.57391
18	0.095172	1.515266	−0.61044
20	0.079015	1.562309	−0.64132
22	0.066634	1.601119	−0.66775

表 13.3（续）

24	0.05694	1.633667	-0.69061
26	0.049213	1.661342	-0.71056
28	0.042955	1.685157	-0.72811
30	0.037816	1.705862	-0.74368
32	0.033546	1.724025	-0.75757
34	0.029959	1.740086	-0.77005
36	0.026917	1.754388	-0.78131
38	0.024316	1.767204	-0.79152
40	0.022074	1.778753	-0.80083

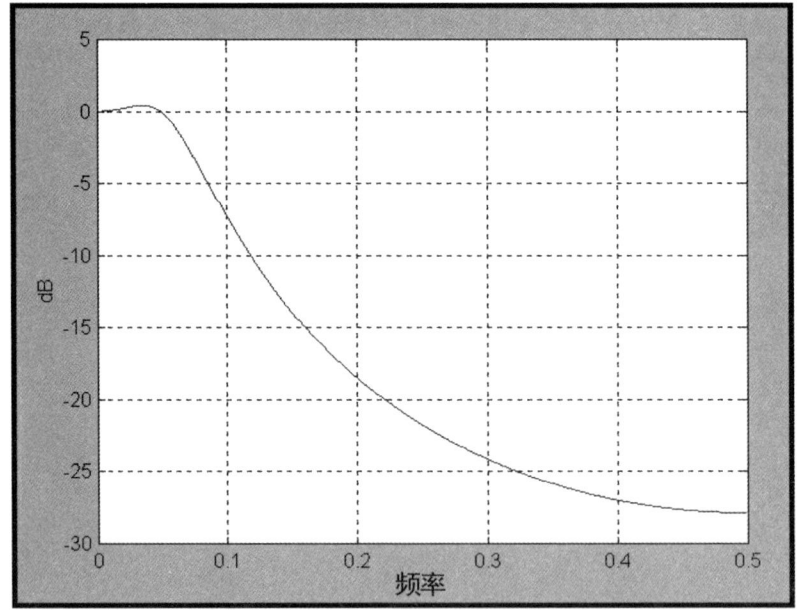

图 13.10　两极超级平滑滤波器的传递响应

```
{********************************************************
              Three Pole Super Smoother
*********************************************************}

Inputs: Price((H+L)/2),
        Period(15);

Vars:   a1(0),
        b1(0),
        c1(0),
        coef1(0),
        coef2(0),
        coef3(0),
        coef4(0),
        Filt3(0);

a1 = expvalue(-3.14159 / Period);
b1 = 2*a1*Cosine(1.738*180 / Period);
c1 = a1*a1;
coef2 = b1 + c1;
coef3 = -(c1 + b1*c1);
coef4 = c1*c1;
coef1 = 1 - coef2 + coef3 - coef4;

Filt3 = coef1*Price + coef2*Filt3[1] + coef3*Filt3[2]
    + coef4*Filt3[3];
If CurrentBar < 4 then Filt3 = Price;

Plot1(Filt3, "Filt3");
```

图 13.11　计算三极超级平滑滤波器的 EasyLanguage 代码

```
/***********************************************************
   Title:   Three Pole Super Smoother
   Coded By:   Chris D. Kryza (Divergence Software, Inc.)
   Email:   c.kryza@gte.net
   Incept:  07/09/2003
   Version: 1.0.0



   ==========================================================
   Fix History:

   07/09/2003 -   Initial Release
   1.0.0


   ==========================================================
   ***********************************************************/


   //External Variables
   var nPrice                    = 0;
   var nBarCount                 = 0;

   var aPriceArray               = new Array();
   var aFiltArray                = new Array();
```
(continued)

图 13.12　计算三极超级平滑滤波器的 EFS 代码

```
//== PreMain function required by eSignal to set_
    things up
function preMain() {
var x;

  setPriceStudy(true);
  setStudyTitle("3-Pole Super Smoother");
  setCursorLabelName("Filt3", 0);
  setDefaultBarFgColor( Color.blue, 0 );

      //initialize arrays
  for (x=0; x<10; x++) {
      aPriceArray[x]             = 0.0;
      aFiltArray[x]              = 0.0;
  }

}

//== Main processing function
function main( Period ) {
var x;
var nA1;
var nB1;
var nC1;
var nCoef1;
var nCoef2;
var nCoef3;
var nCoef4;

      //initialize parameters if necessary
      if ( Period == null ) {
          Period = 15;
      }

      // study is initializing
  if (getBarState() == BARSTATE_ALLBARS) {
    return null;
  }

      //on each new bar, save array values
      if ( getBarState() == BARSTATE_NEWBAR ) {
```

图 13.12（续）

```
            nBarCount++;

            aPriceArray.pop();
            aPriceArray.unshift( 0 );

            aFiltArray.pop();
            aFiltArray.unshift( 0 );

    }

    nPrice = ( high()+low() ) / 2;
    aPriceArray[0] = nPrice;


    nA1 = Math.exp( -3.14159 / Period );
    nB1 = 2*nA1 * Math.cos( DegToRad( 1.738 * 180
            / Period ) );
    nC1 = nA1 * nA1;

    nCoef2 = nB1 + nC1;
    nCoef3 = -( nC1 + nB1 * nC1 );
    nCoef4 = nC1 * nC1;
    nCoef1 = 1 - nCoef2 - nCoef3 - nCoef4;

    if ( nBarCount < 3 ) {
            aFiltArray[0] = aPriceArray[0];
    }
    else {
            aFiltArray[0] = nCoef1*aPriceArray[0]
                + nCoef2*aFiltArray[1]
                + nCoef3*aFiltArray[2]
                + nCoef4*aFiltArray[3];
    }



    //return the calculated values
    if ( !isNaN( aFiltArray[0] ) ) {
            return( aFiltArray[0] );
    }

}
                                                (continued)
```

图 13.12（续）

```
//== Convert Degrees to Radians
function DegToRad( nValue ) {
var nTmp;

    nTmp = nValue * ( Math.PI / 180 );
    return( nTmp );
}
```

图 13.12（续）

表 13.4 三极超级平滑滤波器的系数

Y = C [0] *X [0] +B [1] *Y [1] +B [2] *Y [2] +B [3] *Y [3];

Cutoff Period 截止频率	C [0]	B [1]	B [2]	B [3]
2	1.361195	−0.33625	−0.02682	0.001867
4	0.805867	0.398405	−0.24749	0.043214
6	0.402981	1.08099	−0.60712	0.123145
8	0.22088	1.505892	−0.93465	0.20788
10	0.132326	1.783327	−1.20026	0.28461
12	0.085031	1.976163	−1.41211	0.35092
14	0.057706	2.117205	−1.58246	0.407548
16	0.04089	2.22456	−1.72139	0.455938
18	0.029999	2.308883	−1.8364	0.497514
20	0.022647	2.376806	−1.93294	0.533488
22	0.017507	2.432658	−2.01501	0.564848
24	0.01381	2.479376	−2.08557	0.592385
26	0.011083	2.51902	−2.14683	0.616731
28	0.009027	2.553078	−2.2005	0.638395
30	0.007451	2.582648	−2.24788	0.657784

表 13.4（续）

32	0.00622	2.60856	-2.29001	0.675232
34	0.005246	2.631451	-2.32771	0.691011
36	0.004465	2.651819	-2.36163	0.705347
38	0.003831	2.670059	-2.39232	0.718425
40	0.003313	2.686486	-2.4202	0.730403

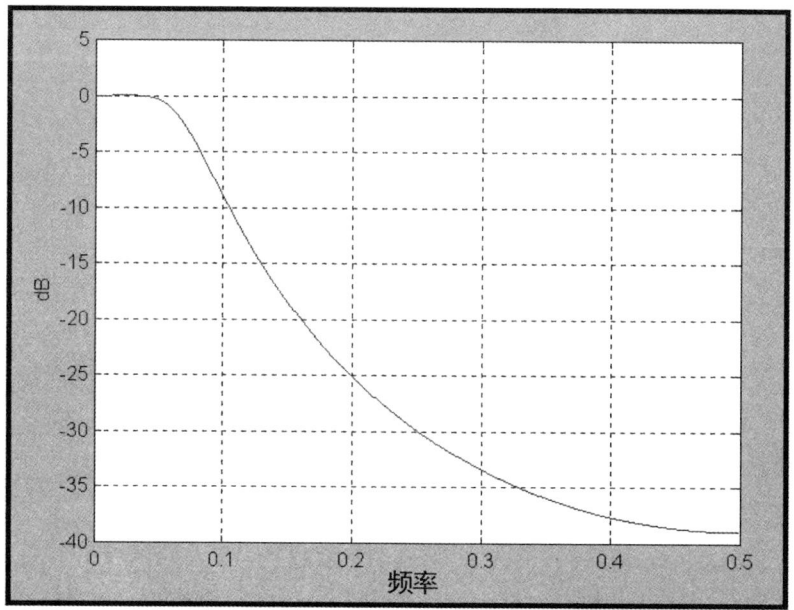

图 13.13　三极超级平滑滤波器的传递响应

需要牢记的要点

- 因为调整滤波器的传递响应中比指数移动平均多引入了一个极点，所以它的平滑性能更优异。
- 调整滤波器的 α 和 λ 参数可以被单独赋值。
- 为了获得一个平坦的通频带响应，α 和 λ 之间的优化关系近似为 $\alpha = \exp(0.16/\lambda)$。

第 13 章 超级平滑器

- 巴特沃斯滤波器是一种模拟滤波器,它在零频处的频率响应是最大限度平坦的。
- 通过对模拟版本的巴特沃斯滤波器进行转换,可以构建一个巴特沃斯数字滤波器。
- 巴特沃斯滤波器可以拥有任意大量的极点。
- 巴特沃斯滤波器的通频带是由单个参数确定的。那个参数就是截止频率,滤波器在截止频率处的衰减是 3 dB。
- 通过保留巴特沃斯数字滤波器的无限脉冲响应(IIR)部分,我们得到了超级平滑滤波器。
- 你可以返回本章查找计算平滑滤波器的公式或它们的系数表。

第 14 章　时间扭曲——无需宇宙飞行

"我只收到《新闻周刊》(*Newsweek*)。"汤姆不停地说。

技术分析中最令人费心的便是努力避免双人拉锯式交易。当把移动平均做得更平滑以避免那些双人拉锯式交易时，由平滑计算而导致的滞后常常使交易信号失去效力。所以，问题的关键就是在平滑程度和滞后长短之间找到一个平衡点。在本章中，我介绍了一种新工具，可以更加有效地解决平滑与滞后的问题。尤其是你将学会构建更平滑滤波器的另一种方法。

移动平均是对采样数据的一种简单处理。它先在过去的 N 个样本数据点上求平均，然后向新数据移动一个样本点，并且对新的 N 个样本点求平均，依此类推。对于每组新的 N 个样本点，只有最早的样本点被去除，而加入一个新的样本点。这种平均计算是在固定数量的样本点上进行的，每次只向前移动一个样本点。平均计算就是这样移动着，工程师们却从不同的视角来观察这种运动。从他们的角度来看，数据是沿着一个固定的延迟线移动，该延迟线上有多个分支，对每个样本点进行处理后输出，然后把分支输出加在一起，便产生了移动平均。图 14.1 中的原理图便描绘了一个 4 日移动平均的这种分析过程。在图 14.1 中，符号 Z^{-1} 表示有一个单位的延迟。当使用日线数据时，延迟就是 1 日。以 Z 变换表示的滤波器响应如下：

$$H(z) = 1 + Z^{-1} + Z^{-2} + Z^{-3} \tag{14.1}$$

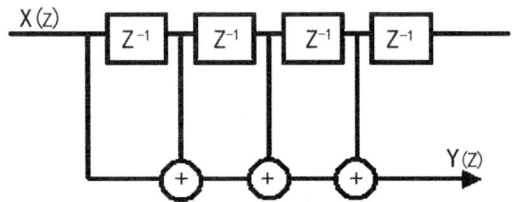

图 14.1　移动平均的原理图

在 EasyLanguage 语言中，移动平均的计算公式如下：

$$Filt = (Price + Price[1] + Price[2] + Price[3]) / 4 \tag{14.2}$$

也就是说，对从最新的数据样本点开始的连续数个较早的数据样本点求平均，便得到了滤波输出。工程师们都喜欢分支延迟线的理论，因为通过改变样本点的相对振幅，可以设计出更加通用的有限脉冲响应（FIR）滤波器。举例说明，在我们的 4 样本点例子中，如果我们希望中间两个样本点比最近和最早的两个样本点具有两倍的权重，那么原理图将如图 14.2 所示。

在 EasyLanguage 语言中，FIR 滤波器的计算公式如下：

$$Filt = (Price + 2 * Price[1] + 2 * Price[2] + Price[3]) / 6 \tag{14.3}$$

这与图 4.1 所示的消除 2 日和 3 日周期性分量的滤波器完全相同。价格上面的乘数被称为滤波器的系数。注意滤波器总是要向系数的总和规格化。在做了这种规格化之后，如果所有样本点都具有相同的值，那么滤波器输出将与输入相同。在工程术语中，直流或零频（DC）增益等于单位1。通过把 FIR 滤波器延长，我们可以获得更好的平滑效果。然而，FIR 滤波器的滞后近似等于滤波器长度的一半。于是，对于传统滤波器来说，如果我们希望更加平滑，那么就必须接受额外的滞后。

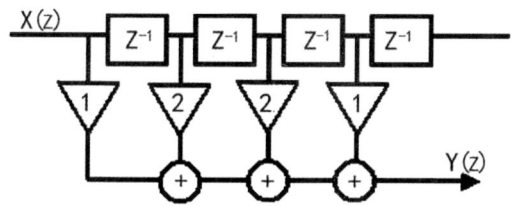

图 14.2　一个四元滤波器的原理图

传统滤波器使用 Z 变换来描述滤波器的传递特性，其中 Z^{-1} 表示一个单位的延迟。用于变换运算的正交函数非常多。其中之一源自拉盖尔多项式（Laguerre Polynomials）。k 阶拉盖尔传递响应的数学表达式是：

$$H(z) = \frac{1-\gamma}{1-\gamma Z^{-1}} \left[\frac{Z^{-1}-\gamma}{1-\gamma Z^{-1}}\right]^{k-1} \qquad (14.4)$$

拉盖尔变换可以看作一个 EMA 低通滤波器（第一项）与一连串全通元件，而非单位延迟元件的乘积（后面的 $k-1$ 项）。所有项都具有完全相同的阻尼因子 γ。我们是通过分析它们的频率响应得知它们是全通网络的。当频率为 0 时，Z^{-1} 项的值为 1，所以该元件的值为 $(1-\gamma)/(1-\gamma) = 1$。类似地，当频率为无穷时，$Z^{-1}$ 项的值为 -1，所以该元件的值为 $(-1-\gamma)/(1+\gamma) = -1$。该元件在 0 到无穷的所有频率上都具有单位增益，所以是一个全通网络。但是，从输入到输出的相移却是随频率变化的，使得滞后成为频率的一个函数。滞后变化的程度随着阻尼因子的取值不同而不同。例如，当 γ= 0.6 和 γ= 0.8 时的滞后（或群延迟）如图 14.3 所示。

所以，我们可以利用拉盖尔元件而非单位延迟元件设计一个滤波器，它的系数同 FIR 滤波器一样，也是 ［1 2 2 1］/6。不同之处在于我们扭曲了延迟线之间的时间。拉盖尔滤波器的原理图见图 14.4。

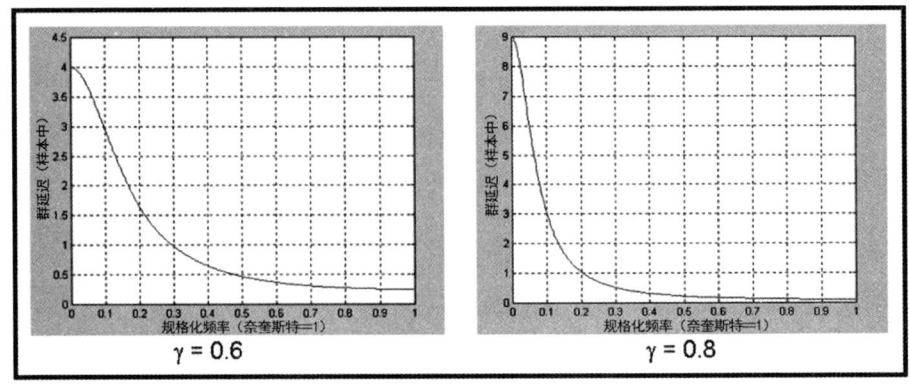

图 14.3　全通网络的滞后是频率和阻尼因子的函数

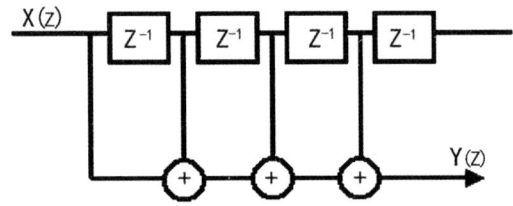

图 14.4　拉盖尔滤波器的原理图

一个四元拉盖尔滤波器的 EasyLanguage 代码和 EFS 代码分别见图 14.5 和 14.6。L0 是第一部分的输出，就是一个 EMA。接下来的三部分在形式上是完全相同的。对拉盖尔延迟线的这四部分求和的方式，与对 FIR 滤波器的线性延迟线的求和方式完全一样。拉盖尔输出就是 Filt 变量。我们同时还计算出了同长度的 FIR 滤波器，以做比较。

```
Inputs:    Price((H+L)/2),
           gamma(.8);

Vars:      L0(0),
           L1(0),
           L2(0),
           L3(0),
           Filt(0)
           FIR(0);

L0 = (1 - gamma)*Price + gamma*L0[1];
L1 = -gamma*L0 + L0[1] + gamma*L1[1];
L2 = -gamma*L1 + L1[1] + gamma*L2[1];
L3 = -gamma*L2 + L2[1] + gamma*L3[1];

Filt = (L0 + 2*L1 + 2*L2 + L3) / 6;
FIR = (Price + 2*Price[1] + 2*Price[2] + Price[3]) / 6;

Plot1(Filt, IFiltI);
Plot2(FIR, IFIRI);
```

图 14.5　拉盖尔滤波器的 EasyLanguage 代码

股票和期货的控制论分析

```
/************************************************************
Title:         Laguerre Filter
Coded By:      Chris D. Kryza (Divergence Software, Inc.)
Email:         c.kryza@gte.net
Incept:        06/19/2003
Version:       1.0.0


==============================================================
Fix History:

06/19/2003 -   Initial Release
1.0.0


==============================================================
************************************************************/


//External Variables
var aL0                      = new Array();
var aL1                      = new Array();
var aL2                      = new Array();
var aL3                      = new Array();
var aPriceArray              = new Array();

//== PreMain function required by eSignal to set_
   things up
function preMain() {
var x;

    setPriceStudy(true);
    setStudyTitle("LaguerreFilter");
    setCursorLabelName("Filt", 0);
    setCursorLabelName("FIR", 1);
    setDefaultBarFgColor( Color.blue, 0 );
    setDefaultBarFgColor( Color.red,  1 );

       //initialize arrays
    for (x=0; x<5; x++) {
            aPriceArray[x]       = 0.0;
            aL0[x]               = 0.0;
            aL1[x]               = 0.0;
```
(continued)

图 14.6 拉盖尔滤波器的 EFS 代码

```
                    aL2[x]              = 0.0;
                    aL3[x]              = 0.0;
        }
}

//== Main processing function
function main( Gamma ) {
var x;
var nFilt;
var nFIR;

        //initialize parameters if necessary
        if ( Gamma == null ) {
                Gamma = 0.80;
        }

        // study is initializing
   if (getBarState() == BARSTATE_ALLBARS) {
     return null;
   }

        //on each new bar, save array values
        if ( getBarState() == BARSTATE_NEWBAR ) {

                aPriceArray.pop();
                aPriceArray.unshift( 0 );

                aL0.pop();
                aL0.unshift( 0 );

                aL1.pop();
                aL1.unshift( 0 );

                aL2.pop();
                aL2.unshift( 0 );

                aL3.pop();
                aL3.unshift( 0 );

        }
```

图 14.6（续）

```
aPriceArray[0] = ( high()+low() ) / 2;
aL0[0] = (1.0-Gamma) * aPriceArray[0]
    + Gamma*aL0[1];
aL1[0] = -Gamma*aL0[0] + aL0[1] + Gamma*aL1[1];
aL2[0] = -Gamma*aL1[0] + aL1[1] + Gamma*aL2[1];
aL3[0] = -Gamma*aL2[0] + aL2[1] + Gamma*aL3[1];

//calculate LaGuerre filter
nFilt = ( aL0[0] + 2*aL1[0] + 2*aL2[0]
    + aL3[0] ) / 6;
//calculate FIR filter
nFIR = ( aPriceArray[0] + 2*aPriceArray[1]
    + 2*aPriceArray[2] + aPriceArray[3] ) / 6;


//return the calculated values
if ( !isNaN( nFilt ) ) {
    return new Array( nFilt, nFIR );
}

}
```

图 14.6（续）

拉盖尔滤波器和 FIR 滤波器的滤波结果如图 14.7 所示。记住两个滤波器都具有相同的长度。FIR 滤波器只有 1.5 日的滞后，并且只对价格数据进行了中等程度的平滑。而拉盖尔滤波器的平滑作用要好得多，并且具有较显著的滞后。你可以通过减小阻尼因子来降低平滑程度和缩短滞后。当阻尼因子被减小为 0 时，拉盖尔滤波器与 FIR 滤波器完全相同。这是控制移动平均计算效果的一种简单方法，而且在计算时只使用了少量数据样本。

我们的研究并非以传统滤波器而结束。正如我喜欢说的："真理与科学总会战胜无知与迷信。"如果我们可以利用非常短的滤波器产生很强的平滑作用，那么接下来我们也应该能够利用非常短的数据长度设计出非常优秀的指标。使用较短的数据长度意味着我们能够设计出对价格变化更加敏感的指标。我们将使用拉盖尔 RSI 作为一个示例。

韦尔斯·韦尔德对 RSI 的定义如下：

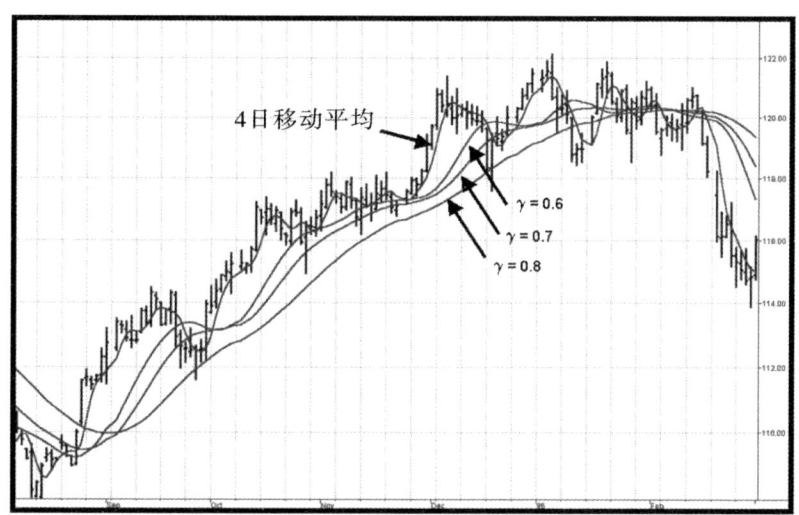

图 14.7　与传统四元 FIR 滤波器相比，四元拉盖尔滤波器的平滑作用显著增强

RSI = 100 - 100/（1+ RS)

其中 RS = 收盘涨幅之和/收盘跌幅之和 = CU/CD

RS 是相对强弱（Relative Strength）的缩写。CU 是我们所观察的时间段上收盘价变化为正的收盘价涨幅之和。同理，CD 是我们所观察的时间段上收盘价变化为负的收盘价跌幅之和，但在求和时以正数表示。当我们以 CU/CD 代替 RS，并且对 RSI 公式化简后，我们得到：

$$RSI = 100 - \frac{100}{1 + \dfrac{CU}{CD}}$$

$$= 100 - \frac{100CD}{CU+CD}$$

$$= \frac{100CU + 100CD - 100CD}{CU+CD}$$

$$RSI = \frac{100CU}{CU+CD}$$

换句话说，RSI 就是观察时间段上收盘涨幅之和占所有收盘变化之和的百分比。我在拉盖尔时间，而非线性时间之上生成了一个 RSI，只使用了 4 个数据样本点，其 EasyLanguage 代码和 EFS 代码分别如图 14.8 和图 14.9 所示。在这个例子中，我使用的阻尼因子是 0.5，但是你可以调整阻尼因子，使它最适合你自己的数据。

四元拉盖尔 RSI 的一个示例结果被绘制在图 14.10 价格图表的下面。我们同时还画出了 20% 和 80% 信号位线。注意这个 RSI 每次向极值处的偏离都是环环相扣的，并且在每个主要的价格反转处它的恢复速度都非常快。拉盖尔 RSI 的一种典型应用是当指标线掉头向上穿越 20% 位后买入，当指标线掉头向下穿越 80% 位后卖出。当然，就像使用传统的 RSI 一样，我们可以制定更加详细的交易规则。

```
Inputs:    gamma(.5);

Vars:      L0(0),
           L1(0),
           L2(0),
           L3(0),
           CU(0),
           CD(0),
           RSI(0);

L0 = (1 - gamma)*Close + gamma*L0[1];
L1 = - gamma *L0 + L0[1] + gamma *L1[1];
L2 = - gamma *L1 + L1[1] + gamma *L2[1];
L3 = - gamma *L2 + L2[1] + gamma *L3[1];

CU = 0;
CD = 0;
If L0 >= L1 then CU = L0 - L1 Else CD = L1 - L0;
If L1 >= L2 then CU = CU + L1 - L2 Else CD = CD + L2
    - L1;
If L2 >= L3 then CU = CU + L2 - L3 Else CD = CD + L3
    - L2;

If CU + CD <> 0 then RSI = CU / (CU + CD);

Plot1(RSI, "RSI");
Plot2(.8);
Plot3(.2);
```

图 14.8　计算拉盖尔 RSI 指标的 EasyLanguage 代码

```
/***********************************************************
Title:          Laguerre RSI Indicator
Coded By:   Chris D. Kryza (Divergence Software, Inc.)
Email:      c.kryza@gte.net
Incept:     06/19/2003
Version:    1.0.0


===========================================================
Fix History:

06/19/2003 -   Initial Release
1.0.0


===========================================================
***********************************************************/


//External Variables
var aL0                              = new Array();
var aL1                              = new Array();
var aL2                              = new Array();
var aL3                              = new Array();
var aPriceArray                      = new Array();
var nRSI                             = 0;

//== PreMain function required by eSignal to set_
    things up
function preMain() {
var x;

    setPriceStudy(false);
    setStudyTitle("LaguerreRSI");
    setCursorLabelName("RSI", 0);
    setDefaultBarFgColor( Color.blue, 0 );
    addBand( 0.80, PS_SOLID, 2, Color.black, -55 );
    addBand( 0.20, PS_SOLID, 2, Color.black, -56 );

        //initialize arrays
        for (x=0; x<5; x++) {
                aPriceArray[x]   = 0.0;
```

图 14.9　计算拉盖尔 RSI 指标的 EFS 代码

```
                        aL0[x]              = 0.0;
                        aL1[x]              = 0.0;
                        aL2[x]              = 0.0;
                        aL3[x]              = 0.0;
        }

}

//== Main processing function
function main( Gamma ) {
var x;
var nCD;
var nCU;

        //initialize parameters if necessary
        if ( Gamma == null ) {
                Gamma = 0.50;
        }

        // study is initializing
   if (getBarState() == BARSTATE_ALLBARS) {
      return null;
   }

        //on each new bar, save array values
        if ( getBarState() == BARSTATE_NEWBAR ) {

                aPriceArray.pop();
                aPriceArray.unshift( 0 );

                aL0.pop();
                aL0.unshift( 0 );

                aL1.pop();
                aL1.unshift( 0 );

                aL2.pop();
                aL2.unshift( 0 );

                aL3.pop();
                aL3.unshift( 0 );

                                                        (continued)
```

图 14.9 (续)

```
}
aPriceArray[0] = close();
aL0[0] = (1.0-Gamma) * aPriceArray[0] + Gamma
    *aL0[1];
aL1[0] = -Gamma*aL0[0] + aL0[1] + Gamma*aL1[1];
aL2[0] = -Gamma*aL1[0] + aL1[1] + Gamma*aL2[1];
aL3[0] = -Gamma*aL2[0] + aL2[1] + Gamma*aL3[1];


nCU = 0;
nCD = 0;

if ( aL0[0] >= aL1[0] ) {
    nCU = aL0[0] -aL1[0];
}
else {
    nCD = aL1[0] - aL0[0];
}

if ( aL1[0] >= aL2[0] ) {
    nCU = nCU + aL1[0] - aL2[0];
}
else {
    nCD = nCD + aL2[0] - aL1[0];
}
if ( aL2[0] >= aL3[0] ) {
    nCU = nCU + aL2[0] - aL3[0];
}
else {
    nCD = nCD + aL3[0] - aL2[0];
}


if ( nCU + nCD != 0 ) {
    nRSI = nCU / ( nCU + nCD );
}

return( nRSI );

}
```

图 14.9 (续)

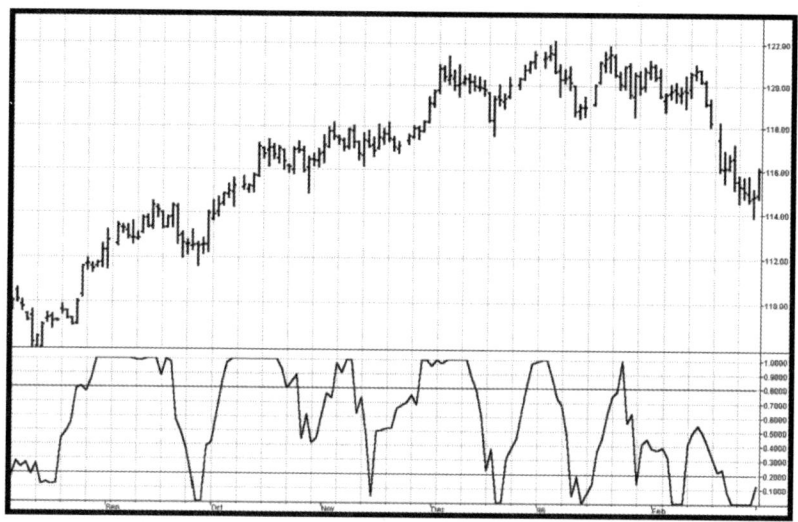

图 14.10　拉盖尔 RSI 对价格变化反应迅速

需要牢记的要点

- 拉盖尔变换提供了一种时间扭曲，使得低频分量的延迟远大于高频分量。
- 时间扭曲使我们可以用少量数据设计出非常平滑的滤波器。
- 我们也可以使用时间扭曲设计指标。
- 时间扭曲指标反应更迅速，原因是我们使用了更少的数据。

第 15 章 评估交易系统

"我发现了前三个错误。"汤姆直截了当地说。

使用技术分析交易基本上有两种类型——随意型（亦称判断型）和系统型（亦称机械型）。随意型交易者能够或者已经利用他们的技术赚到了大笔金钱。他们把自己的生活经验、对市场的知识和技术指标融合在一起，然后做出交易的决定。实际上，在本书中我已经用了很大篇幅讲解可用于工作的新指标。然而，系统型交易者却不需要对市场了解得非常多，或者说不需要很多的经验，他们依靠的是计算机程序根据交易规则自动产生的交易信号。他们有信心使用计算机化的系统，因为业绩统计数据可以通过回测产生。但并不是说模拟的业绩是完美的，在模拟业绩和实际业绩之间可能存在很大的差异。例如，模拟交易不涉及金融风险，不涉及承担风险的能力，也不涉及在面对亏损时坚持使用某套交易系统的能力。订单的执行问题，比如滑动量和佣金，只能以允差率（allowance factors）的方式考虑在内。另外，仅仅因为随机事件，就可使得交易系统的未来的业绩与历史业绩出现显著的不同。由于回测时难免会受到事后诸葛亮的影响，所以生成的业绩报告具有很大的欺骗性。本章内容便是帮助你现实地评估你的交易系统，而不是产生欺骗性的统计数据。

许多人认为金融市场中的投机就是赌博。他们的想法得到了《漫步华尔街》(*A Random Walk Down Wall Street*)[①] 等畅销书的强化。虽然这种想法很明显是错误的、不诚实的，但却一直延续下来。比较认真的交易者会分析基本面，比如价格/收益（P/E）比、销售业绩、公司负债等等，只是稍稍注意一下技术分析。本章讲解的技术使用一些游戏概念，不仅展示了使用技术分析交易系统的优点，而且会使你形象地观察到你的系统的预期资金增长曲线。

当你把自己辛苦赚来的钱置于风险之中时，你需要知道一些重要的统计数据。最大资金回撤（Maximum Drawdown）这个数据非常重要，因为它加上所需的保证金，便是你应该在账户中存入的最小资金，从而在合理的概率范围内避免追加保证金。连续亏损交易数可以考验你使用当前系统交易的胆量。知道每笔交易的平均利润是重要的，因为在你开始为自己赚钱之前必须先缴纳交易费（佣金和滑动量）。

如果不考虑特定系统的所有细节，那么有两个统计数据可以用来评估我们所预期的系统未来性能。它们是获利交易百分比和获利因子（Profit Factor）。获利交易所占的比例当然越高越好，但是如果你在获利交易中所赚的利润比在亏损交易中的亏损要多，那么获利交易百分比不需要大于50%，你便可以总体获利。获利因子是毛利润（Gross Winnings）与毛亏损（Gross Losses）的比值。按照游戏中的说法，它被称为获利概率（Payout Probability）。利用百分比盈利和随机数发生器确定一笔交易是盈利还是亏损，对每笔交易施加获利概率，然后对随机选择的交易求和，我们可以对交易系统产生的资金增长曲线获得比较现实的预期。只有此时才可引入随

[①] 伯顿·马尔基尔（Burton G. Malkiel）：《漫步华尔街》(*A Random Walk Down Wall Street*)，纽约：W. W. Norton & Co.，1973–2003。

第 15 章 评估交易系统

机处理方法来确定系统的性能。获利和亏损不是随机出现的。

我们可以设计一个资金增长模拟程序，然后在 Excel 电子表格中绘制出资金增长曲线。首先我们需要插入两个重要的统计数据。在单元格 A1 中输入 "%盈利"，在单元格 A2 中输入 45。在单元格 B1 中输入"获利因子"，在单元格 B2 中输入 1.5。45 和 1.5 只是初始值。单元格 A2 和 B2 中输入的是系统统计数据，你可以改变这些数据来观察它们对资金增长曲线的影响。

在单元格 A3 中输入 "=RAND()"。这将产生一个随机数，它在 0 和 1 之间具有均匀的概率密度。通过在单元格 B3 中输入 "=IF（A3＜＄B＄1/100,＄B＄2,0）"，我们对该随机数与获利概率进行比较。这条条件语句是说，如果随机数落在获利概率之内，那么将获利概率（获利因子）赋值给这笔交易，否则给这笔交易赋一个 –1 的值。这是这笔交易的结果。在单元格 C3 中输入 "=B3。"把第 3 行的所有内容复制到第 4 行。然后把单元格 C4 的内容改为 "=C3+B4"。这将对 C 列的交易进行求和。然后把第 4 行的所有内容复制后粘贴到第 5 行至第 500 行。现在 C 列数据变成了只使用获利交易百分比和获利因子得出的随机交易的资金增长数据。你每次按下 F9 键使电子表格重新计算，都会使该资金增长数据发生变化。

为了更容易观察，我们可以绘制出资金增长曲线。要想在 Excel 中绘制资金增长曲线，首先选中单元格 C3 至 C500。然后单击图表向导，并且输入所需数据。首先，在标准类型中选择折线图，然后在右侧子图表类型中选择折线图。单击"下一步"。然后单击"完成"。你的图表绘制成功了！现在你可以随便试验你的交易系统所预期的资金增长了。只要按下 F9 键，便可使电子表格重新计算。你将得到一条新的随机资金增长曲线，因为所有随机数字都改变了。根据你的需要，你可以重复多次以获得你所预期的感觉。图15.1和15.2只是我使用默认统计数据得出的两个例子。注意，虽然我使用完全相同的统计数据，但是资金增长曲线却显著不同。我们从中得到的教训是，当不知道某个系统销售商的获利因子和获利百分比时，不应该盲目地接受他们的资金增长曲线（真实的或合成的）。

把单元格A2的值改为50，把单元格B2的值改为2.0，看一下出现了一条多么优美的资金增长曲线。MESA软件公司（MESA Software）是少数提供这些统计数据的系统开发商之一。你可以在网站www.mesa-systems.com（译者注：与作者联系后确认本网站已经停用，可以登录本书提供的另一网站）上看到我们的一些系统的回测资金曲线。接下来我们分析一下获利交易系统的下限统计数据。根据我的经验，在单元格A2中输入42（获利交易百分比），在单元格B2中输入1.5（获利因子）。

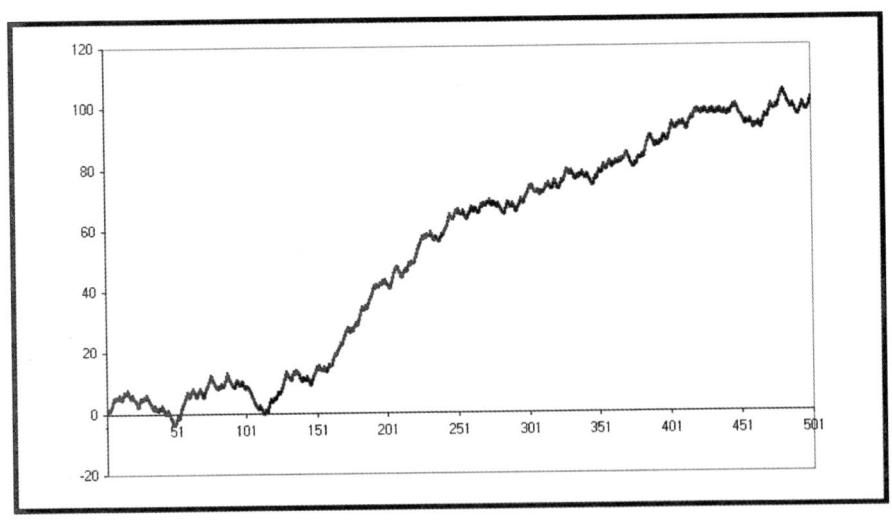

图15.1 获利百分比=45%，获利因子=1.50时的资金增长曲线

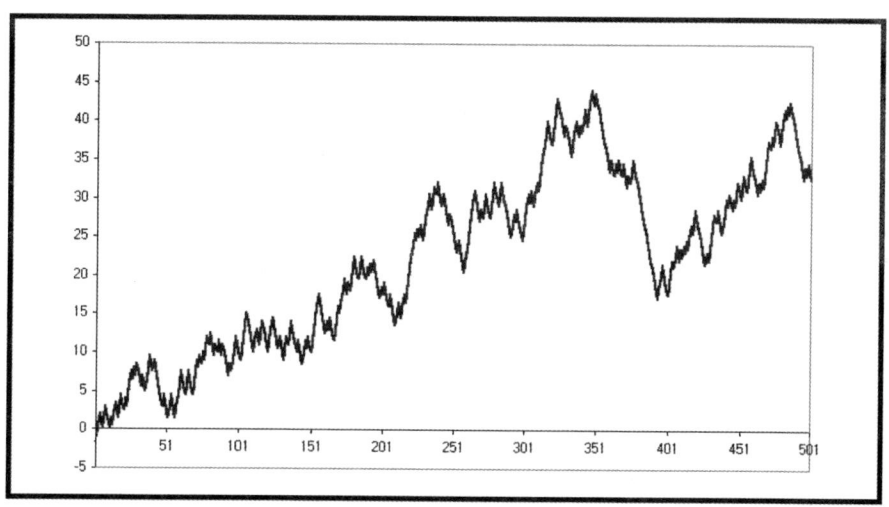

图 15.2 获利百分比=45%，获利因子=1.50 时的另一条资金增长曲线

需要牢记的要点

- 只要知道一套交易系统的获利因子和获利交易百分比，我们就可以绘制出该系统的蒙特卡罗（Monte Carlo）模拟资金曲线。
- 真实资金曲线只是蒙特卡罗资金模拟曲线所有可能中的一条。
- 蒙特卡罗模拟可以用来评估任意交易系统的预期业绩。

第 16 章 领先指标

"领先指标是非常棒的。"汤姆有预见地说。

有两种基本的领先指标：因果滤波器和非因果滤波器。因果滤波器决定于数据，而非因果滤波器几乎可以根据其他任意基础进行预测，包括直觉感受。第 11 章所讲的正弦波指标便是非因果滤波器的一个例子。本章的目的是分析因果型预测滤波器的局限和优点。一个基本的原理是，因果滤波器不能预测特定事件，因为它们的值恰好是取决于那些事件的。也就是说，因果滤波器不能预测瞬态响应。但是，它们的确是稳态响应的可靠指标。

所有移动平均都存在滞后。在图 16.1a 中，我们用虚线绘制了一条移动平均线，与原函数（实线）形成对比。在连续的趋势中，这两条线之间的差值 d 是一个常数。同理，滞后 k 也是一个常数。我们把原函数与它的移动平均之差加到该函数之上，便得到了领先指标。加上该差值之后所得的指标与原函数相比具有负滞后，如图 16.1b 所示。负滞后使得该滤波器成为一个领先指标，领先的时间长短恰好等于原移动平均的滞后。

由于领先指标的领先量取决于移动平均的滞后，所以把指数移动平均作为它的平滑参数 α 的一个函数来分析它的滞后是有指导意义的。假设原函数每个样本点的增量为 1。该函数值在第 I 个样本点处将为 I。如果移动平均的滞后为k，那么在第I日移动平均值将为（I-k）。同理，该移动平均在第（I-1）日的值将为（I-1-k）。把这些值代入计算指数移动平均的公式中，我们得到：

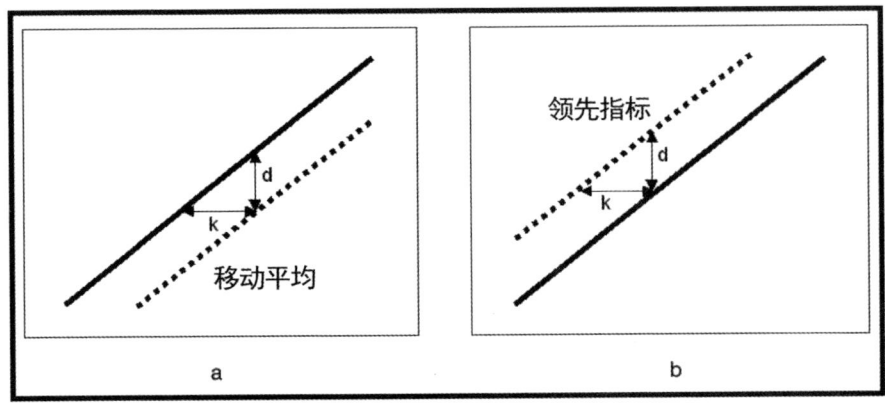

图16.1 领先指标的构建方法

a. 一个滞后为k，与原函数的差为d的移动平均。

b. 在原函数之上增加移动平均差便产生一个领先量k。

I-k＝α*I+（1-α）*（I-1-k）（16.1）

用延迟k表示α，我们得到如下关系式：

α＝1/（k+1）（16.2）

反过来用α表示k，我们得到关系式：

k＝1/α-1（16.3）

通过公式16.3我们可以计算出我们的领先指标的预期领先量。在第2章中我们已经讲过，传递响应是输出与输入的比值。于是，领先指标的传递响应可以写作：

$$H(z) = \frac{输出}{输入} = 2 - \frac{\alpha * Z^{-1}}{1 - (1-\alpha) * Z^{-1}} = \frac{2 + (\alpha - 2) * Z^{-1}}{1 - (1-\alpha) * Z^{-1}} \quad (16.4)$$

但是获得领先函数是需要付出一定代价的。那个代价就是噪声增益。令公式 16.4 中的 $Z^{-1} = 1$，我们便得到零频（常数输入）增益。经过代数运算，我们求出该滤波器的增益为单位 1。也就是说，如果输入为常数，那么我们将从滤波器中得到与输入完全相同的输出。这种输出不可能领先输入，因为输入之中不存在趋势。令 $Z^{-1} = -1$，我们便得到奈奎斯特（Nyquist）频率（最高频率）处传递响应的值。此时，2 日循环的滤波器增益是 $(4-\alpha)/(2-\alpha)$。于是噪声增益从 $\alpha = 0$ 时的 2 变为 $\alpha = 1$ 时的 3。如果领先 3 日，从等式 16.2 可以得出 $\alpha = 0.25$，于是噪声增益为 2.14，略高于 6 dB。图 16.2 所示为 $\alpha = 0.25$ 时噪声增益随频率的变化。

噪声增益可不是什么好事。我们可以在领先指标滤波器之后加一个指数移动平均来降低噪声增益。正如我在前面说过的，所有移动平均都存在滞后。于是，如果我们选择移动平均的系数 α 所带来的滞后量小于领先指标的领先量，那么我们仍然可以得到一个具有净领先量的函数。举例说明，我们选择 $\alpha = 0.33$ 的指数移动平均，它只有两日的滞后。在 $Z^{-1} = 1$ 时它的衰减是 0.2，比领先指标的噪声增益要大。复合滤波器的净增益见图 16.3。虽然在 20 日周期（频率 = 0.05）附近仍然有些噪声增益，但在大部分频率范围上该复合滤波器都有一个净平滑作用。

股票和期货的控制论分析

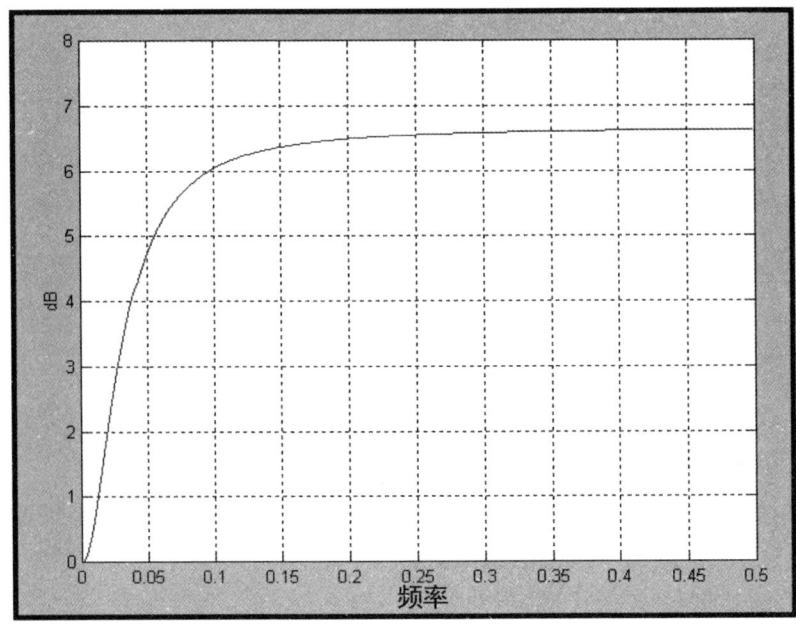

图 16.2　领先指标的噪声增益

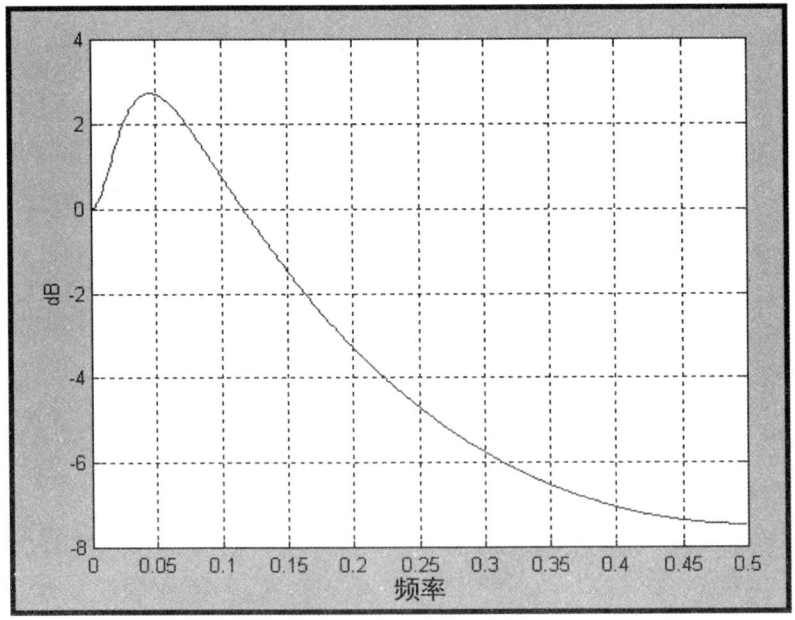

图 16.3　领先指标的净增益

在复合滤波器中仍然存在领先特性，如图 16.4 所示。正如我们所预期的那样，领先量在频率非常低时为 1 日。也就是说，趋势指标将领先 1 日。但是，对于 20 日周期附近的周期性分量，该复合滤波器的滞后大约是 2.5 日。同时，在更高频率处的滞后逐渐趋近于半日。对于这种滞后响应的解释如下，该滤波器会领先 1 日预测出一轮趋势的持续，而对于突然的变化会大约滞后 0.5 日，而对于可以用 20 日正弦波拟合的平滑变化，它的滞后约为 2.5 日。这就是物理规律——你不可能在没有付出的情况下得到任何东西。因果滤波器在某些频段的频率响应上具有预测能力，但并非是所有频段。不存在魔法预测指标。

计算几个领先指标的 EasyLanguage 代码和 EFS 代码分别见图 16.5 和 16.6。在这些代码中，我们将领先指标与 $\alpha = 0.5$ 的指数移动平均进行对比。这个指数移动平均的滞后只有半日。在图 16.7 所示的例子中，我们可以看出，当市场在上升趋势和下降趋势中时领先指标和指数移动平均的相对位置。领先指标的 α 作为一个输入变量，便于调整。举例说明，如果 $\alpha 1$ 降低为 0.15，那么就可以更清楚地辨识出该趋势的持续。给该指标更大领先量时的影响见图 16.8。

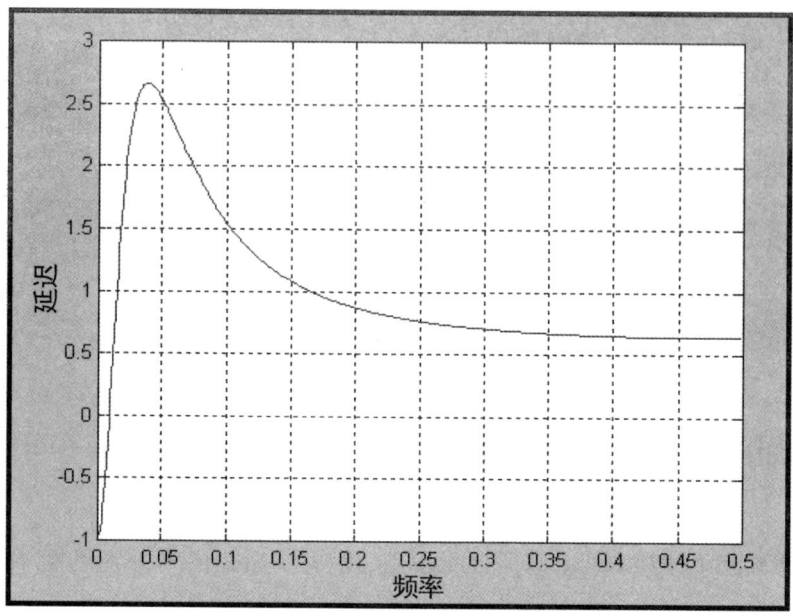

图 16.4 这样构成的复合滤波器具有低频领先特性

```
Inputs: Price((H+L)/2),
        alpha1(.25),
        alpha2(.33);

Vars:   Lead(0),
        NetLead(0),
        EMA(0);

Lead = 2*Price +(alpha1 - 2)*Price[1]
    + (1 - alpha1)*Lead[1];
NetLead = alpha2*Lead + (1 - alpha2)*NetLead[1];

EMA = .5*Price + .5*EMA[1];

Plot1(NetLead, ❙Lead❙);
Plot2(EMA, ❙EMA❙);
```

图 16.5 计算领先指标的 EasyLanguage 代码

```
/***************************************************
Title:   Leading Indicator
Coded By:   Chris D. Kryza (Divergence Software, Inc.)
Email:   c.kryza@gte.net
Incept:  09/02/2003
Version: 1.0.0


========================================================
Fix History:

09/02/2003 -    Initial Release
1.0.0


========================================================
***************************************************/


//External Variables
var nPrice                  = 0;
var nBarCount               = 0;

var aPriceArray             = new Array();
var aLead                   = new Array();
var aNetLead                = new Array();
var aEMA                    = new Array();


//== PreMain function required by eSignal to set_
   things up
function preMain() {
var x;

  setPriceStudy(true);
  setStudyTitle("Leading Indicator");
  setCursorLabelName("Lead", 0);
  setCursorLabelName("EMA", 1 );
  setDefaultBarFgColor( Color.red, 0 );
  setDefaultBarFgColor( Color.blue, 1 );

        //initialize arrays
  for (x=0; x<10; x++) {
```

图 16.6 计算领先指标的 EFS 代码

```
            aPriceArray[x]           = 0.0;
            aLead[x]                 = 0.0;
            aNetLead[x]              = 0.0;
            aEMA[x]                  = 0.0;
    }
}

//== Main processing function
function main( Alpha1, Alpha2 ) {
var x;

        //initialize parameters if necessary
        if ( Alpha1 == null ) {
                Alpha1 = 0.25;
        }
        if ( Alpha2 == null ) {
                Alpha2 = 0.33;
        }

        // study is initializing
    if (getBarState() == BARSTATE_ALLBARS) {
        return null;
    }

        //on each new bar, save array values
        if ( getBarState() == BARSTATE_NEWBAR ) {

                nBarCount++;

                aPriceArray.pop();
                aPriceArray.unshift( 0 );

                aLead.pop();
                aLead.unshift( 0 );

                aNetLead.pop();
                aNetLead.unshift( 0 );

                aEMA.pop();
                aEMA.unshift( 0 );
```

(continued)

图 16.6（续）

第16章 领先指标

```
        }

        nPrice = ( high()+low() ) / 2;
        aPriceArray[0] = nPrice;


        aLead[0] = 2 * aPriceArray[0] + ( Alpha1 - 2.0 )
            * aPriceArray[1] + ( 1.0 - Alpha1 )
            * aLead[1];
        aNetLead[0] = Alpha2 * aLead[0]
            + ( 1.0 - Alpha2 ) * aNetLead[1];

        aEMA[0] = 0.5 * aPriceArray[0] + 0.5 * aEMA[1];


        //return the calculated values
        if ( !isNaN( aNetLead[0] ) && !isNaN( aEMA[0] )
            && nBarCount > 20 ) {
                return new Array( aNetLead[0], aEMA[0] );
        }

}
```

图 16.6（续）

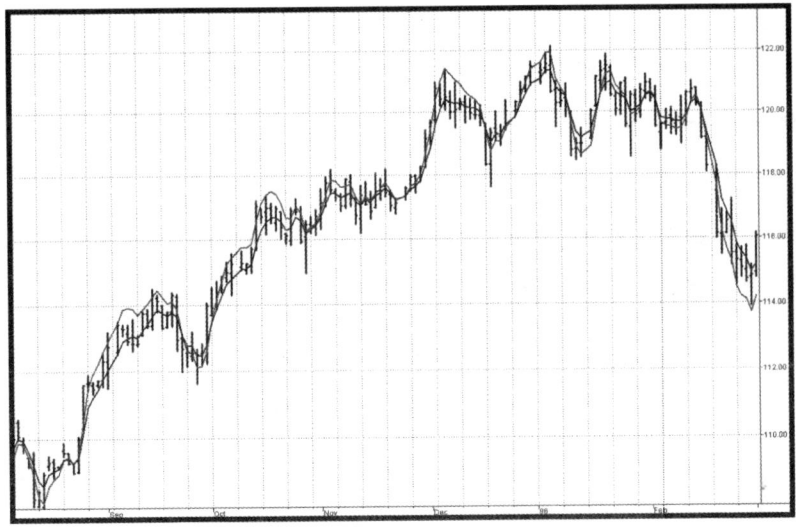

图 16.7 领先指标（α1 = 0.25，α2 = 0.33）和 EMA

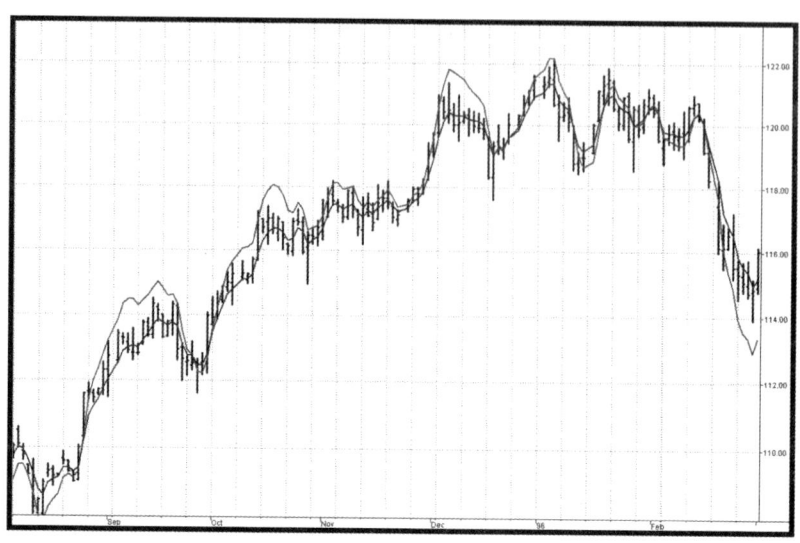

图 16.8 领先指标（α1 = 0.15，α2 = 0.33）和 EMA 提供了趋势延续的更清晰的画面

需要牢记的要点

- 在价格数据之上加上价格和指数移动平均之差将得到一个领先指标。
- 领先指标总存在噪声增益。
- 用另一个指数移动平均对领先指标进行平滑，能够减少噪声增益的影响。
- 在低频处，我们可以通过选择计算系数使指标具有一个净领先量。
- 领先指标在价格反转点处具有滞后。

第 17 章　简化简单移动平均的计算过程

"有一个主题必须放在最后。"汤姆最后说。

一个长度为 N 的简单移动平均（SMA）是先求 N 个值的累积和，然后除以值的个数 N。这一过程在每条棒线处重复。还有比这更简单的吗？虽然从理论上讲非常简单，但是计算较长移动平均的代码可能比较冗长，因为项数太多了。在代码中使用循环求和可以减少这种麻烦。但是循环在某些程序中比较难以实现，比如 Excel。另一种简化方法是去掉最早的那个值，而加入一个新值。但是，这至少要计算一次长移动平均的初始值。本章我将讲解两种计算 SMA 的简便方法。

在 Z 变化标记中，我们用 Z^{-1} 表示一个单位的延迟。传递响应是滤波器的输出除以它的输入。于是，一个 8 日 SMA 的传递响应可以写作：

$$H(z) = (1+Z^{-1}+Z^{-2}+Z^{-3}+Z^{-4}+Z^{-5}+Z^{-6}+Z^{-7})/8 \qquad (17.1)$$

等式 17.2 是用 EasyLanguage 语言表示的相同计算过程，其中用 [N] 表示延迟 N 日。

$$SMA = (Price+Price[1]+Price[2]+Price[3] \\ +Price[4]+Price[5]+Price[6]+Price[7])/8 \qquad (17.2)$$

公式 17.1 是一个简单的有限级数，可以整理为更加一般化的分式形式：

$$H(z) = \frac{Y(z)}{X(z)} = \left[\frac{1 - Z^{-(N+1)}}{1 - Z^{-1}}\right] / (N+1) \qquad (17.3)$$

其中 $Y(z)$ 是滤波器输出，$X(z)$ 是滤波器输入。

如果 $N = 7$，则公式 17.3 与公式 17.1 是完全一样的，所以是一个 SMA。当对公式 17.3 进行交叉相乘时，我们得到：

$$Y(z) = X(z)\left[1 - Z^{-(N+1)}\right] / (N+1) + Y(z)Z^{-1} \qquad (17.4)$$

公式 17.4 提供了一种方法，只使用几项便可计算任意长度的 SMA。用 EasyLanguage 语言表示公式 17.4，我们得到：

$$SMA = (Price - Price[N+1]) / [(N+1) + SMA[1]] \qquad (17.5)$$

如果认识到我们不必一次完成所有的滤波，那么我们可以得到另一种 SMA 编程技巧。更确切地说，我们可以对滤波器进行级联。也就是说我们可以过滤前一个滤波器的输出，然后再用一个滤波器过滤当前滤波器的输出，依此类推。级联滤波器可以用 Z 变换的乘积来表示。所以，级联滤波器的 SMA 传递响应可以记作：

$$H(z) = (1 + Z^{-1})(1 + Z^{-2})(1 + Z^{-4}) \cdots (1 + Z^{-2^{K-1}}) / 2^K \qquad (17.6)$$

举例说明，如果 $K = 3$，我们将得到一个 8 日 SMA。作为一个试验，

第 17 章　简化简单移动平均的计算过程

我们把公式 17.6 展开：

$$\begin{aligned} H(z) &= (1 + Z^{-1})(1 + Z^{-2})(1 + Z^{-4})/8 \\ &= (1 + Z^{-1} + Z^{-2} + Z^{-3})(1 + Z^{-4})/8 \\ &= (1 + Z^{-1} + Z^{-2} + Z^{-3} + Z^{-4} + Z^{-5} + Z^{-6} + Z^{-7})/8 \end{aligned} \quad (17.7)$$

公式 17.7 表明，级联滤波器展开后与 SMA 是完全相同的。在 EasyLanguage 中，级联滤波器可以记作：

$$\begin{aligned} &\text{Value1} = \text{Price} + \text{Price}[1] \\ &\text{Value2} = \text{Value1} + \text{Value1}[2] \\ &\text{Value3} = \text{Value2} + \text{Value2}[4] \\ &\text{SMA} = \text{Value3}/8 \end{aligned} \quad (17.8)$$

需要牢记的要点
- 一个 N 日 SMA 可以写作类似于指数移动平均的迭代形式。
- 一个 N 日 SMA 可以记作 K 次迭代二元平均，其中 $N = 2^K$。

结束语

稍等——还有更多！

在本书的简介当中我曾经说过,我的目标是通过引入现代化的数字信号处理理论来革新交易艺术。我希望得到你的认同,即我已经开发了一些相当有效的新型交易工具。更重要的是,我希望这些新的交易工具已经带给你一个全新的视角,使你可以更好地观察市场,更好地使用技术分析。通过阅读本书,或许你的观点已经有所改变,从认为技术分析不好,到认为它非常地实用。我的工具加强了技术分析的实用性。

《股票和期货的控制论分析》这本书的阅读分几个层次。在第一个层次,你得到了交易系统的代码,使用它们你可以立即开始交易。这些系统的历史业绩与价值数千美元的商业系统的性能不相上下,甚至超过了它们的性能。在较高一个层次上,你已经真正拥有了新的分析工具,比如费希尔变换、CG振荡指标、RVI、测量主循环周期的希尔伯特变换鉴频器,以及把众多理论结合在一起的独特方式。这些指标和自动交易策略,从一个全新角度观察市场,所以会优化你的现有工具。我请你再读一遍本书——或许不止两遍——以便达到最高层次。在那一层次,你将对市场和我们的分析过程都有一个深刻的理解。

如果你已经读过我的前一本书——《火箭技术的交易应用》(威利公

司，2001年），那么你会注意到我强调了一些相同的主题。我甚至使用了类似的术语。比如，我在第2章讲解的瞬时趋势线。瞬时趋势线是滞后几乎为零的一种平滑滤波器。所以，它代表着一种进步。由于消除滞后对交易者极其重要，所以这些思想是对我之前工作的改进。

另一个例子，第9章中所讲的希尔伯特变换循环周期测量方法，是对以前讲过的三个鉴频器的实质性改进。这种改进是通过减少计算滞后的两项创新来实现的。第一项创新是价格周期性分量的恢复，这在去趋势的计算中至少减少了4日的滞后。第二项创新是使用中值滤波器来实现逐个样本点的相位变化的评估。前一种方法需要数据样本的乘积。由于数据包括信号和噪声，所以产生的乘积形式为 $(S+N)(S+N) = S^2 + SN + NS + N^2$。也就是说，现在这个乘积有三个噪声项必须被滤除，而非原始数据中的一个噪声项。滤波过程将产生滞后。所以，避免需要数据样本乘积的方案会降低最后结果中的滞后。

第13章中所讲的超级平滑器，也是对高阶巴特沃斯滤波器的改进。只有在读了关于调整的资料后，我才认识到巴特沃斯滤波器包含有限脉冲响应（FIR）分量和无限脉冲响应（IIR）分量，而且FIR分量可以被去除，使滤波器的通频带只留下一个接近最大平坦的振幅响应。我们不但保留了巴特沃斯滤波器的可取特性，而且由于去掉了FIR分量，减少了数日的滞后。结果便是我们所讲的超级平滑器。

本书绝不是数字信号处理技术在交易中的最终应用。例如，埃勒斯滤波器仍然处于不断研究、创新和改进的过程中。经过不断努力，我希望设计出更加准确的市场模型，使交易者创造更多利润。我希望你能与我一道探索准确度与精密度更高的市场模型。请登录 www.mesasoftware.com 查看我的最新技术文章。你可以用很多方式来使用这些工具提升你的交易业绩。例如，使用相同的周期绘制两极超级平滑器和三极超级平滑器。一套交易系统立即跃入你的眼帘，交易信号便是这两条信号线的交叉。我希望听到你成功的消息，并邀你分享在市场探险中所到达的新境界。

更多信息

对我来说，研究是一个持续不断的过程。有关我的研究的最新报告将以技术论文或研讨会 PPT 的形式发表在我的网站上，网址是 www.mesasoftware.com。

使用 Tradestation 的交易者可能不希望逐字键入代码，同时尽力避开对指标和策略痛苦的调试过程。如果是这样的话，那么你可以把我所提供的 EasyLanguage 档案文件（ELA）直接导入你的 Tradestation 2000I 平台。当导入 Tradestation 7.0 时，这些文件可以自动转换。同样，eSignal 用户可能希望获得 EFS 代码的电子版本。购买这些 ELA 或 EFS 文件有两种途径，其一是登录我的网站 www.mesasoftware.com，其二是按下述方式联系我：

MESA Software

MESA Software 软件公司

PO. Box 1801

1801 信箱

Goleta, CA 93116

戈利塔，加州 93116

电话：(800) 633-6372

使用 NeuroShell Trade 平台的交易者可以联系沃德系统集团（Ward Systems Group），以便获得指标和系统的 DLL 文件和模板。

交易好运！

约翰·F. 埃勒斯

关于作者

约翰是 MESA 程序、SIERRA HOTEL 和 MESA 债券自适应交易系统的作者,是 R-MESA #1 S&P 即日交易者的联合作者。他是一位电气工程师。他获得了密苏里大学(University of Missouri)的电气工程学士学位和电气工程硕士学位,并在乔治华盛顿大学(The George Washington University)获得博士学位,专业是电磁场与电磁波和信息理论。退休前他是美国一家大型航空航天公司的高级工程师。他  从 1976 年开始便是一位私人交易者,并且是从基本面分析开始的。由于他的工程背景,他很快被市场的技术分析所吸引。他开始质疑 14 日 RSI 或其他时间段 RSI 的魔力。他的结论是,指标的参数值并不是唯一的,交易者应该使用测得的循环周期来调整参数,以适应当前的市场行情。

他在 1978 年参加一个研讨会时发现了最大熵谱分析(Maximum Entropy Spectrum Analysis,英文缩写为 MESA)。他很快便将该理论简化为一个用于交易的计算机程序。当时那个程序是为 S-100 计算机写的,他把源代码卖给了几个志愿用个人电脑做技术分析的勇敢的交易者。他把代码转换后用于苹果电脑,以便利用它的图形处理能力和通过调制解调器获取数据的能力。现在的 MESA 仍然使用原来的最大熵计算引擎,加强了处理和推导自适应指标的能力。许多特性,比如用于指标的高级 DSP 算法和先进的图形处理已经被加入技术分析，以提升程序的可用性。

约翰已经发表了大量关于技术交易的文章，并且是这一主题的世界级发言人。他的方法非常独特。任何技术必须首先在理论波形上测试通过，然后才可在实际数据上试用。他已经将希尔伯特变换改编后用于交易，于是可以用先进的数据信号处理技术设计新的指标。